FULL FAITH AND CREDIT

L. WILLIAM SEIDMAN

FULL
FAITH
AND
CREDIT

*The Great S&L Debacle
And Other Washington Sagas*

TIMES **T** BOOKS

RANDOM HOUSE

Grateful acknowledgment is made to the following for permission to reprint previously published material:

Universal Press Syndicate: Excerpt from a Mary McGrory column by Mary McGrory. Copyright © 1990 Universal Press Syndicate. All rights reserved. Reprinted by permission.

The Washington Post: Excerpt from the editorial "Bailing Them Out Is Better" from the September 11, 1987, edition of *The Washington Post*. Copyright © The Washington Post. Reprinted by permission.

Library of Congress Cataloging-in-Publication Data

Seidman, L. William.
   Full faith and credit : the great S&L debacle and other Washington sagas / L. William Seidman. — 1st ed.
       p.   cm.
   Includes index.
   ISBN 0-8129-2134-8
   1. Savings and Loan Bailout, 1989–   2. Savings and loan associations—State supervision.   3. Federal Deposit Insurance Corporation—History.   4. Resolution Trust Corporation (U.S.)—History.   I.   Title.
HG2152.S44   1993
332.3'2'0973—dc20   92-56846

Manufactured in the United States of America
9   8   7   6   5   4   3   2
First Edition

DEDICATED TO ALL THE LOYAL AND HARDWORKING
EMPLOYEES OF THE FDIC AND THE RTC

"It is the sense of the Congress that it should affirm that deposits up to the statutorily prescribed amount in federally insured depository institutions are backed by the full faith and credit of the United States."

> —Public Law 100-86—August 10, 1987
> 101 Stat. 657
> Title IX
> Sec. 901

"The full faith and credit of the United States is pledged to the payment of any obligation issued after August 9, 1989 by the Corporation, with respect to both principal and interest. . . ."

> —U.S. Code Annotated
> Title 12
> Banks and Banking
> Ch. 16 FDIC 12 sec. 1825(d)

Acknowledgments

To Jacqueline Pace and Patrick Hanraty, whose valued editorial assistance is responsible for any merit this document may have, while all of the errors, omissions, miscalculations and verbosity are solely the responsibility of the author.

With thanks, too, to my publisher, Peter Osnos, my editor, Henry Ferris of Times Books, and my agent, Peter Matson.

Lawrence Malkin, chief U.S. correspondent of the *International Herald Tribune*, worked most closely with me editing the final drafts, and his help was invaluable.

And to friends and colleagues for their encouragement, Roger Watson, Alan Whitney, Paul Fritts, John Stone, David Cooke, and Roger Porter.

To Susan Kinsman and Donna Mahon for their support staffing.

And lastly, with special thanks to my wife, Sally, who not only provided valuable assistance but also endured the process.

Contents

"My friends, there is good news and bad news."

"The good news is that the full faith and credit of the FDIC and the U.S. government stands behind your money in the bank."

"But the bad news is that you, my fellow taxpayers, stand behind the U.S. government."

These "immortal" lines, used in practically every speech I had given since I became chairman of the Federal Deposit Insurance Corporation, were very much on my mind as I entered the West Wing of the White House (and received a welcoming salute from the Marine guard at the door—indicating the president was in-house). The good news was that, at last, I would have a chance to talk with the president's chief of staff about the condition of the economy and the financial system. The bad news was that all of the news I had to deliver about the financial outlook was bad and getting worse. But better the president know now what loomed ahead, so he could "be prepared" to deal with adversity. "Always prepared," not "unprepared," is the hallmark of success, even in politics, and hopefully in the Bush White House.

So on the morning of February 2, 1990, John Sununu, former governor of New Hampshire and President Bush's chief of staff, greeted me with one of the world's limpest handshakes in his office in the northwest corner of the West Wing of the White House. It was the biggest office in the building, and looked even bigger than the president's own Oval Office. As he hoisted his short, plump frame into his chair, the chief looked most pleased with himself as he con-

templated his morning kill—the soon-to-be-deposed chairman of the Federal Deposit Insurance Corporation—me.

After a short conversation on banks in which he showed no
interest, he quickly imparted his message with a smile. It was
that the White House wanted me out of my job in "sixty
days, ninety days at the most." More on this later.

Operating in our nation's capital is often perilous and bi-
zarre, and Sununu's unkind behavior was just a particularly
good (and bad) example.

Another example came when I discovered that the windows in my office could be opened, I opened them. The
office faced the White House grounds, where presidential
helicopters came and went. One day as the president took
off, I was standing in awe by the window. An armed helicopter suddenly zoomed toward our office building and took
aim at the new chairman gaping out of his window. Two
Secret Service men raced into the room and shouted, "We
got him." Another assassination plot foiled! You are best off
in Washington keeping your window and your mouth shut.

And then there was the wild-eyed Wyoming man, a purchaser of FDIC property from a liquidated bank. He arrived
at our office and announced that he intended to kill the
chairman if we did not straighten out misrepresentations
made to him by our salespeople. He had a gun, too. After the
police took him away, we looked into the matter. To my dismay, his cause was just. The bureaucrats were attempting to
cover their own mistakes by stonewalling him. Perhaps the
chairman should have been shot.

So government service is full of surprises, both pleasant
and unpleasant, and full of people who can be similarly described. In fact, my chance to serve the government in Washington is still a surprise to me even when I reflect on it years
later. How that came about and what happened while I was
"inside the Beltway" spans the three administrations of Presidents Ford, Reagan, and Bush. This book focuses on the
financial crises of the latter two, when I served as chairman

of the Federal Deposit Insurance Corporation from 1985 to 1991.

Why write about these experiences? Of course, I share the goals of most memoirists: to immortalize my contribution to society; even scores with my enemies; provide financial security for my old age; confirm the taxpayers' worst suspicions about their government; and generally leave a record of my adventures for the benefit of future historians. Perhaps some useful points can be made for those interested in how our government works, and how those in public service can best attempt to accomplish their missions for the common good.

Al Casey, my successor at the Resolution Trust Corporation, advised me not to write a book when I left office. He said, "Bill, you have two friends left in Washington. You write a book, and you'll lose both of them." Nevertheless, this is an account of my experiences during some of the most tumultuous times in our country's financial history. It recounts how I learned the hard way about how Washington works. If it helps others avoid some of the mistakes of the past, it will serve the purpose of any good history and make life easier for others who follow.

FULL FAITH AND CREDIT

"Luck Is Where Opportunity Meets Preparation"

You might say that my Washington experience began on one of the most famous places along the Santa Fe Trail, the spot where Kit Carson and the Sundance Kid planned at different times how to impose their wills on the West, and where, as a result, shoot-outs were regular events. I was in Cimmaron, New Mexico, continuing a long search for a ranch (which my wife and I eventually bought nearby), when I was called to the phone.

"The White House is calling." It was the summer of 1973, and those unbelievably resourceful White House operators had located a middle-aged accountant in the Wild West, and thus introduced me to the efficiency of government. Richard Nixon had just been triumphantly reelected by one of the largest majorities in history. He was firing his present cabinet officers and replacing them with appointees who had business experience, whom he considered more efficient. Penn James, who was in charge of the personnel search, said the Department of Housing and Urban Development was in disarray and they needed a "financial man" to straighten out the agency.

As the conversation proceeded, I realized that we were not actually discussing the position of secretary, but undersecretary. Under the president's new system, the secretary of

HUD was to become a "supersecretary" who, along with three other supersecretaries, would move to the White House to run the government for the president. I never quite understood this complicated scheme, which was probably just as well because it never worked out anyway. But even the office of undersecretary sounded like an important position to me at that time.

I had spent most of my life as an accountant and eventually became managing partner of the family firm, Seidman and Seidman, which my father had helped found to serve the furniture industry in Grand Rapids. Since joining the firm in 1950 after wartime destroyer service, law school and business school, I had helped it grow into a major national firm at second level behind the Big Eight accounting firms—of which, by the way, there now are only six, while Seidman and Seidman has become BDO Seidman and has moved up to number eight or nine. One of my management innovations was now pushing me out of my job. I had requested, and the partnership had agreed, to limit terms of all managers of the firm. I was completing my sixth year as the managing partner, which under our constitution was the maximum time permitted in the job.

This was certainly an important landmark in my life, but how did the White House know that a second-tier CPA was about to become unemployed? It turned out that the skillful Penn James had asked a large number of executives around the country who might be available to serve in the businessman's cabinet. Among those they had talked to was my good friend and college roommate, George Munroe, then chief executive of the Phelps Dodge Corporation. We had kept in touch, and he knew about my imminent retirement from the firm and had suggested me as a potential candidate. Following an old Mormon adage, "Luck is where opportunity meets preparation," I told Penn James I would be pleased to come to Washington and talk things over with the White House.

I never ceased to be amazed, then and throughout my career in Washington, that this exalted organization talked, worried, was restless and angry, and had all the other human characteristics. On reporting to Washington, I was told to meet with Fred Malek, assistant to Penn James, who was conducting the initial interviews. I was somewhat disappointed (and brought down to earth) that the president did not meet me at the airport himself. I began to learn the rules of protocol and hierarchy in Washington while I sat in the Old Executive Office Building for an hour or two before Malek got to me. Malek, later a senior Marriott Hotel executive and George Bush's campaign manager in 1992 until he was eclipsed by Bush's friend James Baker, was a very brisk and efficient member of the White House staff. He had been trained under the "Germans"—Bob Haldeman and John Ehrlichman, Richard Nixon's chief of staff and chief domestic adviser. Haldeman had a zero-defect rule, which meant no mistakes in the operation of the White House. Business schools now call that total quality management, but the idea is a less than perfect fit when it comes to politicians.

The next step was to meet with James Lynn, the new HUD secretary who had displaced my old friend and mentor from Michigan, George Romney. As it turned out, Lynn was a Harvard Law School graduate as I was, and almost my age. He was easy to get along with and was looking forward to being one of the new supersecretaries operating from the West Wing of the White House, one of Washington's most hallowed locations. He said he would be very pleased to let me run the department; the less he heard about it from then on, the better. He obviously was eager to move into the higher realms of public policy.

It wasn't long before Penn James informed me that I was the favorite for the job. Then began the tortuous checks into my background by the Federal Bureau of Investigation, the Securities and Exchange Commission, and other government agencies. They were becoming increasingly intensive at this point because Watergate was creating suspicions about anyone in or near government. Old controversies between one of our firm's clients and the Securities and Exchange Commission were dredged up and had to be reviewed. After a couple of months, Jim Lynn told me that the investigation would take longer than they had previously thought.

While the investigation continued, strange things were happening in the Nixon administration. As if the president didn't have enough trouble with Watergate, his vice president, Spiro Agnew, was forced to resign for accepting favors in government service and not paying income taxes on them either. When Agnew resigned, Nixon had to find a vice president who could be approved by the Congress at a time when he was coming under increasing suspicion. At the same time, President Nixon was also looking for someone he thought would not be viewed as an attractive enough candidate to replace him, in case Congress decided to impeach and remove him. Not an easy task, but as usual, Nixon managed it. He selected Gerald Ford, Republican minority leader in the House of Representatives; he was a well-liked legislator whom Congress would find hard to turn down as one of its own. In the past, Gerald Ford had been mentioned only as a vice presidential candidate. A football player at the University of Michigan, a graduate of Yale Law School, a congressman for twenty-five years and minority leader in the House, his highest ambition was to become Speaker of the House (requiring of course a Republican majority in the House—an unlikely event, as history has proven).

To help with his Senate confirmation, Ford brought in his former law partner and one of my closest friends, Philip Buchen, from our hometown of Grand Rapids. He was a talented lawyer who had been law review editor at the University of Michigan, and whose legs had been left virtually paralyzed by polio. But he was a handsome man with a beautiful wife, and they took to Washington immediately. The confirmation process went well, especially since nothing like it had ever happened before. Gerald Ford became vice president of the United States and Philip Buchen became his legal aide.

However, I was still hanging out on a limb. I had just about decided that there was little use waiting around much longer because the Watergate scandal had become red hot, and it was becoming obvious that no one nominated by President Nixon, even someone as meritorious as I, could be confirmed. This turned out to be a very lucky break. As I was packing my bags to leave, thinking about one of the shortest Washington careers on record, Philip Buchen called. The new vice president, my old neighbor in Michigan, was trying to organize his office and badly needed help. The mail was piled up higher than the windows, and Buchen said the organization needed the services of an experienced manager. Ford's office was then being run by Robert Hartmann, an aide to Ford in the House and an excellent speech writer, but no great administrator and a man with a short temper. Buchen wondered, would I take a few weeks before returning to Grand Rapids and help the vice president get his operation underway?

Would I do it? Of course! I had never before even talked to a vice president of the United States, let alone been in his office. Gerald Ford was a man I had known for years and greatly admired. Right away, people started saying that he was one of my closest friends, and although that was not true, I soon learned it was wise not to dispute the point when he was so described.

In November 1973, I went over to the vice president's office in the Old Executive Office Building on Seventeenth Street and Pennsylvania Avenue, next to the White House. A relic of a simpler age, this pillared gray architectural monstrosity was almost beautiful. The building had held all of the departments of State, Army, and Navy, which decamped to the Pentagon and Foggy Bottom as the United States became a world power. The White House staff quickly filled the vacuum, and by 1973 there were only a few choice rooms left for the very disorganized offices of the newly appointed vice president. The first task was to clean up the mess that Spiro Agnew had so precipitously left behind, and part of it was an unexpected pleasure. We inherited cases of Scotch whiskey that had been presented to Agnew by numerous supplicants as they met with him in his office overlooking the White House. We figured that they belonged to the government, so we appropriated them for official use. There was also a great deal to be done setting up the substantive side of the vice president's operation, coordinating his staff, doing advance work, and, of course, answering the mail.

Early on, my education on how Washington works began in the most traditional form: a turf battle. Controversy erupted with the office of the chief of staff, Robert Hartmann. Our problems were the normal ones—who reported to whom, and who had direct access to the vice president. Ford had made Hartmann his chief of staff, and Hartmann expected all who wished to speak with the boss to do so through him. However, as a precondition to accepting my new position, I had asked for, and been assured of, direct access to the vice president. We worked out our problems with a typical Ford compromise, a dotted line on the organization chart indicating that I had direct access to the vice president, but only after informing Chief Hartmann. Like almost all politicians, Ford thoroughly disliked being involved in staff infighting. Lesson number one: get your staff turf controversies settled without involving the boss!

I had been in Ford's office less than a week when I had my first experience with that Washington fixture, the press leak. Someone in the Nixon administration had accused Ford of trying to ease Nixon out. We knew this was not true, but we also knew that many reporters thought that it was. The old Washington hands in our office suggested that we immediately counterattack by finding the first available reporter and saying that the source of the leak, probably some White

House staffer, was taking bribes, had wandered off the marital reservation, or some similar piece of scandal, regardless of whether it was true. Of course, such an outrageous story never would have been printed, but the mere threat of it would have reached the original source, and this seemed to be the way things were done in Washington. This tactic came from a world of duplicity that was quite shocking to a newcomer from Grand Rapids, Michigan.

Actually, leaks are not without their uses. Inside information passed to responsible members of the press is used to help argue your case in public. A leak also can deliver a message, often an unwelcome one that would be impossible to deliver in person, to other agencies or higher-ups. That includes the president himself, since the White House staff stood shoulder to shoulder in phalanx around the President, often preventing him from seeing people. One way to speak to him was to have a dialogue through leaks to the press. You knew the president read the papers because he often started a discussion by saying, "I read in the *Post* that . . ."

Early on, it became very clear to me that the press played an important role in government, since my job in the vice president's office also included the oversight of press relations and speech writing. A large number of reporters wanted to meet me, not so much because of my job working for the vice president, but because it was becoming increasingly clear that Watergate might put us in the White House. Requests for interviews, lunch dates, and straightforward requests for information began to arrive. Invitations to be taken to lunch were extended from newspaper reporters, job seekers, lobbyists by the score, and all the other players that make up the Washington scene. It was the sort of introduction every Washington novice strives for, and early signs of "Potomac Fever" emerged. The Washington scene was exciting and challenging. And while my position clearly imposed a financial drain, the real compensation was being part of the major league.

To all these people, I would talk only about policy and administrative questions. It was against the rules for us to talk about Ford becoming president, because we had to guard very carefully against creating any suspicion that we were trying to push Nixon out and move Ford in. However, the press was looking for answers to such questions as: What was going on inside? Who argued for what at a particular meeting? Who lost the argument? Who was gaining power, and who really was the secret Rasputin? They soon discovered that I never answered such questions and was willing only to explain and support the public positions of the administration. They began yawning politely and turned to spending their expense-account lunch money elsewhere. My luncheon schedule soon became much less crowded because I didn't really know how to play the game of "Inside the Beltway Politics."

Presidential, vice presidential, and similar high-level aides should always strive for anonymity lest they upstage the very people they have been picked to serve, and that is what I tried to do while working for Gerald Ford. It has been said in Washington that if you do not appear in the press you might as well be dead. But whether or not you need the press depends on your job in government. If you appear only occasionally, you are alive, but still not a person of importance. As an assistant to the president, you can serve most effectively without publicity. But as the head of an agency or as a cabinet officer you need press visibility to stay viable.

It is through the press that your image is created with the rest of official Washington. Few people in that busy town actually have much personal contact with officials outside their immediate circle, let alone many of their more distant colleagues. But everyone responds to what they read in the newspapers or see on television. Those who don't appear in the media and explain forcefully what they stand for and what they are trying to accomplish might just as well have passed away, because politically they already have. For anyone who is operating in Washington as the head of a regulatory agency or with a special mission such as drug czar, the press is vitally important because it literally creates reality.

In the old days, if you were the White House chief of staff, it was presumed that you would have nothing to do with the press. Your mission was to make the White House work, and the public perception of that was supposed to be dominated and indeed created by the president himself. But we have chiefs of staff who have come to believe that they are assistant presidents (at the very least) and ordained to shape the White House image (and their own along with it). Donald Regan and John Sununu probably paid as much attention to how they played on television as to making their operations work efficiently.

The press is also an invisible reporter attending all meetings, because somebody is sure to say what happened. Including even the federal prison system, this is the greatest force for honesty in government that I know of. Our nation's capital has a free and aggressive fourth estate, which inevitably worms its way into practically every secret in Washington. Sometimes it will expose you later, as in Watergate, and sometimes the next morning, much to your surprise when you open *The Washington Post*. As the unseen member of every meeting, the press tries to keep at least some of the participants aware of the public interest and the need for honesty. Of course the press is not always right, and it has its full share of people who are more interested in advancing their careers than the public good, but they are not in the majority. The fact that the press was in attendance, if not actually there, tended to make many of the meetings I attended operate at a much higher level of seriousness. This was especially true after the release of the Watergate tapes. The cynical sound of White House meetings, with expletives deleted from the most ordinary phrases, reminded us that whatever we said in public service might become widely known and enter into history even before the history books could be written.

Among those who had learned this lesson best was President Ford. He never said anything in a meeting unless he was willing to express the same general idea in public. The only times I ever heard him say things he would rather not have appear in print were on fairways and greens, when things were not going well with the little white ball. Most experienced politicians will not say anything in a meeting that they do not expect to see in the newspaper the next day. And that is why in many critical meetings that involve officials and the president or the leaders of Congress, the participants are noncommittal and appear to be doing anything but leading. They do not want to commit themselves by an incidental remark or an inadvertent statement made without proper review by the staff and associates.

As a result, most substantive discussions tend to take place at the staff level, where whatever was said represented the view of staff and thus did not commit the principals. So if the press makes high-level meetings less interesting but more honest, it also raises the tone of the lower level debates, where the public interest is hammered out on a continuing basis.

On August 9, 1974, Richard Nixon gave in to the cumulative evidence called Watergate, and resigned. Gerald Ford was sworn in as president of the United States in the East Room of the White House as Nixon's helicopter took off from the big backyard. I remember standing in the aisle as Ford walked up to be sworn in and finding it hard to believe that I had suddenly ended up working in the White House. It was even more amazing when one of the many military ushers who populate such occasions steered me to a seat in the front row, a privileged spot ten feet away. Suddenly we were in charge of the government. We had done little fighting or maneuvering for places on the White House staff because we were too afraid of appearing to be confident that Nixon would be leaving office. It was not our place to do anything that appeared to help him on his way.

For the sake of appearances if nothing else, we had been virtually immobilized in preparing for the presidency. Phil Buchen did have a secret group planning what Ford would do when he took over, and ultimately I knew about its meetings, although none of the regular vice presidential staff was involved. That way, there could be no reports of the normal fights for position and power that potential presidents always carry with them. Once Ford was sworn in, however, Donald Rumsfeld, a young ex-congressman and Nixon White House staffer who was one of Ford's old friends, soon got himself appointed head of the transition team, forswearing any job in the Ford administration. To no one's great surprise, he soon emerged with the job of White House chief of staff—although the title itself came later—which is a warning for all presidents-elect. When you are organizing a team to decide who gets what job, do not pick the people who want the jobs, make them take a pledge of abstinence, and make them keep it.

As we were preparing to leave the Old Exec and move next door to the White House, Tom Whitehead, a top White House staffer in communications who was on his way out, gave me some sage advice as a friendly gesture. "Bill," he said, "The first thing you do at 1600 Pennsylvania Avenue is get your name on the A list." Officially known as the VIP list, it entitles those on it to the best White House perks—the senior dining room, a chauffeured limousine to and from work, invitations to the key social functions, and the treasured right to play on the White House tennis court. Not knowing how to apply for the list, I simply took out a piece of White House stationery, directed that my name be placed on it, and gave the request to my secretary, an experienced Washington operator, with instructions to send it to "the ap-

propriate office." My name remained on the list throughout
my tenure in the Ford White House. After all, who wanted to
challenge the president's friend? (In fact, the list as such was
abolished by the Ford White House, and the perks were accorded by title; as an assistant to the president, I found my
title more than sufficient.)

Properly handled, these perks could be a powerful tool in
maintaining discipline among the always fractious staff of
egos that surround any president. Although this is getting
ahead of the story, at the end of my White House tenure,
some of the senior staff received a request from incoming
President-elect Jimmy Carter. He asked us to write him a
letter "giving me the benefit of your experience and your
thoughts about how we can run the best White House ever."
My letter was four pages long, filled with thoughtful suggestions about promoting efficiency, protecting the president
from unexpected political calamities, enhancing the position
of minorities, and balancing the federal budget. To conclude
on what I thought was a lighter note, my letter suggested
that he never forget the fact that controlling who played on
the White House tennis court was a powerful presidential
tool to enforce discipline and reward accomplishment. My
letter ended by intoning, "Do not neglect the power of the
tennis court."

To everyone's amazement, some months into the Carter
term, a memo from the president was leaked to *The Washington Post*. It proclaimed that no one was to play on the White
House tennis court without the express permission of the
president, and this rule was to apply whether the president
was "at home or abroad."

One of the first important decisions Ford made as president was to appoint a vice president. He chose Nelson
Rockefeller, former governor of New York State and leader
of the liberal wing of the Republican party. Ford asked him
to serve as head of domestic and social policy for the White
House, and as his first major assignment told him to devise a

plan to reform the nation's health care. True to form, Rockefeller hired the best experts and drafted a report. It was
delivered to Donald Rumsfeld, whom Ford had made his
chief administrative assistant. Rumsfeld, who was not a
strong supporter of the Rockefeller appointment as vice
president, cut the billionaire down to size. He marked up
Rockefeller's entire report with marginal notes, questions,
and comments, declaring it unfit and unready for the president's attention. This was a new experience for Rockefeller,
but he took it back, reworked it, and returned it to Rumsfeld,
who indicated it still was not good enough to give to the
president. Having already dropped Rockefeller into the slot
with all the rest of us White House flunkies, Rumsfeld was
not about to yield his power to a mere vice president.

At this point, Rockefeller decided there had been enough
hazing and decided to see the president in person. He simply telephoned Ford and said that he was not going to live
with this system, going through Rumsfeld to get to the president. The president told him he would instruct Rumsfeld
that Rockefeller could see him anytime he wanted, and furthermore, could send things directly to the Oval Office.
However, in the "big" White House everything has to be
logged, and even the vice president has to get on the schedule. Consequently, on the wall of the chief of staff's office in
the northwest corner of the West Wing of the White House is
a television monitor that records who goes in to visit the
president and where the president is. The chief of staff could
easily keep track of who was going in and out of the president's office, thus keeping tabs on both his good friends and
rivals. And even with Ford's open-door policy, the appoint-
ments secretary supervised the schedule to maintain order,
and the chief administrative officer supervised the schedule
and the paper flow. Never underestimate the power of whoever runs the inside machinery of the operation.

The liberal Rockefeller was dropped from the Ford ticket
in the 1976 campaign against Carter at the insistence of con-

servatives. At the time, rebellious conservatives were gaining control of the Republican party and trying to nominate Ronald Reagan to replace Ford. While it is very clear that the conservatives cost Rockefeller his job as vice president, his disaffection also helped cost Ford New York State in the 1976 election. Although turf battles can be fun and games, they can also turn into very serious business. Dealing with them early in an administration is one of a president's most disagreeable duties, and it is something that almost every executive hates. However, the White House works better when the president is aware of these battles and quells them early on with appropriate discipline.

2

Seeds of the S&L Disaster

One of the principal problems inherited by the Ford administration was inflation. Its immediate cause in the United States was the quadrupling of the price of crude oil by the Arab states in 1974, which pushed up the consumer price index by more than 11 percent. Academic economists have filled libraries trying to explain its fundamental causes and cures, ranging from the obvious one of printing too much money to the more subtle one of psychological hysteria as people race to buy ahead of rising prices. Whatever the real reasons—and there are many— we were stuck with the problem and had to do something about it.

During Richard Nixon's last days, the Congress recommended that the president hold a national conference involving all the major sectors in the economy, asking them to "put aside their domestic and political differences and work together in the spirit of discipline, compromise, and sacrifice for the common good." Early in his administration, President Ford decided to put all his weight behind this proposal from his old friends and colleagues in Congress. He had not yet parceled out the titles to his staff for the White House, but I had served him in a rather undefined portfolio ranging from developing issues to running the advance team. Consequently, he asked me to take charge of the project and act as director of what was to be known as the Conference on Inflation.

We turned it into a major extravaganza. We had subconferences all over the United States, and rented the largest ballroom in what now is the Washington Hilton for the grand finale. Secretary of State Henry Kissinger said to me, "If you survive this, Bill, you will be able to accomplish anything you wish to do in life."

Unfortunately, the best remembered product of the conference was the slogan "Whip Inflation Now," which was translated onto millions of celluloid-covered buttons as WIN. While it grew out of the spirit of shared sacrifice that animated the original proposal, it had little if any effect on stopping inflation, which is a brute economic fact not especially amenable to moral suasion. The buttons themselves collected dust in cartons, drawers, and other cubbyholes in the Old Executive Office Building during the Ford and into the Carter administration that followed, when they suddenly vanished. The Carter people tell me this had nothing to do with inflation, which had only grown worse. It developed out of a delicious scandal involving the dignified Wilbur Mills, chairman of the House Ways and Means Committee, who was discovered to have taken up with a stripper named Fanne Foxe. WIN was suddenly converted into an acronym for Wilbur Is Naughty, and the buttons at last were in some demand.

We all learn over the years that when someone's brainstorm turns out badly, to make sure everyone knows that it wasn't yours and that you had nothing to do with it. So, as far as the record was concerned, I opposed WIN every step of the way. Alan Greenspan, who was chairman of the president's own Council of Economic Advisers at the time, also insists to this day that he had nothing to do with the idea. Just in case you wondered, WIN was dreamed up by the financial columnist Sylvia Porter and pushed through by anonymous lower-level staff people. No one remembers who they were, which is of course what anonymous staff people are for. Even President Ford seemed to love the idea at the time, although his memory of it now could not be less clear.

Another lesson I learned by chairing the Conference on Inflation was how to limit the oratory of a long-winded politician while he is still holding the center of the stage. On the final day of the Conference, and at the final hour, the president was scheduled to speak before an audience of over a thousand people. But first, Senator Hubert Humphrey was scheduled to speak for the Democrats for fifteen minutes. While the president waited in the wings, the senator spoke for twenty-five minutes and showed no signs of slowing up. At my request, the Senate majority leader, Mike Mansfield, passed Hubert a note that read, "The president is ready to speak. Please come to an end." Hubert took the note, looked at it, crumpled it up, and continued with his speech. As the conference director, however, I had the power to control the public address system. The microphones were turned off, then back on. Hubert finally got the message and sat down.

The president came on, and with him came yet another lesson about how things are done in our government. Decision making in the White House is not always the well-organized and -staffed process I had envisioned it as an accountant back home in Grand Rapids. Often, too often, action stems from a presidential pronouncement no one suspected was coming, including at times the president himself. This was the case at the final session of the conference, when to my complete surprise the president announced that "within ten days," he would make recommendations on controlling inflation, reflecting the fine work of the conference. The Congress promptly invited him to deliver his message to a joint session.

Seven days later the conference staff had assembled a huge pile of papers with its own recommendations and those of the scores of committees that met all over the country under the auspices of government agencies including the Treasury, the Council of Economic Advisers, and others to which we had farmed out the work. We did not lack for suggestions as to what the president ought to say but, as might have been surmised from their varied parentage, many of the recommendations were diametrically opposed to each other. For example, one group claimed that prices were being forced up by rising wages, and that of course was attributed to unions and what their critics described as the monopoly position of labor. Unions, for their part, accused greedy industrialists of raising prices well beyond the level they needed to cover their labor contracts. Whether it was rising farm prices or expensive airline tickets, the reports carried the same kind of mutual finger-pointing.

On the eighth day, I found myself sitting in my office at 7:00 P.M. struggling to bring enough order from this intellectual chaos to devise a coherent anti-inflation program. Most of that night and the next day was spent writing the speech presenting the president's program. It may have been one of the most boring speeches ever delivered to any joint session. It espoused the prudent economics of tight budgeting, which was fundamentally sound. The President announced he would oppose spending on any new programs until the budget deficit was under control, which was an entirely new approach to government by any president. He started the deregulatory movement by suggesting that government regulations caused higher prices and by advocating the deregulation of the airlines and the trucking industry. The president also recommended numerous other anti-inflationary measures large and small, ranging from removing production controls on corn and rice to the WIN program itself, thirty-one proposals in all. On a good day Congress can usually absorb about three. It was not a speech, it was a treatise. This effort ended my career as a speech writer for President Ford. From then on, speeches were written by writers who understood less about a subject, and thus could view it from a broader perspective.

We did come to realize what makes inflation such an intractable political problem. While the Conference stressed that inflation hurts everyone—and in the long term, it does—the fact remains that inflation affects different parts of the economy very differently. The economist Arthur Okun, who recognized that, as the chief economic adviser of the Johnson administration, he bore some responsibility for inflation, remarked after he left government service that the principal social damage caused by unexpected inflation is that "it separates the sharpies from the suckers." Creditors and retirees were big losers because they loaned their savings to people who bought real estate, which increased in value while the money repaid to the savers had depreciated in value. Among the biggest losers were the institutions that served as intermediaries, the savings and loans: the cost of their deposits soared to double the income they earned from fixed-rate home mortgages.

As we all learned in Finance 101, one of the riskiest financial ventures is to borrow money on a short-term basis (in an S&L passbook, for example) and lend it on a long-term basis (in a thirty-year mortgage). The simple fact is that the savings and loans had always taken a tremendous interest-rate risk. They gambled that short-term interest rates would always be lower than the long-term mortgage rates, and until the great inflations of the 1970s, they won their bet. Moreover, they hardly worried about it, because the law set the rates of the deposits. But when inflation arrives, interest rates go up, and there is no law that people have to keep their deposits in S&Ls at low rates. So the S&Ls are in trouble unless they pay higher rates, and then they are in double trouble because they are paying more for money on deposit than they are receiving in interest income. The way to cure the problem was to stop inflation now (SIN)—no buttons, though.

We thought we had solved the inflation and S&L problem in the classic manner. Cutting government expenditures and putting the budget on the path to balance by vetoing numerous spending bills had lowered the inflation rate by half, to about 6 percent, and interest rates came down with it. For a time, President Ford's stream of vetoes played its intended role in this cycle by lowering expectations that reduced government deficits would reduce inflation. The S&L problem was fixed, but not for long. Inflation was re-ignited under the Carter administration deficits, and real estate prices and interest rates soared. The S&Ls were back in trouble. The inherent interest rate risks of the industry had not been cured by the Ford administration because S&Ls still borrowed short and lent long.

Another issue that provided valuable experience during my first Washington job was what become known as "deregulation." It later became one of Ronald Reagan's four major economic objectives; he believed, as did I, that government was stifling business and the taxpayer and that the economy would thrive if the dead hand of regulation was lifted from the enterprising spirit of the American people. The deregulation movement really got its public (as opposed to academic) start in the Ford administration at the Conference on Inflation, which had led to concrete proposals by the president. The conference blamed rising prices partly on regulatory restraints and recommended a close study of them in transport, communications, banking, and a number of other industries. Among those involved in the Conference were Roderick Hills of the White House legal staff, later head of the Securities and Exchange Commission; Paul McAvoy, a member of the Council of Economic Advisers and a Yale faculty member on leave; Alan Greenspan, chairman of the Council of Economic Advisers; and me. Greenspan had been nominated by President Nixon and had been left in limbo by Watergate. When Ford became president he asked me to interview Greenspan; and with my strong support, Ford reinstated his nomination. Without that support, Greenspan's very successful career might have been altered.

The administration of President Jimmy Carter followed us with deregulation policies for the airlines, trucking, and to some extent, communications, but not for the financial industry. So I was there when deregulation was born and was a strong advocate of it. I was also there when we figured out what was really wrong with the interest rate risks borne by the S&Ls in an inflationary economy, which we sought to cure by cutting inflation and not by dealing with the congenital defect. However, the misguided use of deregulation came later, when it was applied to the S&Ls by the Reagan Revolution. Much of the Reagan administration's deregulation was of great economic benefit, but applying the doctrine to the thrift industry, where in fact it really had little relevance, was a colossal error. Thrifts do not operate in the free market that is essential to competition, but in a market underwritten by the full faith and credit of the U.S. government and its insurance funds. When the play of the market cannot regulate activity, government controls must operate instead, or there will be no control at all, with disaster sure to follow.

Perhaps because, in part, the Conference on Inflation was viewed at the time as a close escape from potential public relations disaster, the president named me his assistant for economic affairs, which meant a full plate of problems. I became one of the six or seven assistants who reported directly to him. That meant, at least in theory, that we could go and see the president without having to ask the permission of anyone else in the White House (as noted, it was not as easy as that in practice). The rather mundane title "assistant to the president" turned out to be the highest in the White House, and there are few better positions from which to observe Washington at work.

Each president has his own style of decision making. Richard Nixon wanted a memorandum from everyone involved, with a note on top giving the view of his chief of staff. He generally seemed to favor making a decision based on paper, supplemented by discussion with only his closest associates. Ronald Reagan, in my more limited exposure to him, enjoyed meeting with the various proponents. It was said that from time to time he lost interest and dozed off, but the fact of the matter was that, like many things with Reagan, he was taking in a lot more than people gave him credit for. Like a good executive, he was concentrating on the important things that really mattered to him. The way he organized his White House, particularly in the early years, when James A. Baker was chief of staff, Edwin Meese was chief counsel, and Michael Deaver was chief image maker, indicated a desire to get a lot of views before he made a decision.

The Bush White House did not appear to do as much to present the president with alternative options and advocates, at least in the domestic area. George Bush tended to ask his staff to provide him with a solution. In fact, after one meeting at which his staff had been arguing vigorously among themselves, he is reported to have said, "Why don't you guys get together and get this straightened out before you bring it to me." The Bush administration never once invited me or the other regulators as a group to meet with the president or his senior White House staff and discuss the problems of the banking industry, which turned out to be the cause of the single most expensive new program launched during his four years in office: the rescue of the savings and loan industry and its millions of depositors.

That was not the way Gerald Ford liked to get his information before making a decision. Almost all of the Ford administration's economic policies were developed through the president's Economic Policy Board, which was run by me as its executive director. We met in the White House, more precisely in the Roosevelt Room across the hall from the

Oval Office, nearly every weekday morning at 8:30 A.M. During President Ford's first year in office, we actually met every single working day in order to create the continuity by which you can weld together a team. The regular participants were the administration's cabinet-level economic officials and Alan Greenspan as the president's chief economic adviser. We dealt with the country's many economic problems: the worst recession since the Great Depression; the financial failure of New York City; the first collapse of Pan American Airlines; the national coal miners' strike; the repercussions of the major oil embargo by OPEC; and many, many others that flowed through us to the President.* Even the director of the CIA, George Bush, had to come through our board because half of the CIA's activities were research related and much of this involved economic conditions around the world. We asked the agency whether the Soviet Union was in danger of collapsing under the weight of its inefficient economy. The CIA's answer was: Not likely!! Wrong, but we were all wrong about the strength of the Soviet economy—except that the noneconomist secretary of state, Henry Kissinger, confidently predicted that the bureaucracy would choke the Soviet economy to death "one of these years." It takes one to know one, you might say, because Henry was a world-class expert on bureaucracies and how they operated.

President Ford delighted in personally listening to advocates from both the private sector and from government. He encouraged argument to the point of vehemence, steering the debate by asking pointed questions but rarely if ever revealing his position. The nation's economic players had access to the White House, and members of the Economic Policy Board heard them out with the president. Everyone in the business world who had a message to deliver or a cause to espouse came to the board and met either with me or with

* For a detailed account, see *Presidential Decision Making: The Economic Policy Board,* by Roger Porter (Cambridge University Press, 1982).

William Gorog, my deputy for international affairs, or with
Roger Porter, my deputy for domestic policy. The president
regularly saw businesspeople, economists, labor leaders, and
farmers whenever he felt their voices would help him make
his decisions. He saw coal miners when strikes were threatened, shippers about international trade, and scores of others about problems whose urgency they felt demanded
presidential attention.

My job was that of an "honest broker," which is what *The
New York Times* formally dubbed me in an article on the operations of the Economic Policy Board. My formal title was
executive director of the Economic Policy Board. The director called the meetings, set the agenda, and distributed the
minutes as well as the papers that had been prepared by
members setting out their often rival views. It was my purpose to ensure that all views on every issue were fairly presented to the president. Ford never gave me any instructions
about designing the system. It was organized in the way I
thought would best suit him. With our Grand Rapids background, we seemed to have a lot in common in the way we
looked at things, and he approved of using the Economic
Policy Board for making decisions. Ford loved discussion
with people who brought something fresh and interesting to
the table. He abhorred personal innuendo. One day someone made an uncomplimentary remark about Tip O'Neill,
the speaker of the House of Representatives, the main stan-
dard-bearer of the Democrats at the time and our opponent
on many issues. The president indicated in no uncertain
terms that we were not to say disrespectful things about the
speaker.

The board ironed out disputes on many minor questions
so as to save the president's time and concentration for major issues, but its purpose was definitely not to reach a ho-
mogenized bureaucratic consensus at the lowest common
denominator. Quite the contrary, it existed principally to
clarify differences on major policies so the president could

make the fundamental political decisions that were his alone to make. From October 1974, to the end of Ford's presidency in December 1976, the board held 520 meetings and dealt with 1,539 agenda items. Ford was at 93 meetings, which meant he attended on average once a week, more if he was close to making a decision. My views on any given issue were not at issue in the meetings. What was important was that they did not become public, because that would impugn my honesty, credibility, and above all my openness and accessibility as a channel for brokering all views on behalf of the president. After the board meetings, I would accompany the president back to the Oval Office, and he would give his decision on the subject of the day. He often asked my views before checking the action box on the option paper or sending it back for more work. That is when he received them. An honest broker is not without opinions, influence, and perhaps power—after all, I was often the last person to speak to the president before he made a decision—but if the "honest broker" promotes his own views, his usefulness to the president would have been severely compromised.

In retrospect, this system seems very attractive, and not just to people like me who received such personal satisfaction from participating in it. In 1992, the Carnegie Endowment for International Peace and the Institute for International Economics, two Washington think tanks stuffed with high-powered Democratic and Republican wannabees aching to return to government, drew up their recommendations for the new president to staff the White House and organize his government. Those who did the research for the report agreed that the Ford White House was the best organized of all recent administrations in its ability to lay all the resources of the government before the president and ensure that his decisions were carried out. To be sure, they also said that good organization did not always produce good policy— nothing does. But that is not the point, which is that a council like this can be the best vehicle for giving the president a chance to make informed decisions on the economy. There seldom is a "right" decision, anyway, only some that are better than others.

At this writing, it seems to me that the way we ran our Economic Policy Board serves as a good model for his new Economic Security Council. In what was really his first major act of governance, Clinton introduced his style to the American people and his own administration at the economic meeting in Little Rock, Arkansas, almost two months before his inauguration. He seemed to be particularly well disposed to this open, though often messy process, which gave his economic appointees fair warning of what they were getting into well before the inevitable White House battle for the heart and mind of the new president began. Anyone who so enjoys being an advocate that he cannot stifle his natural temperament is a bad choice as an honest broker. That job demands somebody who will deal with procedure, see his assignment as presenting everyone's views fully to the president, and not spend his time trying to convince people, including the president, that he knows the right answer.

From the start, President Ford decided to involve his cabinet members directly in shaping his policies, so our board was composed not just of staff people, but of the principal economic players. This was a distinguished group of people who knew their own minds and spoke them. The secretary of the treasury, William Simon, a free-market proponent, served as chairman. The other regulars included the director of the Office of Management and Budget, James Lynn (as of this writing the recently retired CEO of Aetna Insurance Company) and his deputy, Paul O'Neill (CEO of Alcoa); Alan Greenspan (now chairman of the Fed); Brent Scowcroft, national security adviser in the Ford and Bush administrations; Frank Zarb, known as the "energy czar" (CEO of Smith Barney Inc.); John Dunlop, former dean of the college at Harvard and secretary of labor; Secretaries of Commerce Rogers Morton and later Elliot Richardson. Arthur Burns, whose experience in government stretched back more than twenty years to the Eisenhower administration, often attended. While a de facto member, Burns did not want to be an official member because his position as chairman of the Federal Reserve Board made it incumbent upon him to stay "independent" of the administration.

Cabinet secretaries such as Carla Hills of Health, Education and Welfare and William Coleman of Transportation would also attend as required. Rarely did any of them pass up the opportunity to come to the early morning sessions in the Roosevelt Room, because then, as now, all Washington officials, even cabinet officers, love to return to their office and tell the staff, "I've just come from the White House." Not only was their input important to help the president make up his mind, but to carry them along with him after he did so. Having been part of the process, participants will tend to support a presidential decision with greater fervor, even if they disagree. They often will do so, because the purpose of the council, and indeed the presidency itself, is not to ratify the sectional interest of each department but to strike a balance between the constituency it represents and the general good. Just as an old adage says that war is too important to be left to the generals, it is too dangerous to leave the Department of Agriculture alone to make farm policy or the Department of Commerce to determine policy for business. Each and every department is perfectly capable of making fine policies for its constituents and advancing their interests —indeed, that is what it is there for—but more often than not these policies will be drafted at the considerable expense of the rest of the country.

Each economic policy decision is related to many other domestic and usually some international considerations. Trade, agriculture, labor, and health care all have their interrelated impact on taxes, the budget, and even diplomacy. When making economic policy decisions, it is best to consult all the departments that may be affected and bring them together for a judgment, because they often do not realize, or do not want to realize, the ramifications of what they are doing. One not so minor example of this was once raised by Paul McAvoy of the Council of Economic Advisers, who questioned the use of our wheat export subsidies under Public Law 480, the "Food for Peace" program, to win the support of Third World countries for our policies and thus win their votes at the United Nations. Secretary of State Kissinger was not pleased with the question and said so. But McAvoy said the government should know how much it costs to buy political influence, and by his reckoning, the cost was in the billions. Questions like these are precisely the ones that should be asked at the Clinton administration's new National Economic Council.

The Economic Policy Board's finest hour may have come in dealing with the Great Recession after it hit in the autumn of 1974. The Ford administration had to change quickly from the president's principal domestic priority of fighting inflation. He had closely identified himself with this goal not only in the Conference on Inflation but in many of his public speeches thereafter. Our primary concern was to examine in detail what the administration ought to do, because neither we nor anyone else had any experience with an economy that was sliding into the deepest recession since the Great Depression of the 1930s while throwing off record increases in prices. A new word was even coined in the press, and it was just as ugly as the phenomenon it described: stagflation.

By and large Ford's advisors, including Simon and Greenspan, advised us to do nothing. They argued that the American economy was resilient and would recover. Moreover, they said, the government was running huge deficits, which blocked action. They described the situation as a classic inventory recession and predicted that the economy would bounce back, perhaps stronger than ever, when business worked off its overaccumulated stocks. In mid-November, the president himself acknowledged that the economy was weakening but said inflation was too high and stood fast on the program he had submitted to Congress.

But outside the council, a great many people had a different view, which was that we had to stimulate the economy with a major tax cut, and forget about the deficit for the time being. It seemed to me that we at least had to start making contingency plans if the economy continued to slow down. By December, I was urging the board to listen more carefully to the views of outside economists urging a shift in fiscal policy. What we did then was to arrange for the Economic Policy Board to invite a large number of those outsiders to a series of our regular economic review sessions just before Christmas. They included Walter Heller, who had been President Kennedy's economic adviser and had introduced the formal principles of Keynesian economics to government in America, and Charles Schultze, a former Democratic budget director who would later become President Carter's chief economic adviser.

These were people who certainly would never have been brought in if the White House was being run by a palace guard of insiders. We also brought in some of the economists from the departments who had different views, such as Sidney Jones from the Treasury Department; and we also sought specific outside advice on what to do, some of which turned out to be crucial. As a result, Ford heard a number of arguments and decided that a major tax cut was necessary. He had already conceded publicly ten days before that the nation was in a recession, and he was still enough of a creature of Congress to recognize the tremendous pressure this would put on him to act. At the economists' meetings, he indicated that the deficit was beyond belief, that he could never have imagined that he would preside over it, and that something had to be done. The only thing he could see to do was to cut taxes.

A stimulative tax cut was proposed early in January 1975 and rapidly put in place. The particular form it took was in fact proposed by two economists who normally would be very far outside the White House loop: Andrew Brimmer, who had been appointed as the first black member of the Federal Reserve Board by President Johnson; and Arthur Okun, a Democrat who had been Johnson's chief economic adviser. In separate memos, both suggested a temporary income tax cut that we eventually agreed would last one year and lower personal income taxes by 10 percent. Once again, advice from individuals outside the economic inner circle saved us from what could have been a political disaster. David Packard, the high-tech entrepreneur who was one of Ford's political confidants, did a quick calculation of how many thousands he would save on his taxes and so informed the president. After some discussion and further calculations by the Treasury, the proposed tax cut was capped at a maximum of $1,000 per person to avoid embarassing windfalls to millionaires like Packard.

The recovery from the 1975 recession was more rapid than that from most recessions. It will never be known whether the economy would have bounced back that quickly anyway, but the fact of the matter was that the president was given choices that Greenspan, Simon, and some of the others probably would not have presented him under more traditional operating conditions, and we did recover.

People are every bit as important as policy and the machinery of government (and often more interesting). Secretary of Commerce Morton was sometimes accompanied by his legal counsel, James Baker. I had interviewed Baker for the job at Morton's request, and recommended he be hired. Subsequently he did rather well in government as chief of staff and then secretary of the treasury for Reagan and secretary of state for Bush. He also developed a reputation as an election strategist. Even though he lost his first national campaign for Gerald Ford, he helped pull him up from thirty points behind Jimmy Carter in the polls to within two percent of victory.

Baker got into the game of running national elections by happenstance. Rogers Morton, was designated to run Ford's reelection campaign while Baker was his chief aide and briefcase carrier. Unfortunately, Morton fell ill with cancer and had to drop out after a couple of false starts even before Ford got the nomination. In desperation Ford decided that he would let Baker run the campaign, because he was a bright young fellow and already knew all of Morton's strategies. Baker was thrust into a role he had never played at the national level and told to run the campaign against Ronald Reagan's forces, which were gaining strength at a rate that clearly imperiled Ford's renomination. Baker with great skill was able to ultimately pull Ford through at the Republican convention by a meager 117 out of 2,257 delegates. He then went on to run Bush's successful campaign for the presidency. But politics is a tough game, and ultimately he lost one that maybe no one could have won, when his candidate stumbled over a weak economy and too many TV shots in his speedboat and golf cart.

Alan Greenspan seldom missed a meeting of our Economic Policy Board even though for several months he was in a delicate state of health. As the president's chief economist, he was deeply troubled by the recession. The sudden downturn following the explosion of oil prices in 1973 had caught everyone, including him, by surprise. It was little consolation to this hyper-conscientious cruncher of economic statistics that none of the score of top economists who had joined him at our Conference on Inflation had predicted that the bottom was falling out of the economy, either. But he took it hard, and one afternoon when we were at Blair House discussing the economy with Chancellor Helmut Schmidt of Germany, it all became too much. Schmidt was urging us to spur the economy by increasing government spending. Greenspan, long a fan of the free market guru

Ayn Rand, became agitated. He maintained a diplomatic bearing, but it was clear he was seething. While walking back across Pennsylvania Avenue to his office in the Old Executive Office Building, Greenspan suddenly collapsed. It would not have been helpful to the Ford administration for its chief economist to have been found flat on his back in the middle of Pennsylvania Avenue. So, as horns honked and passersby gawked, I hoisted him over my shoulder, fireman style, and carried him to his office in the Old Executive Office Building, where he was diagnosed as suffering from a case of nervous exhaustion and a bad back. Greenspan was forced to give us his advice lying down on a couch in the Roosevelt Room for the next several weeks of our daily board meetings.

Although our board operated through an honest broker keeping all important players in the loop, there was a way to beat that game by outflanking it and taking an idea directly to the president before it could be "honestly brokered." It will come as no surprise that the master of this outflanking movement was Henry Kissinger, who was the only cabinet officer permitted to send a regular stand-in. It usually was Thomas Enders, then assistant secretary of state for economic and business affairs. Kissinger at that time was serving not only as secretary of state but also as the director of the National Security Council, which gave him offices at both the State Department and in the White House and almost instant access to the president.

But even Henry finally got on board. What happened then was that Henry started giving speeches on economic topics, a subject even he admitted was not his long suit. So whenever he gave a speech on economics, we would let it be known that Henry was certainly a great statesman, but that he did not seem to have his economics right. The press would carry unnamed White House sources with our comments. For example, he suggested a Western consortium of oil-consuming countries to offset the huge oil price increases instituted by the Organization of Petroleum Exporting Countries. But we raised several questions. Should governments try to set fixed prices for energy? Who would set them, and how could we enforce them? They were never answered satisfactorily. Eventually his idea evolved into the International Energy Agency, headquartered in Paris and serving a useful advisory and information-gathering role but never the strong force for lower prices that the market itself finally turned out to be.

After a period of time marked by press comments noting that the administration questioned some of his economic schemes, Henry finally invited me to lunch with him at the State Department. An invitation like that, accompanied as it was by an offer of sherry before lunch, left no doubt that he meant business.

Henry was a very friendly host. He wanted to talk about how he could keep his speeches from getting bombed. He knew we, at the White House, had been "doing a job" on his economic proposals.

I said, "Why not bring your material to the board like everyone else? Then when you give an economic-type speech we will acclaim it!"

Henry responded, "I have never cleared my speeches with the White House. But for you, Bill, I'll give it a try."

I said, "Good, your speeches will be met with rave reviews, at least from us."

Henry began running his ideas on economic policy past us, although not the speeches themselves. But we were not in the business of correcting anyone's rhetoric, just trying to assure our administration spoke with one voice.

One of our early problems in international finance was the buildup of billions of dollars by the oil-producing countries after they raised their prices and could not put their huge profits to work quickly. Since these bank deposits accumulated during the deep and sharp recession of 1974–75—indeed they were one of its causes—we felt it was necessary to find a way to put these dollars back in the world economy, or to "recycle" them in the jargon of the time. Saudi Arabia, the Arab Emirates, Kuwait, and others, for example, had accumulated multibillion-dollar surpluses that they had not yet learned how to spend in their own underpopulated countries. Meanwhile, countries without oil, particularly in Latin America, were strangling on the new prices and were unable to buy imported goods. There were numerous proposals to organize the recycling under the aegis of governments, but the Ford administration, led by Treasury Secretary Simon, held out for private sector recycling of these petrodollars through the world's commercial banks at market interest rates. Thus the foundation was laid for the LDC (Less Developed Country) debt problem, especially in Latin America.

Recycling worked like this: Saudi Arabia deposited its oil profits in Citibank or Chase Manhattan at the going rate of interest. The big banks loaned the money to Mexico, Brazil, or Argentina (the MBA countries as *The Economist* christened them in honor of the eager young bankers who booked the loans and advanced their banking careers). The Latin borrowers then had enough money to buy goods from the United States and other countries. This put the petrodollars back into circulation rather than letting them sit sterile in the Kingdom of Saudi Arabia. Recycling was thought to be economically beneficial, and the government spent a good bit of time cheering on the banks as they lent more and more funds to the developing countries, with less and less concern for exactly how these loans would be repaid. When the loans came due, the bankers argued, they would just be rolled over at the current rate of interest or paid off by the newly revived economies of the borrowers. The most outspoken proponent of this process was Walter Wriston, chairman of Citicorp, who is said to have summed up the conventional wisdom of the day with a wisecrack: "Countries don't die, they just roll over." His argument was that a country's credit stood behind its debt. We have since learned, to our sorrow,

that this is not always the case. Nor was it a dependable policy even then. A brief survey of the international debts aris-
ing out of two world wars, plus an accounting of the
countries that defaulted on their international bonds during
the Depression, present a deplorable record of the repayment of large foreign debts.

While recycling may have looked good from a macroeco-
nomic view, its purely financial aspect was much more suspect. For example, if the Saudis had loaned their
petrodollars directly to Argentina, the U.S. banking system
would have been fairly well protected because it was the
Saudis who would be taking the risk. But they were smarter
than that; they let foreign banks take all the risk. Their deposits were still protected, but the banks' loans were not. The
whole thing exploded in 1982. Interest rates had climbed
into double digits to help the world sweat out the inflation of
the 1970s; the result was recession, and the borrowers simply
couldn't pay interest to the banks. By this time, the major
U.S. banks had loaned so much to the Third World that the
outstanding loans were the equivalent of three times their
capital. In other words, if the loans were not paid back, almost all of our major banks would have been broke.

Not everyone had agreed that the recycling of petrodollars
was such a great idea. At an Economic Policy Board meeting
one morning, President Ford was in attendance, and so was
Fed Chairman Arthur Burns. Arthur was known for his de-
liberative and often delphic statements delivered through a
cloud of smoke from his pipe (which rarely moved from his
lips). So when Arthur cleared his throat, removed his pipe
from his lips, and began to speak that morning, we all listened.

"These Latin American loans are not recycling," he said.
"Recycling, bah, these are just all bad debts." The rest of us
at the table looked at Arthur as someone who was getting old
and was still thinking in national, rather than international,
terms. But we paid him his due by saying, "Of course, Ar-

thur, that is something to be considered." And then we all promptly ignored him.

The entire Ford administration, including me, told the large banks that the process of recycling petrodollars to the less developed countries was beneficial, and perhaps even a patriotic duty. On the other hand, no one ever implied that the U.S. government would stand behind these loans. In fact, we never really considered the possibility that not repaying the loans might jeopardize the financial system. We thought that if Saudi Arabian dollars ended up in Brazil, the money would be spent for roads, machinery, and equipment, or other things to increase productivity. But as it happened, the money was mostly used to close the payments gap caused by higher oil prices, and therefore to maintain living standards and avoid hard choices by local politicians about future investment. Since the money did nothing to increase output and make the countries richer, the loans did not generate the profits from which they could be repaid. In other words, they were used up rather than invested. Thus, when it came time to get the money back, it was not there. This was the genesis of the Third World debt problem, which almost sank the U.S. banking system.

With the clear vision hindsight provides, it is easy to see that one of the larger problems facing the banking system in the 1980s was the direct result of very large loans to Latin American countries by major U.S. banks. We assumed that a free market would apply appropriate discipline, and in the long run, of course, it always has. But in the short run, many may die in the process of assuring the ultimate rationality and discipline of such a system. Latin America lost a decade of growth under the weight of its debts, and only now are the banks finally winding up the liquidation of their unpaid debts at thirty, forty, or fifty cents on the dollar—one reason they have been so cautious in lending to American business during the recession of the early 1990s. Back in the mid-1970s we in the Ford administration had the chance to deal with creation of the LDC debt problem as well as many other problems in the financial system, but we just did not see the magnitude of the trouble ahead. We saw only the short-term benefits of the loans to our industry and finance. But then, long-range planning has never been an outstanding attribute of our governmental process.

As we can see now, the banks' troubles began when they lost their big corporate customers to the investment-banker-operated commercial paper market early in the 1970s. Our banking laws prevented them from entering this market, so recycling petrodollars was their first big replacement activity; and that turned out to be a dud. Then came the financing of the big management buyouts of the 1980s known as leveraged buyouts, many of which also did not end up too well for the banks. When that line of business finally dried up (or worse) after the 1987 stock market crash, the banks in the late 1980s turned to real estate and bankrolled the Donald Trumps of this world. As one of the banks' principal regulators, the FDIC under my chairmanship advocated permitting the banks to break out of their straitjacket and provide a full line of financial services that could have returned them to lively, competitive health.

The Ford administration's principal economic priority was domestic: ending the recession and returning to stability. We believed the way back to a sound economy lay through cutting federal spending, because the budget deficit was running between $60 and $70 billion. In those days that sounded like quite a lot of money, and it was. If the deficit was only about one-quarter the size of the ones during the recession early in the 1990s, the size of the economy (as expressed by the dollar value of the gross national product) was only about one-quarter the size, too.

In his first State of the Union speech in January of 1975, President Ford minced no words when he said, "The state of the Union is not good." He announced an old-fashioned remedy: he would block all new government programs until the budget was brought under control. I helped write the speech, but it really was the work of Bob Hartmann, who had lost none of his rhetorical skills in following his old boss to the White House. For Ford's swearing-in ceremony, he came up with the great line, "I'm a Ford, not a Lincoln."

As a man of Congress, the president believed that the way to control spending was to control the amount of money Congress authorized. He therefore vetoed a series of authorizations that exceeded the limits he had set in his budget. Over a period of eighteen months, he vetoed more than fifty spending bills. All except one veto were sustained, and that one, raising railroad pensions, was supported by a powerful nationwide lobby. All others were sent back by Congress with a lower figure, which the president was able to sign. This is how the real Washington usually works. Congressmen were not really as upset by the president's vetoes as they proclaimed themselves to be. A veto enabled them to tell their constituents that they voted for more money, blame the president, and thankfully vote for less. Ford knew all along he could count on his vetoes being upheld with the votes of his loyal Republican friends acting as the linchpin of a shifting coalition of those who did not have constituent pressure on particular issues. This stream of vetoes, sustained by Congress, put the budget back on track and probably would have balanced it in two or three years if Ford had been reelected.

One more lesson learned: Our process of government depends on all parties to an issue presenting their views, almost as though they were in court. A group must place its views squarely before the White House, the Congress, or the regulatory agencies if it has any hope of a successful outcome. In plain language, this means that special interests, rather than being adverse to good government, are part of it. This was one of the fundamental ideas of James Madison, the father of our Constitution, although he called it "faction" in his day and designed our peculiarly American system of checks and balances to deal with it. The full and open play of special interests, so long as they do not become overpowering, is absolutely necessary to define the national interest.

One of the greatest difficulties in running an open, democratic government is ensuring that everyone has a chance to speak his piece without allowing any one person to gain enough power through financial or other means to enable him to make powerful demands that can be enforced. We are, in our system of government, continuously dealing with groups that accumulate power through contributions to political campaigns, and trying to limit that power. The press has also developed its own powers, but at least these are exercised in the open (or so we are assured by the media barons) and most times are used to gain influence rather than outright power. The political power of interest groups exercised through campaign finance is usually described by the harmless sounding Washington term, "access," which means the ability to go directly to people in authority and put forth a specific case. In practice, access can mean that a special interest has not only a chance to speak but to wave a financial club. One reason the government continuously passes new laws and issues regulations to deal with political contributions and conflicts of interest is that it is part of a running battle to keep the argument fair and open, so that the system can operate without undue duress. In my own experience, the best-known example of this special access was that enjoyed by Charles Keating, the notorious Lincoln Savings and Loan operator, who when asked whether his large contributions assured him influence over politicians, replied "I certainly hope so." This private access eventually cost the taxpayers billions. (More on that disaster later.)

What surprised me most about the process of balancing out competing interests was the failure of business to present its case effectively. Businessmen have to learn to understand government because of its direct effect on their revenues and profits and learn how to deal with it appropriately. They can use many of the same kinds of skills and information that a sales manager does, equally avoiding bribes and undue influence that would be rejected just as vehemently in private business. I thought that learning how to do this should be a regular branch of business training, and it led to one of my favorite Washington projects.

After President Ford had lost the 1976 election, I made a speech to the International Conference of Business School Deans explaining the importance of government to the bottom line of practically every business, and criticizing business schools for ignoring its importance. Several deans approached me and asked me what to do about it. I told them to start right on the campuses by teaching their students how Washington works. They laughed and said none of their faculty knew their way around Washington. Moreover, since the subject was not an accepted academic discipline with its own journal and jargon, they warned me that even the most brilliant business scholar on the faculty would be reluctant to take on the study of how business profits relate to government. Then, I suggested that the course could be taught in Washington by some of the vast number of qualified Ph.D. ex-faculty members who have served in government or still are in office.

My wife, Sally, and I subsequently visited a number of universities asking for commitments for this so far nonexistent program, which we had named the Washington Campus. We never called on any academic official without an introduction from potential contributors in the business community; the Bank of America was our reference at the University of California, and a number of computer manufacturers at the University of Texas. We ultimately signed up fifteen schools, including Dartmouth, Cornell, and Georgetown in the East; Michigan, Indiana, Ohio State, and Grand Valley State (of Grand Rapids, of course) in the Midwest; the University of

California at Berkeley and UCLA in the Far West; and North Carolina and Texas in the South.

Member schools send their business students to six-week summer courses on the Georgetown campus in Washington; corporate managers attend short courses during the winter school year. Since the first course was offered in 1977, the Washington Campus has grown dramatically. Republicans taught the first courses, mainly because a lot of them were available, having just been thrown out of office. These included Brent Scowcroft, NSC director under Ford and Bush; Richard Darman, senior Treasury and Budget official under Bush and Reagan; Richard Cheney, Bush's defense secretary; Roger Porter, former White House assistant; Sid Jones, who has served at both the Treasury and the Council of Economic Advisers; and others. They were later joined by Democrats including Stuart Eizenstat, whose White House job under President Carter was similar to mine under Ford, and Kevin Gottlieb, chief of staff for Senator Donald Riegle of Michigan.

One of the program's best features is that it does not require substantial private funding because it pays its own way. We brought in corporate leaders to observe the program, and they immediately were interested in the program for their own executives. Their contributions helped cover both parts of the program, which has had twenty-five of the Fortune 500 companies as clients.

The first point stressed in the curriculum is that Washington is not the enemy. The U.S. government is you. Washington is the congressmen and senators you elect, Washington is the people you pay. Most of them, including the career bureaucracy, are good people trying to do their job. And all can perform best if they are certain that all viewpoints are brought into play in decisions by officials, from the president on down.

* * *

My first sojourn in Washington was a great and lucky event. You might say that my greatest piece of luck was in having parents who saw to it that I was born in Grand Rapids and lived only a few blocks from the family of Gerald Ford. It was because of President Ford that I had the rare opportunity to observe how Washington works, especially under a leader who engaged himself personally in the important problems facing his government. Equally important, I had the opportunity to observe how problems can be created, and then fester, when the system does not work. Little did I imagine that I would be back almost a decade later to help clean up some of the problems we had left behind in our financial system. But when the Carter Democrats—and more important, 52 percent of the American people—wrote a premature end to the Ford administration, it was time to go back to private life. I was determined to get out of Washington, where former White House staffers were a dime a dozen, and worth exactly that. Most of all, it was my ambition to make myself a glaring exception to the almost universally correct statement about people who come to Washington for a temporary appointment to the upper levels of power: "They never go home."

3

Trying to Escape from the Beltway

Before I could actually depart from Washington, an interesting offer came my way that made me think of staying. One of my friends from Michigan, who was a director of National Public Radio, told me that they were seeking a new president. National Public Radio (NPR) is an unusually democratic institution, run by the hundreds of noncommercial radio stations that make up its membership. My friend Pat Callahan of Lansing, Michigan, knew that I had owned television and radio stations and was currently unemployed. He helped to arrange what turned out to be a very pleasant meeting with the Board of NPR, and we both decided we wanted to negotiate a contract. Then politics raised its ugly head.

It seemed that the Carter administration had heard a Republican might become director. The board reported to me that Bert Lance, the director of OMB and a member of the president's Georgia Mafia, had said that any member of the outgoing Republican administration was totally unacceptable because National Public Radio was the administration's communications operation. The board members were very upset, since this was the first time that any administration tried to interfere with the independence of the board. They said that Lance emphasized that he was expressing the deep conviction of the new president. The board's response was that neither he nor the president was in a position to veto its selection, and that his intervention violated the law. The board went on to explain that it was particularly concerned about public radio's finances and needed someone with financial as well as broadcast experience. Its members stood their ground with Lance and said they would continue negotiating with me.

But when I heard about this from Callahan, it was clear that it was my ticket out of Washington. I told the board members I was flattered by their interest and support, but that it really was not wise for them to challenge a new administration, no matter how misguided it might be. Lance and his OMB, after all, had the most important voice in NPR's funding. Thus, with a bit of disappointment, yet a sigh of relief, my talks with the board of NPR ended. Later, the administration put up its own certified candidate, Frank Mankiewicz, who had been Robert Kennedy's press secretary and George McGovern's campaign manager. Under his administration, National Public Radio went broke and had to be financially reorganized.

That experience definitely confirmed my view that getting out of Washington was the thing to do, but returning home to Grand Rapids also seemed to lack challenge. Although my birthplace is a wonderful city, there had to be new worlds to experience. An article in *The Wall Street Journal* about independent television stations indicated a career in broadcasting seemed a real opportunity. Independent stations meant those not affiliated with the networks; at the time these were not significant players in television, but they now are crowding the networks even in some of the major markets—WPIX in New York, KTLA in Los Angeles, and so on. At that time, the government was offering new licenses in a number of smaller cities on a competitive basis because it wanted to build up alternatives to the three networks. The basis of the competition was not an auction, instead the winner was the applicant deemed to be best for some vaguely defined standard of the "public interest."

The process of applying for a license under the constantly mutating rules of the Federal Communication Commission was the ultimate in bureaucratic rule making. Theoretically the idea of giving the license away to the best qualified applicant made sense—but in practice it was nonsense. The FCC developed concepts favoring local ownership, community involvement, financial resources, experience in the industry, and, in later days, minority participation. We put together separate groups to apply for franchises in Albany, New York; Omaha, Nebraska; and Little Rock, Arkansas, and won a piece of the Albany station. TV, of course, is a heavily regulated industry and working in it is an education in two ways. You first learn how much real good you can do in a regulated environment by ensuring fairness on the air and ensuring that all groups are represented in the public debate. But you also learn how much red tape is involved, how many senseless rules seem to be in place, and how much they increase costs. TV was an enjoyable and in many ways rewarding project, but not enough to engage me fully. Had my partners and I stayed in the business, we probably would have made millions and been media moguls today, because independent television that concentrated on alternative programming for its local market was on the rise. Instead, we treated it as a sideline and failed to realize its potential. In my later days as a federal bank regulator, it was useful to remember what it felt like to be a "regulatee." Though even with this sense of empathy, it took a big effort to make a small difference in the way bureaucracy works.

As a firm believer in serendipitous planning, I ended up spending my time, not in television, but in a Fortune 500 company in the mining business. In 1977, I joined the board of directors of the New York–based Phelps Dodge Corporation and later became its chief financial officer. My old friend and college roommate George Munroe had long been the company's chairman, and his many other accomplishments included a Rhodes scholarship, a Phi Beta Kappa key, and a forward position on an early Boston Celtics basketball team.

The complete story of Phelps Dodge in the early 1980s is a tale of near disaster and recovery. Phelps Dodge was the second largest copper-producing company in the United States and one of the ten largest in the world, manufacturing copper products in more than thirty countries. It was reputed to be the oldest company on the New York Stock Exchange, but it was hard to prove that claim. The company had been extraordinarily successful for many years when copper production was essentially controlled by relatively few participants. But the industry changed dramatically, first with technology and then with the nationalization of copper mines, particularly in Chile. Nationalized companies tend to produce in order to create jobs. This meant that the production and thus the price of copper was taken away from businessmen and put into the hands of politicians who were seeking maximum short-term returns from their nation's principal source of revenue. All of this, with a recession piled on top of it, put the company through the darkest days in its history.

One of my first opportunities at Phelps Dodge was using my government know-how to help an industry in difficulty, but this time from the other side of the fence and, for the first time, to lobby for big-time corporate America. There are many similarities between a large corporation and the government. Both demand diplomacy and other skills in interpersonal relationships, and both have their own bureaucracies engaging in the same sort of turf warfare. The politics of both organizations demand that those inside them work together for the common good, whether it is to increase profits or gain public support. They must provide something people will either buy or vote for.

The major difference between operating in the private sector and operating in the public sector is that the private sector produces a defined report card on a regular basis—a profit-and-loss statement with a bottom line that shows plus or minus. The public sector is much more diffused. The bottom line is only an election every two, four, or six years, and that may depend on things that are far more obscure than the actual performance of a government organization. Another real difference is that whatever you do in the public sector is done with close public observation and media attention. That tends to make public operators behave in a more guarded and circumspect manner than they might if they were working behind the normally closed doors of the private sector. However, in recent years, public scrutiny of the private sector has begun to bring it more into the open and make it more like government. Fighting battles with the press is becoming a regular part of private sector operations, although it is still a pale imitation of the way the game is played in government.

Even though my knowledge of mining was limited to distinguishing the top of a mine from the bottom, my job at Phelps Dodge put me in charge of all the staff operations of the company, that is, everything that actually did not mine ore, smelt it, or manufacture it into product and sell it. That meant I oversaw all corporate services: finance, legal, strategic planning, and public and government relations. To help in the government area, we were fortunate to have Charlie Burns as our man in Washington. Charlie was one of the best of a much maligned group, the Washington lobbyists.

Our job was to convince Congress and the administration that our industry needed a special tax credit that would be worth more than $100,000 a year. The particular tax break that we saw as absolutely essential to the future of the company and indeed the country was called safe harbor leasing, a highly technical provision in the tax code. It was essentially an investment tax credit for capital intensive industries. The traditional process industries such as steel, nonferrous metals, and paper, had fallen on hard times and joined together to seek relief from Congress. Many companies in these fields earned no profits and, therefore, could not benefit from a straight tax credit for modernizing their machinery. Normally they would deduct their investment costs against profits and thus reduce their income taxes, but at that time they were losing money and paying no taxes. Safe harbor leasing enabled them to realize on the investment tax credits they earned by, in effect, selling them to companies that could use them. You may argue that it is never good public policy to help troubled industries—and many free marketers who served with me in the Ford administration would argue precisely that. But the safe harbor leasing system helped Phelps Dodge to reequip, recover, and produce copper at prices that were competitive on world markets. Since then, its tax bills have amounted to millions more than the cost of the original tax break that helped preserve this and other basic industries in the United States.

Explaining the technicalities to most members of Congress was a large order, so we had to find the few members of Congress who specialized in this kind of taxation. Given the vast variety of issues before Congress, it is usually staff members who are best informed on this kind of fiscal arcanum. My experience made me realize that the staff is more important than any representative or senator in drafting highly technical language in special issue legislation. This should not be surprising. Members of Congress need to appear to be knowledgeable about every issue in America that might be subject to legislation. But no representative or senator can be expected to have detailed knowledge about all the implications of any piece of legislation, let alone all of them. Unless it involves their particular specialty or constituency, they rely on their staff. As a result, as the world has become more complex, the Congress has increased its staff by the hundreds. Unfortunately, some of these increases are necessary, but the problem is that there appear to be no built-in limitations.

Staff power does not mean that the big decisions are made at the staff level. These decisions are made by the real leaders, the president, the congressional leadership, and the members. But they are made in the company of a few trusted inside staff, normally after discussions with a vast number of lobbyists and others with an interest. The supposedly minor decisions, such as the definition of a safe harbor lease that can involve very big money indeed, are usually made by the staff. In the executive branch, we dealt with the Department of the Interior, the Treasury, and the White House staff. Usually one person is your government contact, and in the Carter White House it turned out to be Stuart Eizenstat, assistant to the president, and on the Hill the Ways and Means Committee's senior Republican, Representative Barber Conable, who later became president of the World Bank. To my surprise, I found the average member of Congress to be a reasonably capable individual who often was very competent at a specialty. (Some are ignorant about almost everything, but they are very few.) On the other hand, finance seldom lies within the average legislator's area of competence, since financial issues usually do not have high political visibility. Therefore, these issues tend to be even more staff directed.

Lobbying always raises the issue of where sound advocacy ends and improper influence begins. No line is more difficult to draw, nor more important to the effective operation of our government. Each person involved in the process has to draw that line for himself. Public disclosure of the activities of both lobbyists and congressmen affords the voters the opportunity to determine whether, in their opinion, their officials and the lobbyists they confronted drew the line in the proper place. When examining campaign contributions especially, it is not always an easy line to draw. But as the landmark Supreme Court opinion says in trying to describe pornography, it is difficult to define, but you know it when you see it. Citizens can, and do, recognize undue influence and improper advocacy when they see it.

Some of the time, acting as a lobbyist was enjoyable. After all, in my view our cause was just. I understood something about how government operated, and it was a pleasure to use my past experience for the benefit of my employer. When you are dealing in politics you are dealing with people, and by and large the people on the tax committees were good to work with because they were some of the brightest in the Congress. The idea that lobbying is a sin is erroneous. Like all lobbyists I was simply an advocate of what was right and good for the country, and incidentally also benefited my employer, Phelps Dodge. Our basic position was that these special tax provisions were equitable for all taxpayers because they would help the country preserve a basic industry. Others would argue that this was the worst sort of special interest legislation. Whoever was correct, the bill was passed in open session after full discussion and review.

In pressing for special legislative favors, the only argument that really works is one that is made in the public interest. Almost every exercise of power by government results in a benefit to some, but at the expense of others. (At least I have never found any policy decision that resulted in a universal benefit; that would be like finding the alchemists' secret or the economists' free lunch.) The lobbyist must recognize, and clearly and candidly let Congress and others know, who will lose and who will gain as the result of his requests. The worst thing that a lobbyist can do is attempt to mislead a congressman by failing to reveal the hidden results of a piece of legislation. My short career as an advocate before the Congress made that one thing very clear to me. Politicians, like the electorate, want a straight story and all the facts—and this includes the arguments against the proposal. Just like the rest of us, they hate to be fooled.

My experience at Phelps Dodge also included dealing with some of the toughest unions in the country: the United Mine

Workers and the United Steel Workers. Out of that came some bitter labor controversies. But by the time they took place, I had left to become dean of the Business School at Arizona State University, although I remained on the board of the company. In dealing with the unions, it was obvious that they were highly politicized organizations, often acting with what seemed to be irrational behavior dictated by internal union politics. For example, a major strike against Phelps Dodge in Arizona grew in large part out of a contest for the presidency of the union, with one candidate trying to outdo the others in promises to the rank and file. This forced a strike over an automatic cost-of-living clause in the union contract. However, for the company that sold its product in the world market, cost of living adjustments in the United States were not relevant to world prices.

The dispute was a disaster not only for the union but particularly for the Hispanics, many of whom were the major employees of the company. Law and order disappeared as the company hired replacements for the striking workers, and the governor called out the National Guard to keep the mines and smelter producing. Eventually the union was voted out as the workers' bargaining agent. I had done a lot of work with unions in the past because of their heavy representation in Michigan, and this confirmed my experience that all too often they lose sight of the fact that their future depends on the success of the company. No matter how strong the union, if the company comes on hard times and cannot succeed, it is the end for both.

My five-year commitment to Phelps Dodge ended in 1982 while the industry and the company were still in a recession. Much of my job had involved improving our financial efficiency, a grandiose term for cutting costs. A lot of what had to be done was completed, and my salary made me one of the most expensive executives; so it seemed appropriate for me to announce that in the interest of further economies, it was time to move on to something else.

Right on schedule, my friend Penn James called, as if he knew of my decision, which he didn't. He asked if I would consider being the deputy secretary of state for economic affairs in the Reagan administration. My old boss, Gerald Ford, called to urge me to go to Washington and talk with Al Haig, who was secretary of state. At first Haig had grand plans, but once he became involved in an unsuccessful effort to try to head off the Falklands War, he became too upset to give his post his attention. Before we could discuss it in any further detail, he was locked in a battle with the White House that he soon lost, at which point his resignation was accepted.

Shortly thereafter, a head-hunting firm called. Was I interested in becoming dean of the Business School at Arizona State University in Tempe, Arizona? I doubted that a small desert town would be my choice—and where was Tempe? But my interest was in something new, and a visit to the campus was arranged. To paraphrase the song from *Cabaret:* the campus was beautiful, the people were beautiful, the weather was beautiful. Furthermore, Tempe is actually part of Phoenix. The intriguing part of the situation was that the Arizona State University Business College was a large but young and still growing institution in need of a lot of "deaning." This meant it needed to organize itself for the next phase of its development, which in turn meant raising funds, establishing itself with the business community, and blocking out its own areas of special expertise. I had few formal qualifications—no Ph.D. and no experience in educational administration—but the job looked like a challenge and fun.

Arizona was in the middle of a land boom that was big even for that state, where boom and bust were a way of life. The S&Ls and the banks were contributing mightily by making large real estate loans that would later prove to be unsound. As an innocent bystander, I was aware that real estate prices were skyrocketing, loans were easy to come by, and S&L executives were becoming leading citizens in town.

Deans have to keep track of who is getting rich to find the big donors for their schools. Even some of our faculty were becoming millionaires, as their little farms on the edge of the desert turned into plots for potential development worth $25,000 an acre.

My connections with the Arizona business establishment took me into banking. As a very young accountant I had audited banks, but otherwise my previous relationship with bankers consisted mostly of borrowing money, complaining about their occasionally haphazard service, and noting with envy that most bankers were held in much higher esteem than certified public accountants, while not working as hard. Because of the deanship in the autumn of 1982, Jim Simmons, chief executive of the United Bank Corporation of Arizona, arranged my appointment as a real live and fully responsible director of the bank holding company he chaired. At that time, I gave little thought to any potential liability as a bank director. Nor was the difference between the responsibility of a director of the bank holding company and of the bank itself clear to me. But I would learn!

A bank is a very special kind of company chartered by the state or the federal government to do something no other business can do: collect, hold, and lend out other people's money at a profit. Only banks can have their deposits insured by the government and use the extremely complex and efficient payments system that moves billions of dollars around the country in seconds to grease the nation's commerce. (Imagine if you were a businessman in California and received a check for something you had sold to another business in New York—but could not use the money to pay your own bills until the check had gone back to New York to verify that the customer's money was really there, and your own bank was then informed of that fact—all via the U.S. mails!)

A bank holding company is legally defined as a standard kind of company that becomes very different when it decides to own this special institution called a bank. The directors of the bank holding company, a corporate animal that exists hardly anywhere else in the world, are responsible for protecting and fostering the investments of the stockholders and bondholders and ensuring that they get a fair return for risking their money. The directors of the bank are responsible for running a safe and sound banking operation. It is not hard to see how the two different responsibilities (and the two boards of directors) can come into conflict. The Federal Reserve, which oversees bank holding companies but not most banks, has for many years advanced the doctrine that bank holding companies must operate for the benefit of the banks they own, and that holding company directors, who often are also directors of the banks themselves, must put the obligations of the bank first. It is not hard to see why this doctrine has long been heavily disputed and was stretched to the breaking point during the bank failures of the 1980s. Whose money should the directors try to save first? The depositors' of the bank or the stockholders' of the holding company?

Only later when the banking crisis worsened and I found myself in the middle of it at the FDIC did the dilemma of these conflicting obligations make itself painfully clear.

Because CEO Jim Simmons seemed competent and I owed my appointment to him, he generally had my support on the board. Thus, like most bank directors, I began by providing more support than independence. This experience soon taught me how difficult it is to exercise independent control and judgment as a board member. Simmons was a good friend of all the directors, and we were reluctant to criticize him or his senior staff members, including the auditors and lawyers who were part of his team.

At several board meetings the directors raised pointed questions. Should the holding company be buying this or that piece of land? Should the bank be adding more branches when the trend in the industry was to consolidate them? Should our real estate lending continue to expand?

But whenever management came down hard for what it wanted—and most of the time it knew exactly what it wanted —whatever doubts I might have entertained as a director were overcome by the judgment that it was best to give management the benefit of the doubt. After all, it was in the front lines! Occasionally we directors did vote to override management. But the fact remained that management knew so much more about each issue that it was difficult for outside directors to learn enough to offer even intelligent argument unless they spotted something that was obviously reckless, negligent, or dishonest. That is why directors, and not only in banks, have often been so slow to act against management, waiting until the losses are so pervasive that it may be too late to save the company.

After I left the United Bank Corporation of Arizona to return to Washington, the bank was sold to the British-owned Union Bank of San Francisco. Price Waterhouse, the big accounting firm that was the Arizona bank's outside auditor, was sued by the new owners for a less-than-adequate audit. In a landmark suit, the bank won an over $300 million judgment against the accounting firm. However the case was later sent back for retrial.

The United Bank Corporation of Arizona was ultimately resold to Citicorp. As I looked at the record of the lawsuit, it became clear, much to my chagrin, that the bank which I thought I had served so diligently as an independent director had been guilty of a great many unsafe and unsound lending practices not revealed to us directors. But how an outside director could have learned about this is beyond me. If a bank officer is trying to cover up something it is very difficult to obtain answers without relying on the bank's own lawyers and auditors. The only other way would be for an outside director to run his own audit, and not only is that not a practical alternative but it would likely produce another failed audit.

As directors of the holding company, we received the reports of the state and federal regulators. But no real live regulator ever sat down with our board to discuss his observations during the three years that I was a director. Instead, they discussed their reports only with officers of the bank itself, although rules of the Federal Deposit Insurance Corporation required them to meet all directors. As directors, we responded quickly, or thought we did, to the bank examiners' requests for better documentation on loans or forecasts of income, better balance between interest rate risks and obligations, and even better verification of expense accounts. Of course we did not personally verify that all the reforms had actually been put into effect. No single director could do that. We relied on management and outside auditors.

At the FDIC, we directed our bank examiners to meet with directors of both our banks and their holding companies. My experience as a director made me ask myself how my behavior would have changed if I had known all that I later learned at the FDIC. I certainly would have had a much tougher and more independent attitude, and would likely have been a real pain to management. Remembering my own experience as a director, once at the FDIC I tried to hold directors to standards of an average individual exercising ordinary prudence. But it was not easy to apply a more merciful standard with the FDIC legal bureaucracy so ready to sue, an eager Congress looking for redress from the villains, and a press corps hunting for scapegoats.

One of the first things we did after my arrival at the FDIC was to develop a little blue book of about eight pages, describing a director's duties in the simplest possible English, intelligible to even the least educated of bank directors. With my fellow FDIC board member C. C. Hope taking the lead, we persuaded the other regulators to agree to join in publishing our new booklet. The result was a common standard for bank directors and a clearer definition of their obligations, which if performed would help protect them against suits if their bank failed and, even better, would induce diligence so as to make it less likely that the bank would fail in the first place.

In 1984 Arizona Governor Bruce Babbitt appointed me chairman of his newly formed Commission on Interstate Banking, an experience for which I should thank my Democratic friend, since it provided excellent training for a future FDIC chairman. Federal laws had long permitted states to decide which banks could do business within their borders, and almost all kept out banks from other states, thus limiting competition against their local banks. (There was another reason, especially in Western states with a populist tradition: local farmers and businessmen feared the big city banks would siphon away their deposits—which meant their savings—and lend them on Wall Street instead of recycling them to promote their own economic development.) Obviously the prime beneficiaries were the hometown banks, but times were changing. Out-of-state competitors had found ways around the state barriers through bank-by-mail offices, nationwide credit card operations and ties to brokerage accounts operated through the national securities houses. Most states, including Arizona, were considering reforms to regulate these national trends, and those in favor of interstate banking were ready to permit banks to operate throughout the United States, just as chain stores do. To explore the problem, Governor Babbitt created a commission that included all the local interests, large and small bankers, S&L executives, public representatives, and private businessmen.

The commission started off with a bang. At the first meeting, bankers and S&L operators heatedly disagreed. The large banks were split. Half wanted interstate banking, on the theory that they could sell out to larger, big-city banks at a fine price, since Arizona had a red-hot economy at the time. The other half preferred independence and protection from competition, especially from those awful New York and California banks.

Almost all the small banks were vehemently opposed to opening the state to interstate banking. They argued that the bankers from California, New York, and Illinois would come into their state, take out the local deposit monies put there by Arizona's good citizens, and ship the money immediately to Brazil or Argentina. Further, they would replace local citizen leadership with temporary hired hands who would be uninterested in the local community.

Because the principal savings and loans were already permitted to operate in other states, they were less vociferous. Like some of the bankers, the S&Ls were hoping that the big city bankers would come to town and pay top prices for the S&Ls in the booming Sunbelt.

While the committee was meeting during 1984 and 1985, the real estate markets in Arizona were moving even higher, and its economy was growing faster than any other state. Arizona was the envy of the country. As knowledge of the committee's study spread through the banking industry, some of the largest banks did indeed receive very attractive offers, all based on the expectation that the committee would recommend interstate banking in Arizona. Five of the six largest institutions eventually received buyout offers; not surprisingly, their representatives on the committee became increasingly stronger advocates of interstate banking. The smallest banks, with no buyers and more competition in sight, continued to oppose it in any form. Meanwhile, some of the medium-sized banks began to talk with potential purchasers, and they began wavering.

After a year of meetings, the members were dug in. It looked like an entire year had been spent accomplishing nothing, and that, as chairman, I would deliver only a fractured commission and produce only an ineffective report. At that point, our report to the governor could be summed up in two unhelpful words: "We disagree." Consequently, the

committee needed to throw a long pass for a big score, and
there would have to be a compromise that would take into
account the small banks' fear of being swallowed up. We
needed something to help the governor act; he favored some
form of interstate banking because he believed the competition would be good for consumers.

We needed to go for broke, and I announced that our next
meeting would be our last, since we had been debating for a
year with no results. Faced with a deadline, some of the
members began working out a compromise during a recess.
We would recommend interstate banking, but with a transition period. No outsider could buy a bank in Arizona that
had not been chartered before the committee made its report; that ban would remain in place for at least five years.
This meant only existing banks could be acquired; and that
would give them a corner on the market at the high prices
they expected, but only for a limited period. Hoping that
lightning would strike and they would sell out and become
millionaires by the five-year deadline, most of the small bank
presidents became convinced that this compromise was in
their interest, or at least was the best deal they could hope
for. The committee unanimously voted to recommend interstate banking on these terms, and Arizona became the first
state in the Sunbelt to do so—in fact, the first state in the
union except for the two icebox states of Alaska and Maine.
These have always allowed outsiders to come in because they
know so few really want to set up banks there, as opposed to
the salubrious climate of the Sunbelt.

The Arizona legislature voted overwhelmingly for our
plan exactly as we had proposed it, and the governor signed
it into law. Within a short period, five of the six largest banks
were sold to big city banks. When the real estate recession
hit, these acquired banks would almost certainly have failed
in the banking crisis that followed, just like the largest banks
in Texas. Had they failed as independents, the biggest loser
would have been the insurance fund of the Federal Deposit

Insurance Corporation. But they did not fail because they were supported by the banks that acquired them, such as Citibank, Chase, and Security Pacific. (In fact, all the major S&Ls in Arizona had failed by 1990.) Almost certainly, nothing that I would do later as chairman of the FDIC saved its insurance fund as much money as my interstate banking committee did in Arizona. So our committee's work resulted in legislation that was good for Arizona, good for the financial institutions of the United States, and good for the bankers of Arizona, but perhaps not in that order. Certainly the shareholders of the banks came off best; they sold out before the dam burst.

4

Return to Washington: A Room with a View

ven out in Arizona, Washington beckoned. Roger Porter, my old friend and colleague from the Ford administration, was working in the Reagan White House,
and he suggested the president appoint me co-
chairman of a White House conference on productivity in
1983. This project had been wished on the administration by
a Democratic Congress, which wanted to investigate why the
efficiency of U.S. industry was declining—a topic the White
House staff found a political nuisance. (Everything was supposed to be fine in the "city on the hill.") Ronald Reagan
addressed the conference in a twenty-minute speech we had
written for him; the Great Communicator saw the text only
an hour beforehand, yet he delivered it as if it were his own.
He even pronounced my name as we do (Seedman), and
made it sound as if we were the best of friends. While he
appeared pleased with the words of his White House conference staff, his in-house PR group was not enthusiastic.

The final report, delivered in April 1984, blamed the decline in productivity on poor management, insufficient savings, low capital investment, government interference in
private business, declining educational standards, and lack of
cooperation between labor and management. All these ideas
are a part of the political rhetoric of the early eighties; but

even though the report ended on the optimistic note that business was finding ways to reverse the trend, that was not good enough for the presidential image makers who were just then starting to rev up a reelection theme of "morning in America." The White House communications staff buried the report by withholding any official backing and merely issuing it to the press without comment late one Friday afternoon. As it turned out, the report predicted a strong recovery in manufacturing productivity, which in fact did occur by the end of the decade.

About that time Roger told me that the Treasury Department was looking for a new chairman of the Federal Deposit Insurance Corporation to succeed William Isaac. A Republican who was well liked in Congress, he had been appointed by Jimmy Carter and was therefore anathema to the Reagan administration. This was not a high prestige job, but the fact remained that every day, banking was looking like more of a challenging and interesting field. Roger wanted to put in my name as a long shot. My first reaction was negative. It wasn't exactly clear to me what the FDIC did, where it was located, or how it could affect banking; it certainly could not compete with the climate or scenery in Arizona. But my second reaction was, if they want to talk, let's talk. After three years of academic politics in Arizona, I had come to prefer the Washington style. The disagreements were no more intense, and the stakes were higher. Moreover, Arizona State University was growing into a major research institution, with an increasing need for private funding. My rapport with the president of the university was less than satisfactory, and that would become increasingly burdensome in my effort to raise enough money to keep improving the school of business.

But it was my wife, Sally, who cast the deciding vote for Washington. She had come to love it because of the cultural life and the interesting people there. Thus, I found myself talking to Assistant Secretary of the Treasury Thomas Healey, who was in charge of selecting a chairman for the FDIC.

He did a wonderful job of outlining the problems: bank failures had recently increased to almost sixty a year and the banks were groaning under bad loans, such as their hundreds of millions stuck in Latin America. He did not realize this would culminate in the worst banking crisis since the Great Depression, but he did warn me that the job would combine much grief with little glory and that it was of increasing importance to the safe operation of the U.S. banking system.

The administration wanted someone with a financial background, mature judgment, and experience of how Washington operated, my qualifications exactly. Moreover, the fact that I was at the normal retirement age of sixty-five was not held against me, since there could hardly be discrimination against the elderly with a president several years beyond sixty-five. Secretary of the Treasury James Baker had been consulted and was reported to have made one of his typical astute remarks: "He's fine, but Bill Seidman is too smart to take a job like FDIC chairman." But he appeared eager to have me take the job. So did Paul Volcker, an old friend who was chairman of the Federal Reserve Board. In encouraging me to accept, he warned that its difficulty would increase with the growing number of bank failures. Steven L. Skancke, a Treasury official who had worked with me on the productivity project (we had even written a book on the subject, *Productivity—The American Advantage*) told me I would be absolutely nuts to take the job. He argued that the FDIC was treated as merely a minor department of the Treasury, even though legally it was an independent agency with its own budget and board members who, strictly speaking, were not part of any administration. That made me prick up my ears.

The FDIC was conceived in 1933 as a result of the bank failures of the Great Depression, and the chief sponsor of the legislation that created the agency was none other than Senator Arthur Vandenberg of Grand Rapids. Senator Vandenberg was a good friend of my father's and is still a political hero in our part of Michigan. The senator espoused the new insurance program at the suggestion of a number of professors at the University of Michigan, including Claire Griffin, one of my favorite teachers when I was a graduate student there in the late 1940s. Griffin was a devoted free marketer, so his support for an industry-financed, government-guaranteed insurance program such as this was completely out of character. But during the Great Depression of the 1930s, many free marketers found themselves supporting things they never would have touched before 1929.

Deposit insurance did not gain universal support immediately. The big banks, which had no trouble safeguarding their reputations for solvency but dealt only with large companies and paid depositors very low interest, opposed it as unnecessary and anticompetitive. Franklin D. Roosevelt at first warned that deposit insurance would reduce the level of caution exercised by depositors, reducing their incentive to choose sound banks over more risky ones. But deposit insurance was strongly supported by smaller banks, who felt they needed it to compete for deposits with major institutions. It was also strongly supported by the savings and loan industry, which ultimately had a separate fund created to insure its deposits. Both were financed in the same way, with the banks or S&Ls paying annual premiums based on the amount of money they had on deposit. The money went into government-administered funds to reimburse the depositors of institutions that failed—not the stockholders or the bank officers, who were meant to lose out just like unsuccessful risk-takers in any business. The FDIC was considered one of the government's most successful inventions. It was to be known primarily for the FDIC sign at the teller's window, and the inclusion of its name in all bank advertising (required by law). Beyond that required recognition, the agency was virtually unknown to the public. It had been profitable since its inception—a most unusual result in government—and had accumulated a huge surplus of about $18 billion in premium income over the amount it had to pay out to the depositors of failed banks.

In its early days, the Federal Deposit Insurance Corporation handled hundreds of Depression failures, but then it settled down for a long period of reduced activity. Bank failures were infrequent, averaging about six per year from 1940 to 1980. This all changed in the climate of deregulation and the inflation-driven real estate market of the 1970s and 1980s. In 1984, one year before my term began, there had been nearly eighty bank failures, the most since the Great Depression. By the end of March 1985, when my name surfaced as a candidate, there had already been nineteen failures. Bank failures were becoming an increasing concern to the administration. Perhaps one of the reasons that my name had been received favorably in the White House and Treasury was that I could well remember the bank holiday crisis of 1933.

My previous experience in Washington indicated that this could be an unusually interesting job. True, the FDIC chairmanship was a poor position if one was interested in prestige and recognition through invitations to White House dinners or even cabinet-level parties. But I had more than my share of the high life as a White House assistant under Gerald Ford, so I could put that aside without any real regret (though it is always enjoyable to have a meal with the president, and his fancy and usually interesting guests).

Four reasons convinced me the FDIC was a find offering a potentially interesting tour of duty in government service. First, it was unusually independent, more so than most government agencies except the Federal Reserve Board, which also raises its own funds and answers to Congress and not the executive branch. The Fed of course is more important and visible because it controls some of the major levers of economic management through the supply of money and the level of interest rates, but the legal position of its seven governors was somewhat similar to the bipartisan board of three directors who run the FDIC. Although nominated by the president and confirmed by Congress, the members of the FDIC's board do not serve purely at the president's pleasure. Before their terms expire, they can only be removed "for appropriate cause," meaning doing something immoral, unethical, or worse. A mere policy disagreement with the sitting administration is not just cause, although this is still legally a very murky area. It was the Bush administration's position that it could remove appointees of independent agencies at will. Since the FDIC is not funded by congressional appropriations but by premiums set by law, the FDIC is not part of the administration's budget and claims it does not fall under the jurisdiction of the Office of Management and Budget. This makes for a great deal of flexibility in operations, as well as jealousy and annoyance inside the OMB.

Second, the institution had its own research staff, which could become an important source of financial data and analysis that might if necessary be marshaled to support a policy developed independently of the legislative and executive branches. Like the Fed, it also was able to pay more than the civil service scale and therefore attract talented people. Third, the agency had about $11 or $12 billion in loans and other assets it had taken out of failed banks (at the time that looked like a big number, but it did not last long). Managing and selling these assets would be an unusual challenge, and where my private sector experience would be most useful. Fourth, the FDIC was the principal bank supervisor for approximately 9,000 state banks, and thus an important regulatory agency as well as an insurer. The bank regulator with the most impressive list of clients was the comptroller of the currency, who supervised the generally larger national banks, which number about 4,000 but deploy twice the assets.

Thus, the FDIC looked like a government agency with an opportunity for innovation and independence—a gem of an opportunity as long as my objective was not fame, fortune, or entry into high society. In 1985, the FDIC was a low-visibility outfit, with little scrutiny from the president, Congress, or the press. In contrast to my work in the White House, with its need to toe the party line, the FDIC seemed to offer a chance to step quietly into an almost nongovernmental operation while still serving the country and trying to make a difference.

In addition, it would be a pleasure to be a part of the Reagan administration. Having started out as a part of the Rockefeller-Romney wing of the Republican party, a faction that considered both Barry Goldwater and Ronald Reagan dangerously far to the right, I had become a belated if genuine admirer of President Reagan. I believe he will go down in history as a president with real leadership abilities. My reassessment of Reagan began when he ran against Ford for the presidential nomination in 1976. My assignment was to study his record as governor of California. I was supposed to dig up as many mistakes and personal shortcomings as could be found. But after two months at the task, I came to the conclusion that Reagan had been a very good governor, and that an attack on his record would not pay political dividends. Of course, as I watched Reagan during his first years in office masterfully handling public opinion and the Congress, it became increasingly clear to me that he was not the mere movie actor-turned-public relations man that his critics portrayed him to be. In reality, he was a hard-driving executive who focused on what he really wanted. So it appeared that good luck had blessed me again. If the president would oblige and agree to my becoming the fourteenth chairman of the FDIC, the appointment would be accepted. The long and often miserable process of becoming an official presidential appointee began.

Of course, no one at the level of FDIC chairman is ever interviewed by the president himself. I had met him several times in planning sessions, including some connected with the speech we wrote for him on productivity. But he certainly did not know me personally; presidents do not know 5 percent of the people they appoint to act in their name. Instead, my appointment was turned over to the White House staff, in the person of Mark Sullivan, who was in charge of verifying my fitness for the job and seeing to it that Congress ultimately approved. Normally that would have been the job of Bob Tuttle as head of White House personnel, but his family had banking and S&L interests and he was disqualified. It was my good luck to draw Sullivan, a competent person who was easy to get along with, which is the exception rather than the rule in the White House personnel office. He was to guide me through the tortuous process required of all presidential appointees before actual confirmation occurs by vote of the Senate. The process leaves many in disarray. It begins with a background examination by the Federal Bureau of Investigation. It was not hard to imagine the FBI agent shaking his head in dismay bordering on disgust. Clearances of presidential appointees are among the most boring tasks in the agency—and he has to draw an appointee named Seidman who has lived or worked in Michigan, Massachusetts, New York, Arizona, Washington, D.C., and Hawaii, with business interests in Colorado, Florida, and New York, and a lot of places in between. Not only that, but this appointee has been out of the country dozens of times to places like Russia, the Mideast, South Africa, and Latin America—and it was necessary for the FBI to check up on his activities in every one of those places. From the FBI's point of view, the one saving grace about the whole thing must have been that my investigation was not marked priority; after all, it was for some nonjob, the chairman of the board of the FDIC, whatever that was.

The FBI check is only the first test. For a period of time before the president formally sends his name to the Senate, an appointee is merely the "chosen candidate." When his name becomes public, often by leak to test the temperature, he is left to swing in the breeze while everyone from the FBI to the press is given an opportunity to object on any conceivable ground—moral, physical, intellectual, or political. If the objections are unexpectedly strong, the White House can say it had not decided on that nomination anyway.

While all this potentially disastrous research was taking place, my work at Arizona State continued. In about six months, the FBI clearance process was completed, and turned over to the president's staff. My name was then sent to the Hill, and the Senate Banking Committee began its process of determining whether I was fit to hold high office.

The awesome power of Congress to make or break a potential appointee was quickly evident. Congress has the power to investigate any prior actions of the supplicant, whether in kindergarten, college, the board room, the bedroom, the front office, or the executive suite. Unfortunately, Congress is not one individual, but 535 members plus thousands of staffers, any one of whom can make the life of an appointee miserable. My particular tormentor was the chairman of the Banking Committee, Senator William Proxmire, Democrat from Wisconsin, famous for his "golden fleece" award for the most preposterous government expenditures, and for spending less on his reelection than any other senator. Proxmire was unique. Totally independent and righteous beyond human capability, he was not particularly inclined to be friendly with me. Why I really didn't know, but my guess was perhaps because I was a former CPA, who, like many CPAs in a major accounting firm, had experienced some violent disagreements with the agency that oversees the accountancy profession, the Securities and Exchange Commission. In the past, Proxmire had been mainly interested in the chairman of the Federal Reserve Board, the secretary of the treasury, or the comptroller of the currency. The FDIC had not been a principal concern. But bank failures were rising, and Proxmire and his chief of staff, Ken McLean (dubbed Senator McLean, because of his great power to influence the chairman), were beginning to have an increasing interest in the FDIC.

The traditional pilgrimage to Capitol Hill started with my courtesy calls on the senior members of the Senate Banking Committee. Senator Jake Garn of Utah, the senior Republican, was a very independent conservative who, like Proxmire, did not have to worry about reelection. A loyal soldier of the party, he was very helpful throughout the unpleasant confirmation process, and we later became good friends. Senator Proxmire, Democratic chairman of the committee, was reserved, but McLean was downright hostile. They seemed to have picked up the scent of a political victory. I soon discovered the problem.

The committee had information involving a famous insurance fraud case known by the name of the guilty company, Equity Funding. About a decade earlier, Equity Funding had collapsed after creating a huge number of phony insurance policies to blow up its stock price. When the fraud was discovered, the stock price plunged, catching even some of the savviest of investors, including Laurence Tisch of Loews and later owner of the Columbia Broadcasting System. Nine months before the fraud was revealed by a former employee, the firm of Seidman and Seidman, of which I was managing partner, had become Equity Funding's auditors. We inherited the insurance company as our clients after merging with Wolfson & Weiner, a small California firm of accountants. This was one merger that did us no good; Weiner subsequently went to jail for covering up his client's crimes.

My first knowledge that something was amiss with our newly inherited client was a call from our California partner, Robert Spencer, summoning me to an emergency meeting in Los Angeles. He took me to the Equity Funding computer center and then to an exact duplicate of those facilities a few blocks away. The latter operated at night, producing phony insurance policies to be placed in the records of the other office down the street during the day. It was an extraordinarily crooked and elaborate system, manufacturing huge profits that did not exist and creating a record of earnings growth unparalleled in the insurance business. The object was not to sell insurance but to produce high stock prices, which of course quickly dissolved into record losses once the fraud was exposed. The company had been a fraud from its inception.

Even though our firm had never completed an audit of the evil Equity, it appeared headed for breakup, my reputation for disgrace, and my career toward selling apples on the street corner. In fact, the firm survived and prospered under the able leadership of my successor, B. Z. Lee of Houston, Texas, who took over when my term as CEO was completed and when the firm was still negotiating with the SEC to reach a settlement on charges of failing to uncover the fraud. The problem was worked out in the usual way, with the firm neither admitting nor denying the allegations against it but agreeing never to do anything like it in the future. Lee also went to work with the other accountants to redeem the firm's standing in the profession. Ultimately, he even ended up being elected president of the American Institute of Certified Public Accountants. He was able to rally the troops to stick with the organization through those trying times. Later, there were much larger frauds, for which the CPAs at other partnerships were blamed for having failed to discover. But at the time, Equity Funding was one of the biggest in history.

Never even having been on Equity Funding's premises while it was operating and never having looked at its books, I had no personal involvement. The SEC took no action against me, but my responsibility as managing partner did some damage to my belief that I was a great manager. Equity Funding was probably the most notable and newsworthy white-collar fraud of its time. After an inside informant brought the details to *The Wall Street Journal,* it broke the story, none of which was any more favorable to auditors than to the actual perpetrators of the fraud. Lawsuits aplenty were filed against the accountants as well as the officers of the corporation. One shareholder's lawyer with a long memory wrote the Senate Banking Committee, saying that he had discovered many nefarious activities by Seidman and Seidman's managing partner and that he wished to reveal them to the committee so that they would not make the mistake of confirming me. Why, after ten years, did this lawyer have so much interest in the matter? A little history would be helpful.

As part of the Equity Funding lawsuits, depositions were taken, and this particular lawyer had taken mine. We spent about a week at it, and came to dislike each other immensely. At one point, the record showed, he began to emphasize his questions by moving around the table and poking his finger in my chest. I told him that if he did not get his finger under control, his arm was going to be broken. My lawyer hollered, "Let the record show that the lawyer for the plaintiff is on our side of the table." Some pushing and shoving took place, and he got the worst of this less-than-championship-caliber contest. He finally returned to his side of the table, and it was evident that we would never be friends.

Nevertheless it was a surprise when, ten years later, he considered the issue important enough to send the committee the entire transcript of the case—and at his own expense, because several hundred pages had been sequestered from the public record by the judge. Senator Proxmire's subordinates leaped with joy and settled down to study the transcript but could find no smoking gun. All of the pertinent information about me was already in the committee's files. (Staffers who examined the transcript indicated that the firm apparently needed to improve its due diligence examinations of prospective partners by merger—a judgment that none could deny.)

The entire confirmation proceedings took about six months. The older you are, the more history exists to be examined, and the longer the process takes, especially when the record has to be read and referred to the SEC, the IRS, and other agencies for possible objections. The hearings themselves therefore were something of an anticlimax. Senator Donald Riegle, a Democrat who would not be expected to be well disposed, made a fine speech commending me as a fellow Michigander. This was the result of the good luck that occasionally makes the difference in Washington. It so happened that Riegle's chief of staff, Kevin Gottlieb, had worked with me on the Washington Campus project and we had become friends. A tried and true Democrat, Gottlieb was also a very capable tried and true Washingtonian, which meant that he knew the utility of having friends on both sides of the aisle. He helped persuade his boss that the president was in any case going to nominate only Republicans, and as one of that breed of cat, I was not all that bad, even though at one time it had been rumored in Michigan that I might run against Riegle for the Senate.

The questions posed at the hearings were generally routine, and my responses could not be called memorable either. But two events stand out. First, it had been the practice of the FDIC to rescue big banks when they failed, holding all depositors harmless from loss, even those with more than the maximum deposit of $100,000 covered by FDIC insurance. This was called the "too big to fail" doctrine and was applied when a bank was thought big enough to jeopardize the entire financial system if it was allowed to go belly up. The FDIC had also attempted to protect all depositors at small banks by selling them to a bigger one that promised to honor the deposits as a way of preserving the goodwill of the failed bank it had bought. This was not possible in all cases, and in those limited and infrequent sales, big depositors in small banks were denied insurance payment on amounts over $100,000 because the FDIC had been unable to sell off the bankrupt bank. Small banks of course could not be rescued whole as "too big to fail" because their failure would not endanger the stability of the banking system.

The small banks saw a gross inequity in the system. Big

depositors in small banks could not be assured that they would be fully protected, while those in big banks were safe no matter what the size of their accounts. The doctrine had developed as a result of the rescue of the Continental Illinois Bank, where not only the depositors but even the bondholders were paid off. The regulators feared that if anyone doing business with this money center bank in Chicago were to suffer a major loss, confidence in the American financial system would be shaken. This differential treatment gave big banks an advantage, which I stated before Congress could not be justified on any grounds. I pledged to work my hardest to level the playing field. But the problem persisted throughout my term, and as later events will make clear, I was regrettably unable to achieve that one goal, although there was some progress. Under later legislation it became much more difficult to designate a bank as "too big to fail," by requiring not only the approval of the FDIC but of the Treasury and the Federal Reserve as well.

The second important event in the hearing was Senator Proxmire's effort to air his doubts about my confirmation. Instead of coming out and saying that he thought me an unacceptable candidate, he read into the record the problems of my firm with the Equity Funding case. He argued that while I was well qualified, the managing partner was responsible for the faults of his firm, even if not personally involved. Who could disagree? Our mistake was merging with a firm that had a crook for a partner. Given the chance, we would never do that again. Proxmire seemed to be positioning himself to criticize my stewardship of the FDIC if something were to go wrong. Then he would be able to point to the fact that he had brought up the record of Equity Funding and say, I told you so. But he also wanted to be able to work with me in office and did not want to come down so hard as to cut off all communication between us and make cooperation impossible.

He was the only member of the Banking Committee who

did not vote for my confirmation, and I resolved at that point to get him to change his view of me. Long afterward, when he had left the Senate and was writing a newspaper column, he wrote one approving my tenure at the FDIC, but he did not mention that he had opposed me at the time. Nevertheless, his initial opposition required a response. I replied in a civilized manner and expressed my view in other ways.

At the time of my confirmation hearings, we were without a dog, since our last dog, a mean little cairn terrier, fortunately had been disposed of in an unusual way. This beast was continually lifting his leg on the furniture inside our house, and when reprimanded by me, would retaliate with a ferocious attack. So when we moved, a friend took a liking to the animal and agreed to take him home. Our friend later moved to South Carolina and lived near a pond in which there was a very large alligator. Lo and behold, one day the alligator emerged from the pond, grabbed the dog, and ate him. When this was reported to us, we had a moment of silence but shed no tears.

We decided to get a large dog to make sure that it would not be molested by any of the alligators in Washington. We chose a beautiful Irish wolfhound puppy and then considered a name for him. Our dogs had always been named after contemporary and newsworthy individuals, for example "Pope" when His Holiness happened to arrive in the United States on the same day that we got a new dog. We considered naming our new puppy Chairman out of respect for my new job, but that would have meant rubbing the chairman's nose in it when he made a mistake. When the events of the day suggested Proxmire would be both topical and appropriate, Sally pointed out that Proxmire was a German name, and our dog was an Irish wolfhound. "Well," I said, "then it's going to have to be a German-Irish wolfhound so that I can proceed down the street, and with a commanding voice and a clear conscience, say, 'Heel, Proxmire,' 'Sit, Proxmire,'

'Stay, Proxmire,' and 'Proxmire, you'll get your dinner when I'm damned good and ready!' " The dog's name is proof that the Washington press does not know everything, because there was no mention of it until long after Senator Proxmire retired.

It was now time to visit the FDIC headquarters at 550 Seventeenth Street, N.W., and introduce myself to my predecessor, William Isaac. Chairman Isaac, a Republican appointed by President Carter, who apparently had wanted to be reappointed, but was denied the honor despite strong bipartisan support in Congress. He appeared reconciled to leaving and accorded me every courtesy. His reluctance to leave was understandable when he showed me his beautiful office. The visit confirmed that the FDIC was literally the place to be in Washington.

The chairman's office had the finest view in the city—a magnificent vista taking in the Washington Monument, the White House grounds, the Jefferson Memorial, the Tidal Basin, the Corcoran Gallery, Robert E. Lee's Mansion, the Department of Commerce, and much more. In Isaac's time, the chairman's office was decorated in blue brocade, and the windows were curtained with an enveloping pale blue shantung that hid the view unless the drapes were pushed back. I could not wait to get the job and take those blue babies down!

As it turned out, the chairman's office was not a great place to work. It was half the size of a basketball court, and the desk was placed with its back to the beautiful sights outside the window. This is a widely used Washington maneuver that forces a visitor to approach by taking a long walk across the room while the august presence studies him the entire way. I had my desk moved to a very small room with the same view next to the grand office, which was then turned into a conference and lunch room for me and my staff.

My own office was furnished with Kachina dolls and Indian rugs brought from New Mexico and Arizona at no expense to the taxpayer. The curtains in the big office did come down and were not replaced. Not a penny was spent for remodeling! The press loves to dig up a nice remodeling bill as an early indication of a new appointee's grandiose fiscal preferences. It was my pleasure to invite the financial reporters for the major newspapers to lunch so that they could examine my office for themselves. Among those who came during my first days in office to witness our frugal lifestyle were: Nathaniel Nash of *The New York Times,* Kathleen Day and Jerry Knight of *The Washington Post,* Monica Langley and Leon Wynter of *The Wall Street Journal,* Barbara Rehm of *The American Banker,* and David Skidmore of the A.P.

Isaac and his staff gave me a huge amount of material to read. I began to study what the FDIC chairman was supposed to do and know, including a whole new glossary: a "purchase and assumption transaction," the "cost test," nonmember banks, and other buzz words of bank regulation. But however opaque the jargon, my reading indicated that my new job would not be boring, nor would it be an easy task, even for an experienced old accountant and government hand like me.

5

In the Beginning—The Chairman Discovers His Fate

The Federal Deposit Insurance Corporation was an agency with a reputation for both efficiency and resistance to political pressure. It also was one of Washington's backwaters as long as banks remained dull, solvent places that closed at three in the afternoon so the tellers could use the rest of the day to balance the books while the officers were out on the golf course drumming up business. Never mind that the public was inconvenienced if it wanted to cash a check. That was before the invention of automatic teller machines and much else that changed banking forever. Have you heard of a man named Frank Wille? While he was a fine fellow, neither had anyone else. He and his wife, Barbara, were social friends of ours, but we had no official contact with him and were only vaguely aware that he headed one of the financial regulatory agencies—even though he was chairman of the FDIC and worked not a couple of hundred yards from me when my job was in the West Wing of the Ford White House.

But change in banking was coming, and it did not come without pain. When I started work as chairman on October 15, 1985, the FDIC's list of banks with major financial problems was growing, from 217 in 1980 to well over a thousand. With the true bureaucratic penchant for euphemism, it was called the "Problem Banks List," and new names were being added all the time. The problems in the larger banks centered on their loans to Latin American countries, a result of the mismanaged recycling process that had begun during the Ford administration and continued unchecked until the crash of 1982, when Mexico announced it could not pay interest on its bank loans. The difficulties of the smaller banks, for which the FDIC had more supervisory responsibility, were concentrated in the Midwest farm belt. An agricultural recession of a severity unparalleled since the Great Depression was forcing foreclosures of thousands of farmers who had borrowed optimistically to expand production with their nation's conquest of world markets. However, they suddenly found themselves trapped between sky-high interest rates that were wringing inflation out of the economy and the world recession that deflated their trade. In the Southwest, banks were squeezed by the collapse of oil prices after the bubble of the early eighties. By region, the banks' health was mixed because this combination of overextension and recession had not yet hit the Far West, the Northeast, or the South, where profits were strong. Looking over the entire country, it seemed reasonably certain that the FDIC was in for interesting and difficult times. We needed to reorganize and prepare for handling unprecedented insurance claims.

Studying the FDIC organizational chart was the first step. It had been changed several times by the previous chairman and had become too complex. We drew up a simple chart, with all the principal division heads reporting to the chairman: Bank Supervision, which oversaw the supervisors that examine banks' accounts; Liquidation, which sold the assets of failed banks; Accounting and Administration, which handled our own cash flow of billions a year in premiums; Congressional Relations, which was becoming increasingly important as bank problems affected the constituents of our friends in Congress; and Research, a somewhat neglected division that had spent a good part of its resources in handling the largest bank failure in the FDIC's history, the Continental Illinois Bank, and very little on real analysis and projection. In reorganizing the agency, we followed the precepts of my own White House productivity studies: "When in doubt cut it out, because every layer of management eliminated is a productivity gain."

While a budget existed, it had never really been used as an active instrument for management. We had no productivity standards—for example, how long does it take to do an examination of a $3 billion bank? The FDIC was just emerging from an era when it really had very little to do. Banks were so heavily regulated that supervising them was not very arduous except in the rare cases of outright fraud. The FDIC dealt mainly with small banks as regulator, and its examination methods were out of date. But as insurer, the FDIC was drawn into the big leagues in the 1980s when banks worth billions started tottering. We knew we had a great deal to learn about the new and sophisticated types of banking operations, the loans to Third World countries, and the leveraged buyouts that were coming into vogue.

One of my earliest announcements was to assure all members of the professional staff that no changes in personnel would be made for six months, which would give me a chance to evaluate them and give them some near-term security while they evaluated the way the agency operated under my chairmanship. Within a year, most of the key players would be gone, and a new team would be put in place to deal with a new set of realities due to the emergence of the banking industry's worst crisis in half a century.

Only a few weeks after my arrival, before we could even build our new structure, we received a visit from some young examiners from the Office of Management and Budget (OMB), which is the White House financial management arm and office of general know-it-alls. Their mission was to examine our budget for the purpose of determining whether we were operating in a manner satisfactory to the administration. The Office of Management and Budget had tried to assert management control over the FDIC's budget in the past, but had never pressed its case because the agency had made money out of its bank premiums and posed no problems for the budget. Because OMB supervises funds appropriated by the Congress, and all of our agency's funds came from the deposit insurance premiums paid by the banks, not from the public purse, there was a real question about its right to supervise our funds and how we spent them. This independence from White House policy and other control had helped to make the chairmanship of the agency an attractive place where an independent board could run the shop.

The examiners told us that they had been instructed by James Miller, director of OMB, that henceforth they would be supervising our budget just like any other government agency that depended—as we did not—on funds appropriated by Congress and approved by the president. They were particularly interested in whether we were reducing the number of bank supervisors we employed, and reminded us of a letter of instruction to that effect which had arrived before I was sworn into office. At one time in the late 1970s the FDIC had reached its peak staff of almost 2,500 bank examiners. The Reagan administration began ordering staff reductions because its deregulation policies were directed at getting the government off the backs of business. The FDIC board had been following administration policy voluntarily.

By 1983 our number of supervisors had shrunk to about 1,400, and it was hard to hire good new auditors because government hiring policies were so cumbersome and the best students went elsewhere (it took nearly six months to make an offer). But the main reason that the number had shrunk was that the Reagan administration held the view that fewer supervisors would be needed when financial institutions were deregulated. They thought that fewer people would be needed to look over the shoulders of the banks. It was my view, and one expressed many times, that deregulation requires more, not less, supervision—for the same reason that deregulated and therefore more cost-conscious airlines require more safety supervision. The more freedom you give bankers to undertake various kinds of risk, the more you have to watch them, especially if your agency is the one that is offering the government's full faith and credit guarantee of the bank's balance sheet by insuring its depositors in case the risky loans turn sour.

My predecessor as chairman, William Isaac, a loyal Republican but a man who could see what was coming in the banking industry, had begun to change direction and start hiring new inspectors. As his term ended, he proceeded, despite the views of the OMB: the prospect of leaving office gives courage to one's true convictions.

My first few days in office convinced me that our banking system and its insurance provider were heading into some very trying times, and that our understaffed supervision division was lagging far behind in its examinations. The OMB was asking us to cut an additional 10 percent, which would have meant another hundred reductions below the number of supervisors we already had. We probably would have to fight them to keep control of our agency, its standards, and the solvency of the banking system.

While the FDIC had not previously been under the jurisdiction of the Office of Management and Budget, occasionally the OMB tried to assert authority, citing what is called the Anti-Deficiency Act. This 1950's statute stipulates that any government agency overspending its budget is subject to discipline by the OMB, which ultimately could include criminal penalties. My general counsel, Jack Murphy, researched our legal position. His report was mixed. He said the statute was not entirely clear and we could rely on a long tradition of not having submitted to OMB's surveillance and budget approval. His opinion was that, on balance, we were not subject to OMB jurisdiction; but if we wanted to test it, our only appeal was to the Justice Department. Ultimately, of course, Justice listens to the White House—not a terribly encouraging prospect. If we wanted to force the issue, it would probably be passed straight to the White House for a decision by the chief of staff or the president himself.

And so began the first of my problems as an independent agency chairman: Should we fight to maintain the independence of the FDIC or should we be "team players" and change the status of the institution? Of course the staff at the FDIC was vehement in its view that the agency's independence was essential to its operating efficiency. They believed that it was critical to maintain the FDIC's record of freedom from the political influence that had afflicted so many other government agencies—most especially our sister agency, the Federal Savings and Loan Insurance Corporation. This agency, which was partly funded by Congress and under OMB control, found itself more vulnerable to pressures from members of Congress and their constituents. The FDIC staff members made this issue a test of valor: Did their bosses have the courage to fight the establishment? But, of course, the controlling issue in the decision that had to be made was what was the best way to run the agency for the protection of the banking system. With the other two members of the board behind me, the entire staff urged me to throw myself in the path of the OMB power grab—even if it resulted in a human sacrifice.

We did not have to look very far to find people who said that I would be fighting OMB for our own personal aggrandizement and freedom. But in the end you do what is needed for the organization and you serve in the job you have sworn to do. In the Ford administration, I was the ultimate loyalist to the president's policies and worked closely with the OMB, which served as his watchdog in ensuring they were carried out. In an independent agency like the FDIC, your duty is to develop and support policies appropriate for the agency, which is a creature of Congress charged with a very specific task. This often puts the agency and its chief in conflict with the administration and its chief management and financial arm. Such conflicts between an administration and the independent agencies are not uncommon. Almost every administration crosses swords with the Federal Reserve over interest rates and what is best for the economy. At some point in its term, almost every administration decides it would like to curtail or eliminate independent agencies. In the Reagan administration, Ed Meese, White House counsel and subsequently attorney general, spent a great deal of time advocating the elimination of all independent agencies because they would not hew to administration policy. That, of course, is why Congress made them independent in the first place.

We told the OMB examiners that we would be pleased to meet with them and give them any information they wanted. We also told them we believed that they had no jurisdiction over us and asked them to return to their offices across the street in the Old Executive Office Building. Not long afterward, a summons arrived from OMB recommending an appearance to discuss the matter further. Accompanied by my deputy, David Cooke, I walked across Seventeenth Street to the office of James Miller in the Old Executive Office Building. During the Ford administration, he had worked for me on problems of inflation in the Office of Price Stability. I had only a vague memory of his abilities, and it was limited to the impression of an aggressive official without a great deal of diplomatic skill. We began our meeting in the usual manner, calm and factual. Our lawyers believed that we were not subject to OMB's budgetary jurisdiction. Miller's lawyers insisted we were, under the Anti-Deficiency Act and he intended to exercise control over the FDIC, period! He was the administration's big gorilla, and he was determined to let us know who was in charge. As we left, Miller put his hand on my shoulder, and said, "Well, Bill, I'm afraid we've gotcha, we've just gotcha."

Walking back to my office, I thought to myself that Mr. Miller had not got me yet. We would seek to make it a long, distasteful job for him. My decision to join the FDIC was based partly on its independence, and that independence was already challenged in my first days on board. What should our next step be? What support did Miller really have? Fortunately, with a few calls I guessed that Miller and the OMB were making their power play primarily on their own initiative. It was not backed strongly by the president's chief of staff, Donald Regan. This was confirmed when I ran into him at a social function and mentioned to him in passing that we were having some arguments with OMB. "Oh, everybody does," he said. He had no special information on our problem or interest in it. If he had, he was certainly outspoken enough to have insisted there and then that we follow orders. But he did not. Miller seemed to be acting mainly on his own. That meant the battle could be waged far out of public view as an agency turf war and not a confrontation on principle with the White House staff and the president.

Unfortunately, the process of brokering disagreements through a formal policy council of the type that was a specialty in the Ford administration was no longer available under Reagan to resolve our controversy with OMB. We conducted negotiations for months in an attempt to find a way to work together on the problem of who had the last word on the size and structure of our agency. Ultimately we reached a stalemate. In a final letter, OMB's deputy director wrote that they could not understand how we could take a position in opposition to the president and labeled me a "disloyal Reaganite." No more derogatory epithet existed in official Washington at that time. But I had been quickly transformed from a policy broker to a fighter. That is not surprising because the job often makes the man. In the Washington bureaucracy they have a good way of explaining how your job and its goals affect your position on any issue; they say, "Where you sit is where you stand."

We knew that an intentional violation of the Anti-Deficiency Act could potentially be a criminal offense, and that OMB was not unwilling to explore this option. The agency had already threatened Chairman Edwin Gray of the Home Loan Bank Board with jail when he overspent his budget to take care of a failed S&L. Maybe they thought it would be a political plus for me to be sent up the river, but that seemed unlikely. We decided that our only option was to take the matter to Congress. Armed with the OMB's uncompromising letter accusing me of disloyalty and worse, we went to see Chairman Proxmire and Senator Garn of the Senate Banking Committee.

Bank failures were on the rise and the committee was increasingly apprehensive about problems in the financial industry, much more so than the administration, which was still fighting its battles over deregulation through the OMB and others. Banking committee members were growing anxious, as politicians normally do when faced with the possibility of being blamed for failure, and they wanted us to increase the number of bank examiners. Meetings were arranged with Representative Fernand St. Germain, chairman of the House Banking Committee, and the ranking Republican member, Chalmers Wylie. In a fine display of placing the country's interest first, Republicans and Democrats in both houses supported the continued independence of the FDIC in a bill to exempt us from the Anti-Deficiency Act. It didn't hurt that Congress generally prefers an independent agency to one under the administration's control, since it can exercise more influence over an independent agency than over one controlled by any administration. But no agency, independent or not, can really avoid the influence of Congress. However, there are many voices on Capitol Hill, and the wise leader of an independent agency will try to ensure that his committee chairman, as well as the majority of the rest, understand his agency's policies and how he is applying them.

Once those at OMB learned that we had jumped ship and taken the question of independence over their heads to Congress, their anger intensified. Miller went to the House and Senate Banking Committee chairmen to protest. There are very few people I would rather have firing at me from the opposite trench in a war like this than Jim Miller. His take-no-prisoners approach was not well received on the Hill, where he tended to treat members of Congress as second-class citizens. The Senate Banking Committee, with Senator Riegle in the lead role, proposed to exempt the FDIC and other regulators from the Anti-Deficiency Act. He did many other important things to help banking but nothing more important to our work than this. Even in defeat, Miller persisted. In President Reagan's message signing the bill, which probably was at least monitored if not actually written by the OMB, the president highlighted our exemption as undesirable, but said it was not sufficient reason to veto the bill. His message read: "I am signing this legislation with a firm understanding that notwithstanding the provisions of section 505 [the exemption for the FDIC], the President retains his inherent supervisory authority under Article II of the Constitution to insure that all Executive Branch agencies are spending appropriated funds in accordance with law."

The administration had been blinded by that word "deregulation," which meant that everyone had to follow the line even if it was misapplied. By the time the idea got down to the middle ranks where we were, deviation of any sort was not permitted. Someone on top who had interested himself in how policy was actually working would have looked at our situation and might have realized that the principle of deregulation did not apply in the same way to an industry like banking, where the deposits that were the very basis of its business were insured by the government. But raising such questions at our level was seen as disloyalty, which stopped another traditional check that exists in the government. Most political ideas encounter practical objections and are modified as they move down the chain of command, but this was a matter of outright ideology that had helped to elect Reagan. The troops at the lower levels wanted to prove their loyalty and allegiance by carrying out the party platform with 110 percent effort.

Such demands for blind obedience are not by any means limited to the government. We all have certainly seen the chairmen of great corporations decree new strategic directions and pay a huge price for not listening to the feedback warning of the possible costs of his decision. During the decade of restructuring in the 1980s, many corporations realized they were dissipating their resources in new and unfamiliar lines of business that had originally seemed profitable. It became common to hear chairmen ordering a "return to roots," which would force the company to concentrate on its core business. Too often, however, the middle managers would get the word and prune away even the profitable shoots. The order of the day becomes: "Get rid of it. Throw it out." (That is what happened at RCA, when it dumped Gibson Greeting Cards in a fast auction. Bill Simon who was standing there waiting, bought it at a bargain, later restructured it, and went public with it for a near $100 million gain.)

The best check for the head man is to install a fearless friend who can question his decisions without fear of being sent to Siberia. Any structure that challenges "group think" is useful, but the essential is a leader who is aware of the danger of being blindsided by the unexpected event or the unargued idea. A real leader has to be ready to listen to and encourage people who are ready to tell him things, whether or not he wants to hear them.

*   *   *

Free, free at least for a time, from the OMB, and its auditors. Still it was clear to me that if we, at the FDIC, did not do a better job of budgeting and management, the argument might well be made that we needed the "tender loving care" of the Office of Management and Budget. Therefore, better management became a top priority.

One way to reduce operating costs is to reduce the staff. Our most likely place for staff reduction was the legal group. Laws of course are the main product of the nation's capital, and the District of Columbia has more lawyers per capita than any state in the union. We at the FDIC were doing our part; at the time of my arrival, we had about 28,000 active lawsuits going and a legal staff of 487 that reveled in litigation.

Most of the suits had been filed to collect loans made by banks that had failed, which meant we were primarily involved in the unpleasant business of collecting bad debts. Borrowers often became reluctant to repay loans after a bank had failed and its assets had been turned over to the FDIC because they reckoned they could get a better deal from the government. Some tried to argue that the government had no right to collect, even though the government had repaid the bank's depositors from insurance funds and was trying to recoup what it could from the bank's assets. Many of them really were hoping that they could persuade their congressional representatives to raise political pressure that would relieve their financial problems. (Remember, the fact that their businesses had gone sour and they could not pay interest on their loans had pulled down their banks, not vice versa.) Consequently, Congress was swamped with calls from debtors, many of whom were past or potential campaign contributors seeking help from their oppressive government and relief from their legal obligations. The borrowers' anxiety was understandable. When a borrower goes to his banker for help in working out his problems, he knows that sacrifices and compromises he makes today will

be remembered by the bank tomorrow when times get better
and he returns for credit. No such goodwill could be stored
up with the hard-eyed bureaucrats of the federal government. The FDIC was acting as a collection agency and not a
bank, and in the debtors' view it was even worse—we were a
government collection agency.

Thousands of lawsuits against these people meant hundreds of millions of dollars in legal expenses. Since most
were farmed out to local lawyers who knew the situation,
much of our legal division's work was the supervision of
other lawyers. However, a sizable group was involved in
"D&O" suits—another nasty business that entailed suing the
directors and officers of banks for failing to carry out their
legal obligations. The policy at the FDIC was to sue all directors and officers of failed institutions on the assumption that
allowing a bank to fail had to be the result of faulty, improper, unwise, negligent, or illegal activities by the directors
and officers. This tough doctrine stemmed from the fact that
for many years only an infinitesimal percentage of the nation's nearly 15,000 banks failed—no more than twenty in
any year since the Depression. It seemed a reasonable pre-
sumption that a bank had to have been grossly mismanaged
in order to fail in a tightly regulated environment with interest rates set by law and the economy generally sound and
predictable.

In previous years when regulation was tighter, banks
had to do something awfully stupid or outright criminal in
order to fail, and very few did. Directors then might be presumed to have been more closely involved in a bank failure,
or else so derelict by inattention or pure laziness that they
deserved to be sued. When banks were allowed to operate
with less regulation, the potential for failure through mistakes was greater.

In the eighties, with deregulation, farm deflation, international competition, and real estate inflation, banks could and
did fail with just poor to average, and not necessarily negli-

gent or even crooked, management. We needed to review our sue-we-must policy, but how were we to decide which suits to pursue and which suits to drop? The FDIC did not have a risk-reward system for evaluating its legal attack machinery. If we believed we were owed money we sued, despite the fact that it was sometimes rather evident that it would cost us more to win a lawsuit than we could possibly hope to extract from the bankrupt debtors whose failure had helped bring down their banks.

My experience as a bank holding company director in Arizona made me very conscious of the potential for managers to influence their directors, and for directors to be unable to detect well-hidden fraud. Their responsibility and thus their liability should be limited to what they could reasonably be expected to do as directors. It was for this reason that we changed the basic policy which, at the time I arrived, was to sue practically every director of every bank that failed: we would evaluate each director's behavior individually and sue only when we could make a cost-effective case based on "real world" negligence or worse.

We developed a system under which each lawyer in charge of every suit had to demonstrate periodically that the money he was likely to collect would exceed by a reasonable amount the likely cost of pursuing the defendant. One of the factors to consider was how deep were the pockets of the defendant. Another was how long each director and officer had actually been in office, and what decisions they might have made that would weigh in the case. In time these policies began to have an effect. The suits against officers and directors dropped by about half. Suits against debtors dropped by about one-third as we dropped those that appeared unwise or unrewarding. Under the leadership of our general counsel, Jack Murphy, who had been in private practice with Cleary, Gottlieb, Steen and Hamilton before coming to the FDIC, we reduced the number of suits to about 12,000, even though bank failures had doubled.

One of the results of our lawsuits against directors and officers was an increasing reluctance on the part of insurers to provide them with protection. Lloyds of London, the principal reinsurance group at risk on most of these policies, had been threatening to get out of the business, as had several of the principal U.S. insurance companies. They were all losing money on it. Lack of insurance kept many well qualified people from accepting directorships. Since regulators depended on the independent directors to keep management operating prudently, our lawsuits were having precisely the opposite effect from our intention, which was to install some discipline in the system.

Murphy and I decided to go to London to meet with the main underwriters and directors of Lloyds. We explained that we were abandoning the old policy of blunderbuss litigation and stressed that we had no intention of suing every officer and director of each failed bank. We illustrated our new procedures of investigating each case and of filing suits partly on the basis of whether they would secure a return to the government. We then showed them our new booklet for directors, which outlined what was expected of them— "maintain your independence from management," "keep informed," "ensure qualified management"—and promised that if they followed its guidance they would be protected from liability. Some of our legal staff did not like the idea because it would be harder for them to win cases, but we held our ground. Our trip helped to bring the insurers back to the marketplace. Of course, as long as there are bank directors who think of their job as some sort of financial knighthood, as an honor and not a duty, there will be litigation; not just by regulators, but by stockholders and creditors as well.

The role of a director, obviously, is to keep the bank operating safely and profitably; his fundamental job is to set policy, hire the right managers, and pay attention to the supervisors' reports. More than half the suits against directors were based on the charge that they had deliberately ignored or not even read the supervisors' reports. Our Blue Book stressed that their duty was to do this, and then to use their own judgment to question management if they thought the bank was not being run properly. Managers always will have more information than directors, but that must never prevent the directors from asking whether the managers have made reasonable business judgments. That is about the best they can do.

After Congress tried to legislate standards in the 1991 Federal Deposit Insurance Corporation Improvement Act, we lost considerable discretion in applying the standards for suing directors. Bank directors were required to certify that their bank's standards of control and business practices met the guidelines that had been set by the regulators. By demanding this in its new law, Congress could in effect paralyze directors in their willingness to exercise reasonable business judgments. That is why I called it the Credit Crunch Enhancement Act of 1991 and recommended that the president veto it.

Experience has taught me that the support of fine colleagues and a staff of great skill and loyalty is essential to your financial health. Because I was chief executive officer with the power to run the place and the buck stopped at my office, staffing was my top priority. No executive can succeed without good people. Good staff cannot save a bad executive, but bad staff can pull down an otherwise competent one. Together we wrestled with some difficult and, to most people, genuinely arcane problems of the banking system, and together we came up with new and innovative actions despite being a bureaucratic government agency.

Many comments are made about how difficult it is for government bureaucrats to change their ways. That was not my experience in the public sector, or the industrial bureaucracies of the private sector, for that matter. Most employees in any organization hunger for a clear sense of direction and a chance to participate in deciding what that direction should be. In most cases they will implement management initiatives, whether they approve of them or not. What people really hate is indecision, politicized decision making, and even worse, no decision at all. Indecisive leadership ensures bureaucratic lethargy. If you do not know where you are going, any road will do.

Early in my chairmanship, the FDIC received a great break with the appointment of a new director to the Democratic seat, a real Southern gentleman from Charlotte, North Carolina, named C. C. Hope. He replaced Irv Sprague, who retired on April 3, 1986, after serving nobly for eleven years. C. C. was an experienced banker and former president of the American Bankers Association. Not surprisingly, more letters from bankers in support of his nomination arrived on my desk than did in any other matter. If C. C. had any enemies, they were not to be found in his old profession. His peers loved him, and for good reason. He was a professional at banking, had great judgment, and was a wonderful master of ceremonies.

During my term, C. C. chaired meetings of staff, bankers, and assorted personnel. He ran these with good humor, old and new jokes, and a firm hand that always tried to limit the length of a meeting long before the participants' eyes glazed over. He also took charge of our educational programs, created many of our best publications, and handled many of our problems with the Treasury Department.

For several years Jack Murphy did an outstanding job for us as general counsel, and then he left to return to private practice with his old law firm. This was one case in which I can testify that both sides benefited from the revolving door that leads in and out of government. When Murphy later appeared before us representing his clients, he was a knowledgeable fellow who knew the business and an honorable gentleman who was easy to work with. This made our job much easier, because the ability and desire of some lawyers to mislead their own government is unfortunately without limitation.

We needed a new director of the Division of Supervision to replace Robert Shumway, since he chose to be C. C.'s new deputy. The increasing number of failures had turned that job from "ho-hum" to "heave-ho." To help decide which of our many experienced professional bank examiners should replace Shumway, each of the regional directors was asked to outline his goals, in three pages or less, if he was picked for the job. The responses were interesting. One experienced old-timer, the head of our San Francisco office, a man who obviously liked living in the "City by the Bay," responded with a one-liner: "I will work very hard to make the division outstanding." He obviously figured that San Francisco was about as close as he wished to be to the chairman. The quality of the responses varied, but most showed that the subject was not one to which they had given much thought.

But one memo was outstanding. It came from the director of supervision in Chicago, Paul Fritts. My first encounter with Fritts was at one of my get-to-know-you meetings with staff from around the country. He had gone out of his way to make it clear that he was a tough professional who believed that banks needed to be more heavily supervised, and that no political appointee was going to change his style. He had heard that my reputation was one of a political compromiser, and he was not enthralled.

It was true that, as the new man on the job, I believed bank supervision could be effective without being adversarial, and I still do. As for the staff, it viewed the new chairman as a Republican from the private sector whose spine needed to be stiffened with respect to an industry about which he had much to learn. Fritts, who manifested this view in spades, thus would not seem to be my first choice as our top supervisor. He had a fine record as a tough but fair bank examiner, and bankers themselves liked and respected him. He certainly did not look like the typical green-eyeshade accountant. He was big and blond and looked more like a Midwestern college football star, which in fact he once had been. His paper was the most thoughtful and recognized the magnitude of the challenges. It was the best, with no competition even close. He proposed a new and more efficient supervisory structure for the FDIC through enhanced training, better coordination with other regulatory agencies, recruitment of better qualified supervisors and more of them, and a more efficient audit process.

But how would we get along personally? He came to visit me in Washington. My initial fear that he would turn out to be a typical long-serving bureaucrat, inflexible and perhaps uncooperative, turned out to be totally wrong. Fritts was universally described as one of the best professionals in the FDIC. In the past, he had had some serious controversies, but that was not a negative. We needed a director who stood up for his views and knew what he was talking about. Fritts did. I put aside my natural inclination to select someone who thought the new chairman was wonderful and took a second look at this no-nonsense fellow. He said that as director he would state his views whether he thought I would like them or not, and he wanted them taken into consideration as part of the decision-making process. But once a decision was made, he promised he would support it, or if he could not, he would resign. No chairman should desire anything more.

Paul Fritts was selected to head the Division of Supervision, and I never regretted it. As soon as he came on board, we began an in-depth review of the health of the banking system, the outlook for bank failures, and the needs of the industry. In 1986 the outlook was gloomy, and problem banks continued to appear. Beyond the Midwest farm problems and Southwest oil problems, we found evidence across the country of increasing bank lending on commercial real estate projects (that now have created such a drag on the economy). Fritts, in his three-page memo for the job, had proposed increasing our supervisory forces and improving the quality of our recruits. We told him to get going, on a crash basis, with his new plans. Over the years almost everything he proposed has been put in place. The academic grades and class ranks of our new supervisors increased dramatically, and our training program was expanded and improved.

Jim Davis, a wily veteran of the agency, continued at the Division of Liquidation, whose job it was to sell assets from failed banks. His intelligence and savvy were impressive, but his division was operating under an outmoded and very expensive strategy. Its basic objective had been to protect the agency from losses and accompanying political attacks by holding on to the assets we had inherited from failed banks until they could be sold at a price that would show no loss to the insurance fund. They were always marketed at the value at which they had been carried on the failed bank's books, no matter how far that diverged from the reality of the marketplace—and since the bank had failed, it was a good bet that its managers had not been too good at judging the market. This strategy first came to my attention when a sales report from the division proudly listed the sale at its original price of one asset inherited from a failed bank that had been held on our books for *fifteen years*. It was a piece of property in Detroit, and I happened to know all about it because it had been taken over when I was chairman of the Detroit branch office of the Federal Reserve Bank of Chicago. So I sort of met it again coming around, to my surprise and horror. The holding cost of carrying this asset was not recorded in the report, or considered. It probably exceeded the money we finally got from selling it.

As a result of this system, practically nothing was ever sold during a recession and very little was ever sold promptly. This was not a serious problem in an agency with very few failed banks, and when the FDIC insurance fund had lots of cash. It also made a cozy life for the good bureaucrats who were naturally interested in holding on to assets, and their jobs with them. But it could be disastrous as the number of bank failures increased. From 1982 to 1985, our inventory of assets skyrocketed from $2 billion to $12 billion. The Division of Liquidation was hiring a thousand new people every six months to oversee the failed businesses, buildings, hotels, and whatever else we inherited. Given the bank failure rate, it anticipated its personnel needs at between 11,000 and 13,000 by the end of the decade. The strategy of holding on to assets would swallow up all our cash very quickly. One thing the private sector teaches is that increasing inventories mean decreasing cash. Cash had never been a problem at the FDIC, with billions in premium income on deposit at the Treasury. But my calculations showed that on the basis of the way we were doing things, if you took the FDIC forecast of bank failures from 1985 to 1990, our cash reserve of $16 billion would be wiped out well before the end of the decade.

We quickly adopted a new and simple strategy—sell, sell, sell! All the assets in our inventory would be for sale, at all times, at current market values. These almost uniformly depressed values were not the values on the failed banks' books. We would determine the new ones by current appraisals. We took our loss up front and set aside reserves to reflect the loss in asset value. We assigned sales goals for the division. We had to reduce our inventory in order to make room for the new assets we were acquiring at an accelerating rate as bank failures increased.

As a result of this change in policy, we planned to reduce the personnel selling assets because we expected inventories to go down, even though we knew that more failures were certainly going to occur. But running any liquidation agency is an inherently difficult management challenge. It is a self-limiting project, because everyone knows that the faster the assets are sold, the sooner the employees will be looking for new jobs. There are obvious incentives for the employees to drag their feet. We tried to counter them by offering special sales awards, for which a lively competition developed, just as in the private sector.

To meet the problem of people worrying about working themselves out of a job, we created a core division of about a thousand and promised them permanent employment even though we might not have a single asset to liquidate. We knew we would always need people ready at a moment's notice to begin the process when an institution fails—and we surely did when we were called in for the S&L conflagration. (You don't get rid of the fire department because the town firebug has been put in jail.) But as the number of bank failures continued to increase, our fast-selling liquidators worried less about running out of assets to sell and working themselves out of their jobs.

Selling assets is especially difficult for a government sales agency. Full public disclosure is a must so that all citizens get an opportunity to bid, and this process must be carried out with a punctilio unknown in the private sector. A public agency also needs a much more complex system of internal controls against fraud. In the private sector, losses are part of doing business; in the public sector, they are political disasters. Noneconomic checks and balances are always a part of governmental sales efforts, and always will be. We had to be able to prove that the government had gained a fair price and none of our people had taken a bribe or showed favoritism. We attempted to streamline the process by setting our own deadlines for replying to bids and by trying to move the responsibility for making final decisions down the line from Washington. Fear of scandal, however, always forced us to stay within cumbersome bureaucratic guidelines.

Our inventory of assets for sale conformed to the 80-20 rule—80 percent of the items made up less than 20 percent of the value of the assets we had for sale. So we decided to sell off our smaller assets more quickly and with less red tape by putting them out for open bidding with no reserve prices. It worked and we got rid of most of them. We made a substantial reduction in the number of people we needed to baby-sit these small assets, which had always needed a disproportionate degree of management for what they were worth.

As an experienced and professional public servant, Jim Davis reversed the old policies and implemented these new ones without complaint and with vigor. His job was to carry out board policy whether he agreed or not. (I never really knew his personal view.) Davis became as effective at selling bank assets as he had been at holding them in the past. In large part that was due to the fact that we had set guidelines for our new policy, which like most policies was applied case by case. Our goals were to maximize returns to the fund and minimize market disruption caused by forced sales. It was a challenge and, while every sale was really a compromise, our inventory did decrease even though bank failures rose from 80 per year to over 200.

Primarily due to the many changes made in liquidation and the rigorous leadership of Steve Seelig, who replaced Davis on his retirement, the FDIC staff declined from 11,000 to 8,000 between 1985 and 1988. (Of course it went back up later when the S&L hurricane hit.) Just as challenging but more complex was the question of what to do with the banks themselves after they failed. The old strategy for "resolving" a failed bank was to give it a fresh start and sell it clean by removing all of its bad assets and turning them over to our Division of Liquidation. Bad assets included nonperforming loans (those on which the debtors had stopped paying interest) and real estate on which the bank had foreclosed. We could no longer afford this and had to develop a new philosophy.

Like the new liquidation policy of selling instead of holding, our new resolution policy contradicted everything that had been gospel for the last thirty years. It was called the "whole bank" policy. We would try to sell entire failed banks, with all the assets on board, mainly to other banks. Bankers usually buy other banks to gain the customers who are depositors of the failed institution. Their deposits, called core deposits, are the primary franchise value of a banking license. To accomplish a sale of a whole bank, we would have to pay buyers to take the bank off our hands, since it was insolvent. Thus began "reverse bidding" for banks.

Instead of the price being bid up, we were trying to bid down the cost. The bidders would submit their bids in terms of how much money they would accept to take the hemorrhaging bank off our hands. The winning bid was the lowest —not the highest—since the low amount represented the lowest cost to the insurance fund. Within a few weeks, our people had adopted the new system, and soon nearly half of all the bank failures were handled as "whole" or "almost whole" transactions. The results were lower inventories, more cash, fewer personnel, and faster decisions all around.

Some critics felt that instead of handling banks this way, we should have closed them down and broken them up, since it was clear that the banking system, especially in places like Texas, had far too many banks anyway. From an insurance point of view, our job was to keep the cost as low as possible to the insurance fund. That was what the law required, and selling whole banks cost the fund far less than liquidating them and paying off the depositors. But even more important, when we sold a whole bank, it simply meant that the buyers bought it, not that they kept it in one piece. (Why should they? It had obviously proven unprofitable in that form already.) The buyers would keep whatever part they wanted and sell the rest. The net result was really not too different, except that the private sector was doing the disposal of the pieces instead of the FDIC, and presumably was acting in more direct response to the market than we could. Very few of the whole bank sales resulted in separate new institutions. Almost all of them were purchased by banks and then merged into the system of the buying bank. That meant there *was* one bank less in the system. The argument that this was an inappropriate way to handle failures really did not make a lot of sense to us.

The argument has more than theoretical validity, at least when it comes to handling the very few large banks that were recapitalized and continued as independent institutions. Closing them would have cut surplus banking capacity with one quick chop. But it would have been an expensive one. The cost of liquidating them would have been many times the cost of selling them as a whole bank. Just imagine the billions it would have cost to liquidate the $40 billion Continental Illinois, when history shows us that assets lose 5 to 15 percent of value just by being taken out of an institution and put on the junk pile for sale. Unliquidated, it cost $1 billion.

We next looked to improve the Research Division, which was headed by Stan Silverberg, an economist and another FDIC veteran. Its basic task had been to provide information for the support of our operations. It collected data for supervisors to regulate banks; for example, it would provide estimates of the cost of liquidating a bank or selling it. The FDIC Research Division had played an important role in handling the failure of the Continental Illinois Bank; not only advising but helping in the negotiations. But we needed much more: a steady flow of data on the current status of the troubled banking industry so we could monitor, and hopefully spot emerging trends before they overwhelmed us. My background as business school dean was finally going to be of some practical value; deans spend a lot of time trying to encourage useful research. The division was redirected and enhanced with the enthusiastic support of all involved—except Stan, who decided to retire. His deputy Dr. Roger Watson took over.

We created a new quarterly analysis of the entire banking industry. It was called *The FDIC Quarterly Review*, and soon became a standard for the industry, used not only by our supervisors, but by insured banks, economists, investors, journalists, and the public. "Publish or perish" is the law of educational institutions, and we adopted a modified version in which we encouraged publication, but only of useful, relevant, and understandable material (in contrast to some of the less relevant work seen in the educational world). The FDIC was particularly well situated for this bank analysis, since the *Quarterly* was based on the "call" reports submitted by banks, which we already had in our computers. The database had always been ours to use, so the industry analysis was a natural. The Research Division also began to publish monographs on the future of banking and surveys of real estate trends, which were full of information on markets gathered from the on-the-spot surveys of our supervisors and liquidators. Under Watson's stewardship, the division soon was recognized as one of the best in the country, up to the standards set by the Federal Reserve Banks.

No management challenge is more basic, and more rewarding, than developing a strategy for changing conditions. The FDIC, in 1985, was the ideal place for that, since the whole financial system was undergoing radical change. Successfully managed agencies develop a strategy and put the right people in place to achieve their goals. Good planning has been defined as "innovating around a general sense of direction," and the FDIC was developing a new sense of direction.

Reflecting back on my first year in office, my view was that the rewards of my new job would be even more satisfying than the beautiful view from the chairman's office. But my enjoyment of the moment came before the culmination of the S&L disaster; the formation of the Resolution Trust Corporation; the problems with the Bush White House and with the president's son, Neil; the near exhaustion of the FDIC fund; and the credit crunch. Things would become much more interesting as the problems in the financial system accelerated. The "room with a view" continued to be the best place from which to operate in Washington, given that the Oval Office, which really has no view at all, was not available.

6

Congressional Relations:
The President Proposes and the
Congress Disposes

One of my first goals as FDIC chairman was to achieve a solid and mutually respectful relationship with Congress. Easier said than done! The Congress of the United States is truly representative of the American people. If you sit in on a hearing, and look over the committee room, you will see the many different social, ethnic, and economic groups of America. Congress is a microcosm of the American people and thus reflects all the political and social turmoil that occurs in a great democracy. Since the Congress disposes of what the administration proposes, all of the administration's agencies spend a lot of time and money seeking to keep on good terms with Congress, which funds them and pays their salaries. While the FDIC was not directly dependent on Congress for funding, it was still a legal creature of the Congress, and therefore responsible to it. Oversight of our performance was primarily a congressional, rather than an executive, responsibility. Our political well-being depended on satisfactory relationships with the Senate and House banking committees. At any time the Congress, with the concurrence of the president, could change the way the agency worked, or even legislate us out of existence. One of my principal jobs as leader of the FDIC was to maintain ap-

propriate relationships with the Congress, and particularly
with the banking committees of the House and Senate.

The old adage that the way to a man's heart is through his
stomach proved useful. We had a very good kitchen in the
FDIC, which served a fine breakfast, and very early on we
started holding breakfasts for members of Congress. (At the
suggestion of Beth Climo, the attractive and talented lawyer
who headed our Congressional Relations division.) The
kitchen whipped up particularly tasty Hispanic dishes, so
Congressman Henry Gonzalez, chairman of the House
Banking Committee, especially enjoyed our breakfast meetings, and that proved a fine grounding for good relations.

Much time was spent on the Hill talking with various congressmen. The senior Republican on the House Banking
Committee, Congressman Chalmers Wylie of Ohio, turned
out to be a classmate at Harvard Law School. We did not
know each other in school, and I discovered our mutual educational experience only when thumbing through a Class of
1949 Year Book. Senator Donald Riegle and I, both Michi-
ganders, even though we were from opposing parties, enjoyed in-depth discussions on the financial and economic
outlook. We sought to get "ahead of the curve," and foresee
the problems facing his committee and our agency. We truly
learned how to disagree without being disagreeable, and
perhaps to our surprise, we found a great many issues to
agree on. Frank and open lines of communication were the
bedrock of congressional relations. In addition, when a
member needed help with a constituent, we moved rapidly
to see that he got it. Many times my staff was instructed that
providing constituent service for Congress was an important
and legitimate part of our job.

But nothing worked perfectly in Washington. I had inherited a good fellow and a very serious bureaucrat in Graham
Northrup, who was Beth Climo's predecessor as congressional liaison. He presided over one of our small but most
humiliating legislative defeats. While he was looking the

other way, the Congress, led by Senator Proxmire and Congressman Jack (old New Dealer) Brooks of Texas, engineered a complete elimination of the FDIC directors' portal-to-portal limousine service, the right to use our government cars and drivers to be transported from home to the office and back. These gentleman had been working on this mean-minded ambush, which was also directed at the Pentagon and even the Supreme Court, long before my arrival. Without cars and drivers, directors of the FDIC suddenly became second-class citizens in Washington. Others, including the postmaster general and the Federal Reserve members, got wind of the punitive strike on their "perks" and lobbied successfully for privileges of their rank. The restriction really did not bother me, since I rode my bicycle to work from my home in Georgetown on a daily basis (a distance of about three miles, mostly downhill, but only in the morning). But what really hurt was the resulting loss of status in the government community.

The limo service was never restored. While it made no practical difference to me, it did affect the other directors, who lived in the suburbs. Northrup decided to retire and was replaced by Beth Climo. Beth knew how to get results. She led many trips to the Hill to talk with the leading members. I told her that "going to the Hill" was among my highest priorities. When she needed me she should let me know, because fighting the FDIC's battles on the front lines of congressional relations was of paramount importance.

During 1985, open warfare existed between the FDIC and Senator David Boren and Representative Mickey Edwards of Oklahoma. These gentlemen were outraged by the way the FDIC handled the failure of the Penn Square Bank (the little oil and gas lending bank that went bust in 1982 after shenanigans that have been fully recounted in the aptly named book *Funny Money*). They were enraged that Penn Square was the first failed institution of any size at which the FDIC had not protected all the depositors. Those with more than

$100,000 on deposit, the maximum amount that Congress permitted us to insure, did not get all of their money back. As a result, they had a very unhappy constituency in their state. First, they demanded the right to examine FDIC records, and then they waged a press campaign against the agency. Chairman Bill Isaac had responded with a campaign of his own, and each side accused the other of bad faith. When I arrived, with our new policy of full and open disclosure of our operations, they were quickly mollified. It meant reversing my predecessor's position, which they appreciated to no end. It showed their constituents what they had accomplished. I told them, "We will provide you with anything you need." They got what they wanted, and no harm to the FDIC followed. While battles over policy with the Congress are unavoidable, no agency ever wins by hiding the facts or misleading the members. Tell it straight and tell it all!

Another inherited problem involved the senior senator from Kansas, Bob Dole. He was supporting an outraged group of Kansas bankers who accused our regulators of being distant, uncommunicative, and harsh in their relations with bankers. The senator said communications had broken down, and there was no one in the state who was pleased with the FDIC. Because of the farm recession, Kansas banks were in considerable trouble at the time and tensions were high. One of my first trips was to Kansas to tell the citizens what the FDIC could do to help work out the problems of the farm banks. I took along copies of some of the harsher letters that had been sent to them, tore them up as they watched, and then promised to turn over a new leaf, a more courteous and less adversarial one. I told them, "We are your regulators and supervisors, but we do not consider you to be the enemy." The executives of the Kansas Bankers Association were astonished when we decided to examine the complaints firsthand, visit the state, and talk to Kansas bankers. We listened to a lot of people, decided that much had to change, and vowed to make it happen. We went to Capitol

Hill, met with the Kansas congressional delegation, and promised that things would change. We subsequently developed the forbearance program to make good on our promise. But basically we changed our organizational attitude. The change was not difficult—most of our supervisors preferred it. It cemented good relations with our new friends in the Kansas congressional delegation.

Though we spent a lot of time on the Hill, only a little of it was with Fernand St. Germain, the House Banking Committee chairman. He was one of the most difficult gentlemen to deal with and seldom deigned to talk to me. For whatever the reason, he appeared to have little time for an unimportant player like the chairman of the FDIC. In the two years that his chairmanship overlapped mine, we probably spoke only three or four times. At hearings, he generally opened by castigating the FDIC in order to make some political point. In the 1988 election he was returned to private life by the voters of Rhode Island in an unusual electoral upset. As his election day neared, he called to tell me he was running ads showing us "working together," but his affection for the law-and-order regulators bloomed too late. He lost probably because of reports in the press that he received thousands of dollars worth of meals and entertainment from a top S&L lobbyist.

Because of our congressional breakfasts, I was well pleased when Henry Gonzalez succeeded St. Germain as chairman of the Banking Committee. He was a great storyteller and a very intelligent gentleman. He was often lampooned in the Congress for his resolutions to impeach presidents or for threatening to slug someone who called him a Communist. He was not your average congressman, because he had no personal wealth, and was a person of absolute integrity. He knew the history of U.S. banking through his committee work—the laws it had passed and defeated. Later, on a visit to his hometown of San Antonio, Texas, I spoke at a testimonial dinner in his honor. He had a wonderful group of children and grandchildren and a very lovely wife, who later provided great hospitality and a fine Mexican dinner.

But in politics one must always remember that no matter how friendly an individual in the Congress may seem, his political imperatives come first. To illustrate: M. Danny Wall, successor to Ed Gray as the chief S&L regulator, began his term in office by estimating that the cost to the government of repaying the depositors of the bankrupt S&Ls would be only $15 billion, instead of the over $200 billion it eventually will cost. Congressman Charles Schumer of New York, who was skeptical of Wall's figures, asked the FDIC for its estimate. We estimated it at close to $60 billion, and rising every day. Congressman Gonzalez liked our work and did not like Wall's, and said so. Unfortunately, we too were soon forced to start changing our estimates of the cost of the banking failures. Our in-house numbers were increasing rapidly. Having a new number every couple of months was embarrassing, but the fact remained that the situation was getting worse, and we wanted to report it truthfully. At one hearing, Chairman Gonzalez expressed annoyance that he could not rely on our estimates because we kept raising them. He said that it began to look like I was turning into "another Danny Wall." Our failure to predict the situation accurately gave Chairman Gonzalez a chance to shoot at "his new friend," the Republican chairman of the FDIC. The political imperative prevailed, and he took a shot.

A principal test of an agency's standing with the Congress is whether or not, and how quickly, a representative or senator will return the chairman's call. Nothing is more important in Washington, in terms of status and effectiveness. Returned calls are golden chips in the tribal rite of Beltway politics. Of course, some congressmen are better at returning calls than others, and the same goes for administration officials, but there is no question that the ability to reach a key legislator at the right moment can change the tide of a legislative battle. No surprise, the most effective way to ensure that your calls are returned is to return calls yourself. It was my absolute rule that every staff call from the Congress would be returned the same day as it was received, no matter what. I personally tried to accept any calls from elected members immediately. When they make a call, senators and congressmen appreciate the ability to get through, particularly when some constituent is standing nearby. It is impressive for them to show that they command respect at the regulatory agencies.

Chairman St. Germain seldom returned my calls, though he sometimes had them returned by his staff. On the other hand, Senator Riegle, chairman of the Senate Banking Committee, and I agreed that returning each other's calls was essential to the success of our endeavors. No matter how busy the senator was, and no matter how difficult the situation might be, he never failed to return my calls. In turn, no call was placed unless it was essential to speak with the senator so as not to abuse the privilege of access.

The most obvious way to keep on good terms with Congress is to do favors for its members by seeing their constituents when they come to Washington. Whenever it was humanly possible, we did the job with political impartiality. The FDIC had such a good reputation for independence and incorruptibility that people were very careful about why they came and what they asked for. Nevertheless, congressmen sometimes sent us constituents who wanted contracts with the agency and who wanted to find out the best way to get a contract. Often my congressional friends from Arizona would call with problems about what was going on in Arizona. But during the entire period of my chairmanship, there were very few requests that were inappropriate. Sometimes the requests required extraordinary efforts, and a question of ethics would arise. We developed rules and regulations in this area, but we always tried to respond when appropriate.

In the first place, we saw very few individuals, and we

never saw anyone who was complaining that his own bank's regulator was being too tough on him. If a congressman called such an individual complaint to our attention, we would reply that it would be handled in the usual way. As a result, we received very few requests for special treatment because it was already well known how they would be dealt with.

However, we did get many calls protesting some rule or interpretation because it adversely affected the operation of the banking system. Bankers would complain, for example, about our rules for valuing bonds or the way real estate values were being pushed down to liquidation prices. Often they came in because they could not get a clear answer at a lower level to their questions about our regulations. All this was comparable to lobbyists presenting their point of view to Congress, and we felt this was a reasonable exchange between a government agency and its clients. Occasionally a congressman or a senator accompanied a constituent, and from time to time our visitors might get close to the line and ask whether what they were actually doing was permitted. Someone complaining about our rules valuing real estate might say, "Now in my case your people are . . ." We would immediately reply: "We do not take up specific cases in this office."

On the other hand, we learned a lot about what was really going on in the real world from listening to people whose banks we were actually regulating. This often resulted in our taking a second look at our rules and how they were being interpreted and enforced out in the field. No one ever met with these individuals without a number of people in the room, so there could be no doubt about what was being said. We made it clear in advance that everything would take place before plenty of witnesses so there would be no misunderstandings later—specifically that the meeting did not constitute a tribunal for judging any particular application of the rules to individual institutions.

All politics being local, one of the many functions of Congress is to serve as an ombudsman for the people. Without a doubt, our elected representatives respond with more speed to their contributors, but they certainly respond to the ordinary voter as well. We got hundreds of letters a week from members of Congress asking us to look into things that affected their constituents. One of the many ways that we built a reputation with the Congress for being a responsive agency was to answer every one of those letters according to a schedule. Every one received a substantive answer, and not some brush-off piece of boilerplate phraseology from our data bank of standard replies. As a result, they were able to say they had talked to the agency, received a reply, and were passing it on to their people at home.

Although congressmen probably got priority attention from us, all letters were answered within a prescribed period. It was roughly thirty days, sometimes less and sometimes more, and although funneling a request through Congress might give it a little edge because we respected its ombudsman role, the answer would always be the same. Quicker, perhaps, but not more favorable.

It is useful to have Congress involved in this process, because by providing good service, regulators get a chance to interact with the people who make the laws and let them know how their legislative creations work in practice. This is essential to the operation of our system, and it goes back to my basic premise that if government deals with people on a reasonable basis and provides them a forum in which to thrash out and settle their disputes amicably, it will avoid the political upheaval that always threatens authoritarian governments, and recently overturned many of them in Latin America and Eastern Europe. Our agency had some bureaucrats whose attitudes, if put into words, would sound something like "To hell with them all—any congressman who tries to deal with us is trying to influence our independence." That was an attitude that had to change, and it did! Our new view was that "any congressman who talks with us represents over 500,000 people and must be accorded respect." In our system, when you start closing out the citizenry, you are in trouble.

The Congress, for better or worse, represents the will of the people and thus must be treated with due deference and respect—though from time to time its individual members behave in a manner that should more appropriately be treated with scorn and leg irons.

Love them or hate them, but do not ignore them!

7
Turf Wars:
No Peace at Any Price

No activity is followed with greater interest in Washington, D.C., than the battle between various agencies for "turf." Turf is a euphemism for power, and particularly for the power achieved in gaining additional control and responsibility at the expense of rival agencies. In order to understand the U.S. banking system, it is necessary to describe the various regulators' areas of responsibility, which represent a constant temptation for them to defend their respective turf. No one can explain the territories of the bank, savings and loan, and credit union supervisory and inspection systems in a short and painless manner, but here is a best effort.

There are two kinds of banks in the United States: national banks, which are chartered by the Comptroller of the Currency under federal banking laws, and state banks, which are chartered by agencies of each state under their own laws. The Comptroller of the Currency is the primary federal regulator of national banks, sets the rules by which they operate, and has the duty to close them down if they become insolvent. Each state has a similar agency with similar powers over banks chartered in the state; its head is usually designated the supervisor or commissioner of banking. The country's largest banks are usually national banks, but there are many more state banks that focus primarily on their own communities. Here the situation becomes more and more complicated.

The Federal Deposit Insurance Corporation insures the depositors of both state and national banks (and, following the collapse of the Savings and Loan Insurance Fund, the S&Ls as well since 1989). The FDIC is designated the primary federal regulator only for state banks, and not even all of them. State banks that elect to be members of the Federal Reserve System (the Fed) are regulated primarily by the Fed. The FDIC was not originally given this role when it was formed in 1933, but it became the primary federal regulator of state banks in order to fill a vacuum and protect the insurance fund. It was assumed that the Comptroller and the Fed would exercise adequate federal supervision of the national banks, and banks that are members of the Federal Reserve System. Thus, there are three separate federal *bank* regulators, the FDIC and the Fed, which are independent agencies, and the Comptroller of the Currency, which is a part of the Treasury Department. Treasury also is the home of the charterer and supervisor of federally licensed S&Ls—the Office of Thrift Supervision (OTS).

In addition, there is a separate regulatory and chartering system for state-chartered S&Ls and banks in each of the fifty states. The National Credit Union Administration serves as federal regulator and insurer for the credit unions, and states have their own charterers as well. So, altogether, there are five different federal regulatory agencies involved in regulating institutions that accept deposits, plus fifty separate state agencies for state banks and S&Ls. On top of all this, a separate regulatory layer was provided for bank holding companies that own a sufficient share of a bank to control it. These parent corporations not only control a bank's stock but may have subsidiaries separate from the bank itself to issue credit cards, make auto loans, and perform operations that are closely related to, but not strictly speaking, banking.

Bank holding companies are under the supervision of the Federal Reserve system, no matter which type of bank the holding company owns. A diagram of this system looks a lot like a plate of spaghetti.

No one said this was simple, and in fact it is about as complex as the financial history of our country. The founding fathers had profound suspicions of centralized control of anything. During the first half century we experimented with a central bank to issue currency, which we called the Bank of the United States, but it was abolished under our first populist president, Andrew Jackson. Frontier farmers and businessmen feared the big East Coast banks would dominate their rural banks and cut off the credit they needed to develop the country. Banks operated independently and unsupervised, and many of them printed their own money.

Every few years a panic would take place, which resulted in a financial crisis with banks failing and depositors out in the cold. Gradually the pendulum swung toward some sort of oversight of the businesses that held other people's money in deposit, but it moved in fits and starts. The Comptroller of the Currency was set up in 1865 to create national banks, which were chartered to prevent state banks from having local monopolies. The Federal Reserve System was formed in 1913 after the panic of 1907. At that time the United States, alone among industrialized nations, had no central bank of last resort to issue money and provide short-term loans should there be a "run" on the banks. Our Federal Deposit Insurance Corporation was formed in 1934 after the banking collapse of the Great Depression.

As the system evolved over the years, it provided ample opportunity for regulatory turf wars of the most exquisite "inside the Beltway" variety. Every common sense proposal to simplify this contraption into a single, independent regulatory agency has been nixed by people defending their bureaucratic empires. In 1949 the Hoover Commission proposed that the bank regulatory system be replaced by a single agency that would operate in much the same way as the Securities and Exchange Commission. The SEC regulates the nation's multifarious capital markets, which are not only as complex and as efficient as any in the world, but also the safest, one reason for their success. The commission's proposal was opposed by the Treasury, which wanted to continue its control over the biggest banks; the Federal Reserve, which felt it needed a regulatory role to supplement its policy function in supplying money to the banking system; and the FDIC, which, like the others, knew the proposal would mean the loss of its regulatory functions.

In 1990 the Bush administration introduced its program for bank regulatory reform. But its suggested regulatory structure would have preserved all the disadvantages of our hydra-headed system. It would have given the large holding companies, as well as all state banks, to the Federal Reserve, and given the national banks and the rest of the holding companies to the Treasury. It eliminated the FDIC from regulation. There would have been two coequal regulators with no way to decide conflicts between them. It was a formula for civil war, nobody was in favor of the plan, and it sank beneath the waves.

Agency disagreements and turf battles are not only about jurisdiction over banks. They can involve regulatory standards and practices as well. A good example (perhaps unfortunate example is more accurate) of a turf war was the battle over setting the amount of capital required to be held by a bank: Should it be different for national banks, member banks, state banks, etc.? State regulators always seek to allow their state banks to be free from unwarranted interference from federal regulators. Few areas provide a better chance to observe how regulatory tangles can impede the operation of government.

One of my first experiences with a serious regulatory war came in the area of international finance, and it demon-

strates how the turf you control influences what you think
about an issue. I received a call to come to the Treasury
Department to meet with Assistant Secretary David Mulford,
whose duties included international finance, where he dealt
extensively with the problem of loans to Latin America. He
had summoned the heads of the agencies overseeing banks
to tell us that our supervisors were inhibiting the administration's campaign to urge banks to make more loans to Latin
American countries, particularly Mexico, Brazil, Argentina,
and Venezuela. Mulford said these countries needed more
money to "work their way out of their debts." All of these
countries' loans were in default. The United States had to
create a rescue plan in August 1982, when Mexico ran out of
money and could not even pay interest on its debts. This
operation was led by Chairman Paul Volcker of the Federal
Reserve with the help of Deputy Secretary Tim McNamara
of the Treasury. He spent hours arguing with David Stockman, the OMB director, for authorization to use government
funds for an emergency loan to Mexico. In one telling point,
he said that if their banks close on Monday, our banks will
close on Tuesday.

The administration and the Fed wanted the private sector
to help rescue the situation. What they really were saying
was that our banks should loan these defaulting debtors
more money so they could use these funds to pay interest on
their old loans, which would keep them from defaulting and
also keep our own banks from going under from the weight
of too much Latin American debt. Latin American treasuries
were busted and unable to service existing loans. Like most
good debtors, their prescribed answer to too much debt was
a little more of the same.

But our supervisory people were certainly not urging U.S.
banks to make additional loans. Mulford wanted us to tell
our people to back off. Given that the loans in question were
in default, it did not seem unreasonable for bank regulators
to discourage more lending. I said it seemed to me that as

good bank regulators, our job was to insure that banks did
not take on more bad loans after the billions they had already
lent to their Third World clients. In my view, that could
mean throwing good money after bad. The bank board I
had recently left in Phoenix, Arizona, had decided to make
no further loans to Mexico and, like many others, decided to
do everything in its power to reduce its outstanding obligations. While I was not familiar with the total government
picture, it still seemed entirely reasonable that additional
Latin American lending should be reviewed carefully.

Mulford made it clear that he was less than pleased with
my remarks, and he showed even less enthusiasm for the
final comment by the FDIC's representatives that we would
"review the matter with our professional staffs." He was
known throughout Washington as one of the toughest and
most arrogant of the government's financial officials, which
unfortunately did not help promote the interaction between
domestic and international considerations that is essential in
forming policy on questions such as this one. In my next five
years at the FDIC, Mulford never spoke to me again.

Perhaps it was too early in my new job for me to speak up.
Still, it did not seem to me that we could agree to go back
and tell our supervisors to urge our banks to make additional
loans to the Latin American countries. Supervisors are in
place to prevent bad loans, not to encourage them. Our supervisors told the banks to use their judgment and treat the
Latin American loans like other loans: If they looked sound,
they should be carried and supported by the bank, and if
unsound, they should not be. The question in such circumstances always is whether by lending more money, a bank
will recover in the long run. There was, of course, a classic
banking argument for continuing the loans. It is what banks
traditionally consider when they hope to nurse their clients
through bad times, and sometimes it works. The big banks,
which had underwritten most of the loans, were ready to do
this, but the small banks were not. The small banks had also

bought pieces of the loans when the big ones syndicated them, and they were not pleased with what they had been sold.

The big banks—and the U.S. Treasury and Federal Reserve—took the view that the small banks should carry their share of the load in bad times just as they had profited in good times. A good point, but it did not take full account of the problem. The small banks probably never should have been part of Latin American lending in the first place. They knew little about the borrowers and had depended solely on their big brothers in the big cities to decide on the credit risks. When it became clear that Wall Street's master bankers had messed things up so badly in Latin America, it was not surprising that the small banks balked at providing any additional credit.

The problem with the less developed countries was that their debts were so large that no one believed they could ever repay them. It did not seem appropriate to provide additional money until we could agree to forgive some of their debt and make it manageable. (The principle was later adopted in the Brady plan.) That is what we actually favored and later proposed. The banks would in effect share the consequences of their bad judgment with their debtors by splitting the difference and cutting the size of the debts to manageable levels. The banks would take the losses out of their profits in exchange for setting up an insurance fund against the remaining debt. Until a viable plan, and not just a stopgap, was worked out among the banks, the government, and the debtors, providing additional money did not appear to be sound policy. The Treasury consulted us no further on the issue and our plow went nowhere.

We reviewed the whole problem with the FDIC's and other regulatory agencies' professional staffs, and every one of them agreed that further lending should be done only when the banks wished to do so and the circumstances made it reasonable. We decided to issue no new instructions to our supervisory staff, despite the request from Treasury that we should loosen our lending guidelines for Latin America.

Thus, right off the bat, my FDIC chairman's job required opposing the administration's requests. I hated to do it, because my goal was to be a "loyalist," and on the "team." When my oath was administered, I fully expected to be a team player, but under these operating conditions, there appeared to be no team and no recognition of the different positions to be played. It is too bad, because things go better when people work together.

My other brush with Mulford came later during a press interview. When asked about him, I referred to him as the James Bond of international finance. The statement reflected my observation that he was a secretive, handsome and able fellow, who looked like he could handle any situation. He was always immaculately and stylishly dressed. When it was printed, the word got back to me that he was highly displeased. It was my thought that I had complimented him; it would have pleased me no end to have been so described, even if inappropriately. I sent him a note to apologize for inadvertently upsetting him but received no reply, which did not surprise me.

Because such disagreements are often due to lack of communication, it seemed a good idea to regularly bring the bank regulators together. We needed an informal institution that would help moderate the natural tendency for conflict— and what better way than to break bread together? So soon after my arrival at the FDIC, I invited all the bank regulators, and officials of the Treasury, for a hearty FDIC breakfast. Present were Chairman Paul Volcker of the Fed; Undersecretary George Gould and Charles Sethness representing the Treasury; Comptroller of the Currency Robert L. Clarke; and Chairman Edwin Gray of the Federal Home Loan Bank Board representing the savings and loans. At that point, we did not invite the National Credit Union Administration chairman, because I did not know enough about the system to realize it was a separate organization that ought to be brought on board.

At the first meeting, I reminisced about the fish tank I had in my office when I served in the West Wing of the White House. It had been there to remind one and all of the occasional similarity between the behavior of schools of fish and workers in the political arena. My fish swam together in schools, like brothers in the bond, until suddenly one would turn and bite the rear end off one of his companions. A similar performance is often observed by those working together in government. Apparent cohesiveness turns into open warfare. Of course, I said, this was unlikely to happen with the stalwart group represented at this breakfast, but it was possible. Perhaps it would be useful to have a place to talk about problems on an unofficial, non-decision-making basis. (There are many nasty rules about making decisions at informal meetings.) Thus began what became known as the regulators' breakfast, a new activity in the federal bank regulatory world, but a practice common in government in other areas. Breakfasts can become a more important part of the operation of the system than anything found in the organizational charts. Ours took place every few weeks, and all of the parties involved must have found them useful enough, because they attended regularly.

At one of our breakfasts, early in my term, the subject for discussion was a call we had all received from John Reed, chairman of Citicorp, the largest bank holding company in the country. He had informed us he was about to create an unprecedented reserve equal to about 30 percent of his bank's loans to Latin America, a reserve to absorb possible losses if the loans were not fully repaid. This meant that the bank was going to show a substantial loss in its earnings that quarter. What it really meant was that the bank was finally acknowledging that it did not expect to collect the entire amount of the loans it had made. Of course, it also was an indication to the debtor countries of Latin America that Citibank was in doubt about its ability to collect on the loans.

Fed Chairman Volcker led off by indicating that he felt Citicorp was being very unwise. He warned that this move would destabilize the delicate international financial situation and make loans harder to collect by advertising to the debtors that the banks expected less than full payment. It would weaken the capital position of all large U.S. banks, since all had Latin American loans; and by marking them closer to their market value, they would cut the value of their assets and their book capital. Volcker had been leading the campaign to keep the debts on the books because he felt that once a public write-down started, the debtors would never stop demanding even more of their loans be forgiven. Most of us felt that since there was no way all of the money was going to be repaid, good accounting and honest reporting required banks to start reserving against losses on the loans; and that was just what John Reed was proposing to do.

Volcker suggested that we meet with Reed and persuade him to abandon the idea. Since the Fed was the regulator most responsible for international banking stability, Volcker wanted all the regulators to follow the Fed lead and help talk Reed out of his radical new approach. Shortly before our breakfast discussion, *Time* magazine had put Chairman Volcker's face on its cover and called him the second most powerful person in the United States because of the Fed's control over the economy, so we all were inclined to follow his leadership. Nevertheless, as an old auditor and accountant and as a new bank regulator, I had to observe that creating these reserves was long overdue, and had long since been accepted in the marketplace.

My suggestion was that Reed be accorded a regulatory Medal of Honor for stepping forward and taking his losses. Volcker strongly disagreed and found my observations somewhat out of order from one so new in the business. He seemed to feel that the entire international financial system would be shaken. I timidly whispered that setting aside a reserve was not going to destabilize the marketplace, and that this view had already been conveyed to Reed, along with the thought that taking this courageous action had proven him to be a leader of men. It seemed to me that the markets had already recognized the need for a reserve for Latin American loans by cutting the price of the bank stocks. Thus, if countries below the border were unable to pay their debts, different accounting entries in the bank's books probably would not make them pay up any sooner or delay their payments any more than they were already doing.

There was a good, healthy disagreement at the breakfast. Since no consensus of regulators was going to be reached, I finally offered to bet Volcker on how Citicorp stock would be affected after Reed made his announcement and the news hit the market. Chairman Volcker predicted Citicorp stock would go down. I said it would go up and offered to bet him a dollar a point. Volcker indicated that, since he had advance knowledge of foreign markets, he had an unfair advantage. First he agreed, but on second thought felt it was unseemly for us to be betting on such grave matters of public policy. Alas, we called off the bet. Citicorp stock did go up a couple of dollars. Volcker was also right, though, on another point. The major countries of Latin America did take note of the reserves, and it reinvigorated their requests for debt forgiveness.

The Latin American loans were so formidable that they had placed the world's largest banks in jeopardy. U.S. bank regulators, given the choice between creating panic in the banking system or going easy on requiring our banks to set aside reserves for Latin American debt, had chosen the latter course. (European banks, which can create "hidden reserves" that reassure regulators but do not alarm the public, had less of a problem. They also had a lower ratio of bad loans.) It would appear that regulators made the right choice. We discussed it often at the regulators' breakfast; it went by a special term—forbearance.

Regulators use forbearance when they exercise judgment in applying normal supervisory mandates. They do this when, in their judgment, to do otherwise would unnecessarily cripple a bank financially. When the Third World debt crisis broke in 1982, regulators were slow to require banks to build up reserves against potential losses; if they had not exercised judgment, seven or eight of the ten largest banks in the United States probably would have been insolvent. It is not hard to imagine what kind of an economic, and then political, crisis that would have created. The regulators had looked over the abyss and decided to take a different path.

Sometimes forbearance (the F word) is the right way to go, and sometimes it is not. In the S&L industry, all rules and standards were conveniently overlooked to avoid a financial collapse and the intense local political pressure that such a collapse would have generated. But in this case there was no visible plan for a recovery, so the result of this winking at standards was, as we know, a national financial disaster. On the other hand, in the case of Latin American loans, forbearance gave the lending banks time to make new arrangements with their debtors and meanwhile acquire enough capital so that losses on Latin American loans would not be fatal. Like medicine and the other healing arts, bank regulation is an art, not a science.

My first experienced look at exercising forbearance occurred in 1985 and 1986. Hundreds of Midwest farm banks were badly squeezed by falling prices and high costs (especially the high interest rates used to fight inflation). As farmers fell behind in interest payments or went bankrupt, banks had to dig into their capital, the cushion of money provided by the owners against too many bad debts. The FDIC minimum ratio was three dollars of capital for every hundred dollars of assets. As losses mounted, many of our banks' capital dropped below the ratio of 3 percent. What should the

FDIC do? Withdraw our insurance cover from any bank that fell below the minimum? When word of that got out, it would be the surest way to bring in depositors demanding their money at once—and bring the bank down with a crash that would resound throughout the local economy.

Both state and national banks in the farm belt were in trouble, and as usual, the regulators were split on the remedies. The FDIC proposed a formal plan allowing banks to operate with capital below the minimum 3 percent as long as they were well managed and operating under a plan to restore their capital. They had to either shrink their loans so their capital ratio would rise, raise new capital by selling stock or convertible bonds, or cut costs and improve profits. The Federal Reserve took a dim view of the way we formalized our forbearance guidelines. They preferred to follow the case-by-case pattern set in the Latin American debt crisis by working with the banks on an individual basis and simply allowing the institutions to operate with lower capital without setting any formal rules.

The Federal Reserve followed the custom of the Bank of England, which had traditionally exercised its authority through typically British informal "understandings," which work well in the tight network of the old boys in the banking fraternity who do most of their business with each other in the square mile of the City of London. The difficulty of adopting this informal system was that obtaining these understandings with hundreds of banks spread across the United States was not practical. (By the way, the British system can have its problems when new and untried bankers set up shop and, as the regulators later find to their horror, they have not been playing by the rules.) Ultimately at a regulators' breakfast, we all agreed that the forbearance program would be put in place, with each agency adopting a common position. Banks would be allowed to operate with their capital below standard as long as they submitted to their primary regulator a satisfactory plan to raise it.

Forbearance worked well with the farm banks. Many would have been closed by a strict application of the 3 percent capital rule, but they were allowed to remain open. Most eventually survived and recovered. We had bet that the classic farm business cycle would repeat itself and lead to recovery—and when the agricultural economy recovered, the banks recovered. One point proved by the farm banks' forbearance was that the success of the program depends on who is doing it and how it is done. When standards were eased on the savings and loans, reduced supervision accompanied the relaxed standards and risky new ventures were financed (particularly speculation in raw land). In the case of the banks stuck with farm loans and Latin American debt, although the standards were relaxed, the supervision was markedly increased, and new risky loans were not added to the problem.

Not every issue could be settled at our regulators' breakfasts, or any other meeting. In many cases, a fight for jurisdiction had been going on for years, and no amount of goodwill over eggs and bacon or yogurt and bran could bring about a friendly solution. These regulatory disagreements had a very unfortunate effect on the operation of the system. During my first year in office we had an unnecessary fight over which regulator controlled the corporations that were owned by state-chartered banks, which themselves were owned by a bank holding company. (Remember, the FDIC and the states regulate state banks, but the Fed regulates the holding companies that own them.) The states' chief regulators and the FDIC asserted they had jurisdiction. However, the Federal Reserve also asserted jurisdiction over the subsidiaries of the state banks if the state bank was owned by a holding corporation.

This was a fine-line legal point that had never been decided by a court—and it was more than just an argument to make lawyers rich. These bank subsidiaries could be vehicles for new and more profitable businesses than traditional banking, and many banks were eager to get into the game—developing real estate, selling securities, selling insurance, and initiating other operations prohibited by the Fed's holding company rules. But these new ventures also could rack up bigger losses as well as profits, and federal regulators felt that it was necessary to set rules for these subsidiaries lest they get out of hand and drain the bank of its profits. Who should set the rules, and what should the rules be? The FDIC believed that operations could be put into a subsidiary and walled off from the insured bank. Transactions between subsidiary and parent would have to be at market value, which admittedly would require continuous and careful supervision. The comptroller of the Currency and the state regulators agreed with us. The Fed disagreed, arguing that clever operators would get around even the most careful supervisors (although perhaps the real reason was that if we were right, and we could supervise the subsidiaries, there would no longer be any role for the Fed).

At a regulators' breakfast we proposed a compromise. Both the FDIC and the Fed would set up the same rules at all levels. Once this was done, the agency that had jurisdiction would become irrelevant. This was my brilliant proposal for avoiding conflicting turf claims, but it worked only in theory, not in practice. All the agencies agreed it was the way to go, but every rule proposed by one agency was unacceptable to another. The bureaucracies were not interested in peace. Many employees in both organizations spent much of their time designing and executing turf war strategies and battles. Under the leadership of the Fed's turf-war commander and chief legal counsel, Mike Bradfield, the Fed drew the line, withdrew from the agreement to set common rules, and stated that it was not really interested in any agreement that did not settle the matter of jurisdiction in favor of the Fed. The battle was reminiscent of the trench warfare of World War I—no victors in sight. In my first two years at the FDIC,

I spent too much of my time in this most disagreeable, unrewarding, and wasteful warfare.

Just one more example of turf disagreements should be
sufficient to illustrate why government is often so horribly
inefficient. This one is complex but useful. The classic contest revolved around how much investment a bank should
have to keep as a safe cushion of capital—the amount of
money the stockholders were prepared to lose if their bank
managers made bad loans. The term of art for this issue was
capital standards. Under the chairmanship of Peter Cooke of
the Bank of England, an agreement on capital standards was
negotiated by the principal banking countries through the
Bank for International Settlements in Basel, Switzerland. It
was a most miraculous achievement in international affairs
and an example to government officials everywhere. Our
chronically feuding breed in the United States had for once
all participated and *agreed*. Unfortunately, the beauty of the
cooperation abroad did not last long at home. The Basel
agreement provided that a bank's capital requirements
would be based on the types of loans it had on its books.
Obviously there was more risk in holding mortgages on private houses than bonds on the government of the United
States, and the former demanded a thicker capital cushion
than the latter. This was called a system of risk-based capital.
In adopting the new standards, regulators abandoned the
common capital standard traditionally used in the United
States for all loans and assets of whatever kind, which is
called leverage-based capital.

Congress approved this agreement on risk-based standards in the 1989 law that also set up the rescue of the savings and loans. Using the international agreement for
guidance, the Comptroller of the Currency was given the
power to set standards for his national banks and for the
troubled S&L industry. But these new standards were not
considered sufficient to protect the FDIC insurance fund.
For example, the new standards stipulated that banks did

not have to hold any capital to protect themselves against losses in their government bonds, which were considered risk-free. But of course government bonds do have some risk, as do all debt instruments. Even though no one doubts the full faith and credit of the United States to pay interest and principal when due, when interest rates go up, the market value of the bonds goes down because the fixed rate is less than the money could earn in a new bond. This is called interest rate risk and is no small matter for banks. In fact, in 1992, with loan demand down and bond interest high, commercial banks had more of their money invested in government bonds than in commercial and industrial loans for the first time in memory. The risk is obvious. Until the boys in the Basel committee came up with a low interest rate risk standard (which they were working on), it was generally recognized that an additional backup standard was needed to cover all assets: our old friend the leverage ratio (ratio of capital invested to total assets).

However, Robert Clarke, the comptroller of the currency, appeared to have fallen in love with the new standards. New Mexico–born, Harvard-educated, and Texas-trained, he had been appointed by President Reagan at the suggestion of Secretary of the Treasury James Baker. He was a very fine lawyer and had a strong backhand (we played the backhand court on our regulators' doubles team). Sally and I became good friends with Clarke and his wife, Puddin (only in Texas), and we enjoyed many memorable times together. The unfortunate tendency of government service to erode these personal relationships will be well illustrated as this tale proceeds.

By law his agency had been awarded the power to implement the new standards, and he naturally did not relish the imposition of another standard that would displace his own. Without slowing down the story for too much technical detail, suffice it to say that unless the new risk standards were overridden by a leverage standard demanding a ratio of at least 6 percent of capital to loans, about nine out of ten small banks across the country would be allowed to reduce their capital cushion at precisely the time when the entire banking industry was being threatened by a rising level of risk. Clarke, normally a cooperative gentleman, consulted with his staff and insisted that 3 percent would be high enough. A few weeks later we met in my office to try to settle the issue. Compromise was in the wind: We agreed on 4.5 percent—halfway between 3 and 6 (what could be fairer?)—and we shook hands on the deal in the interest of a common national front and good government. Not more than two hours later, Clarke called to say that after a further review (with his world-class Treasury turf squad), the deal was off. "Bill," he said, "I went back and talked to my staff, and you know there are times when you can't get a compromise. We will just have to disagree."

The banking industry was stuck in the middle, unsure of what standard should apply. The Federal Reserve, with the wise William Taylor in command of its Supervisory Division, was also unhappy with the comptroller's rigid position. The FDIC and the Federal Reserve reached a compromise with the help of C. C. Hope. The lower capital requirement, Mr. Clarke's 3 percent, would apply only to banks in the safest class—Camel One banks, we called them. Banks are rated by regulators from one (best) to five (worst), based on their *C*apital, *A*sset, *M*anagement, *E*arnings, and *L*oan quality. All other banks would have to have a ratio of more than 4 percent to back up their loans.

In fact there were no Camel One banks with such low levels of capital; banks in this category, such as J.P. Morgan, were far better protected with higher capital ratios. (By definition, that was one reason they had won their top ratings.) So on its face, the proposed rule was preposterous because the 3 percent standard we wrote into the rules to please Clarke could apply only to banks that we all knew did not exist. Still, it illustrated how compromises develop among the turf combatants. The proposed compromise (the 3 percent rule) was presented to the Office of the Comptroller, whose denizens nodded wisely and declared that it certainly was an improvement—but they still did not agree. They were dug in!

What was happening here was of course not just a battle for turf, but a real disagreement over what each regulator thought was right for the banking system. Clarke wanted a capital standard that would allow large national banks under his purview to compete with foreign banks. It is not that turf battles are only about ego and never without merit; the problem is that the response to disagreements is for each regulator to grab his own banks and wall them off from the others. Meanwhile, the industry suffers from uncertainty and uneven rules.

The matter soon came to the attention of Congress. At a hearing, Chairman Riegle of the Senate Banking Committee informed Clarke that he would move to have the Congress set standards if the regulators could not come to a sensible agreement among themselves. (All regulators fear losing turf, but most of all they fear losing it to Congress.) Riegle noted that the Federal Reserve and the FDIC were in agreement, and asked the Comptroller to resolve the situation. Clarke finally buckled and agreed to the standards as proposed by the FDIC and the Fed. What an inglorious story! The net result was a capital standard that was indefinite and inapplicable. It took over a year to achieve this triumph of compromise over rationality. Our banking system would be far more efficient at providing credit if regulatory wars and overkill could be controlled.

Unfortunately, the strains on Clarke's and my personal relationship increased even more over something only tangentially related to turf. Alone among all regulators, Clarke had not put his personal investments into a blind trust. Thus he would know what was happening to them. Trusts were used to clearly avoid any appearance of profiting from his

136

FULL FAITH AND CREDIT

government office. Instead, he traded in junk bonds and even invested in property tax certificates in Colorado while he was serving as comptroller. He told his own office, which found it difficult to call the boss on the carpet for conflicts of interest. But the information was not supplied to the FDIC on our request. Even after the FDIC took over the bankrupt insurance funds of the S&Ls with their inventory of junk bonds, when we asked that his records be filed with us, we were politely but firmly told by the Treasury Ethics Department that it was none of our business.

The whole thing surfaced (as it usually does sooner or later) in the press. Sue Schmidt of *The Washington Post* reported that Clarke was buying and selling junk bonds at the same time that these very bonds were being bought and sold by the Resolution Trust Corporation, the government agency set up to clean up the S&L mess. The matter was ultimately resolved by the regulatory agencies meeting under the jurisdiction of the Treasury. The Ethics Department at the Treasury and the White House ruled that Clarke had not violated the law. He agreed to put his assets into a blind trust and to desist from any further activities that created an appearance of a conflict of interest. Since even the *appearance* of a conflict was itself a violation of the administration's own rules, it seemed to me a somewhat benevolent ruling. They did not even rule that he had created an appearance of a conflict, but rather that he *"might* have created an appearance of a conflict." The average American had a hard time understanding this bit of sophistry, and the government's entire regulatory apparatus got another piece of publicity that it did not need.

I did not participate in the adjudication because of my friendship with Clarke. But it was hard to hide my personal opinion that Clarke's activities did not help the reputation of the RTC, which was already under siege. Clarke, of course, soon learned of my views, and that, sad to say, tainted our friendship.

Shortly thereafter, Clarke's appointment as comptroller was expiring; and beyond all reason, he decided he wanted a second term in the thankless job of comptroller. The country was going into a recession and there was a severe credit crunch, which many attributed to the harshness of our regulators in the field. When Clarke's name arose, it was immediately opposed by the White House chief of staff, John Sununu, who reflected the feelings of Team 100, a group of the largest contributors to the Republican party, about half of whom were big in real estate. Large builders and contractors had benefited immensely from the previously delayed recognition that the banks were loaning money for real estate on the flimsiest of proposals, and they resented Clarke's self-described role as "the regulator from Hell" when he tightened up supervision. Clarke's nomination was batted around for a while until his boss, Treasury Secretary Nicholas Brady, debated the matter with Sununu in front of the president. Brady liked working with Clarke, had no one else in mind, and wanted to continue things as they were. Brady prevailed, and Clarke was named for a second term. In Clarke's confirmation hearings his personal financial dealings were damaging, and that, combined with his regulatory problems, resulted in his failure to win the support of the Banking Committee. Many of his problems could have been avoided if turf considerations had not prevented better cooperation. Even as good friends, Clarke and I, comptroller and chairman of the FDIC, could not avoid Washington turf wars and the resulting damage to the system's effectiveness and our personal relationship.

8

Texas: The Bigger They Are . . .

Most banks fail for a simple reason: they lend money they are unable to retrieve. This sad event occurs when borrowers are unable to repay their loans, and the assets pledged to the banks to ensure repayment are not sufficient to cover the debt. The pledged asset, like an empty office building or a failed business, does not meet the loaned amount because both borrower and lender misjudged what it would be worth if it had to be sold to pay off the loan. Occasionally banks fail because they mismatch their cash needs and their obligations—for example, when they have too much of their cash tied up in nonsalable long-term loans and cannot pay out money when their depositors demand it. This is called "liquidity insolvency."

Banks seldom fail because their management is fraudulent, although there are occasional cases of bankers literally stealing enough to break the bank. Since banks have the ability to create money by making loans, they are an obvious target for those with larceny as their preferred life-style. Banks therefore must be carefully regulated in order to avoid fraud, even though it is the exception and not the rule. In my experience at the FDIC, the cause of the greatest set of bank failures since the Great Depression was not fraud but a set of interlocking policy decisions that loosened regulation, protected banks from competition and gave a full faith and credit government guarantee of their deposits. Most important, it was the decision of many bankers to make commercial real estate lending their new land of opportunity— forgetting, of course, that this is the most speculative of all markets.

During the regime of my predecessor, William Isaac, the FDIC began to emerge from its long period of quiet anonymity as bank failures rose from an average of ten or fifteen a year to 79 in 1984 and 120 in 1985, which included the collapse of one of the country's top ten banks, Continental Bank of Illinois, just before my term as chairman of the FDIC began. In the spring of 1986 my senior staff, Cooke, Watson, Fritts, and Murphy, began its favorite (and most impossible) activity: predicting the future course of banking. We assembled our group to identify those banks that were going to fail over the next eighteen months. The staff agreed that the problems in the banking system in 1986 and beyond were going to be huge but not new, just the old-fashioned kind: bad loans. Large numbers of bad loans suddenly are revealed when the economy weakens. As the saying goes, "It is only when the tide goes out that you can see who is swimming without a bathing suit."

Texas was the focus of the approaching problem. In the Lone Star State, everything is bigger and optimism knows no bounds. In 1985 Texas had 1,935 banks, more than any other state; half of all the banks on the FDIC problem list called Texas home. The first comptroller of the currency in the Reagan administration, C. Todd Conover, had chartered an abundance of new banks in Texas. Supporting the administration's ideals of deregulation and more competition, he chartered almost every bank that could meet the minimum capital standard. But the new banks were often poorly managed, undercapitalized, and had no real prospects of economic success because they could not create a market franchise or were crowded by an established bank that already had it. One way to fight for a share of the market was to make more loans, and that meant both the new and the established banks were drumming up risky business that neither of them had any business being in.

When the Comptroller of the Currency chartered a national bank, the FDIC was required to insure it, which meant that we had no say in the quality of the clients we were bound by law to insure. This lack of veto power proved very costly in Texas. The problem, once again, was caused by turf. The comptroller resisted, with all possible force, the suggestion that the FDIC should even be able to voice its doubts about the risks it was forced to undertake. Through their capital, the shareholders took only about six to ten cents of the risk with every dollar of the loans their banks made—and they made loans very freely in an attempt to attract new business. If the banks failed, ninety cents and more of the risk in every loan was carried by the FDIC, which in the last resort could mean, but to this date has not meant, that the taxpayers would pay if bank premiums could not cover all the failures. Few new banks in Texas were ready for the economic tide to recede. But hard times in Texas came as oil prices plummeted from $30 a barrel to the low teens.

Then, in the Texas spirit of ever bigger and better, banks turned eagerly to real estate lending. Looser laws compounded the problem. At the request of the Reagan administration, in 1982 the Congress removed from federal banking laws all the rules on real estate lending for construction and development projects (C&D). Up until then, builders who wanted a C&D loan had to put down at least 25 percent of the money. The borrowers also had to arrange for a "take out," which meant that they had to refinance bank loans within three to five years through a long-term lender who would then take out the bank by taking over the loan. That long-term lender usually was an insurance company. At the time the rules were changed, new tax incentives were also being provided for real estate developments. This allowed developers to take more liberal depreciation allowances and create tax losses to shelter their other income. In this combustible mixture of liberalized banking and tax subsidies for real estate, construction lending exploded. Large banks and small, new and old, advanced money with no equity from developers, who did not even have to pay interest for the first three years because it was provided in the total amount of the loan.

The Texas banks were unprepared for hard times. Texas had been a locked-up state, with no foreign—which to Texans meant no out-of-state—banks allowed. Texans believed their banks were the most profitable, the best capitalized, and the best managed in the country. Only the first two of those beliefs were correct. They felt they had too good a deal to share. Years of limited competition had left their managements weak and unprepared for a real estate recession.

The construction boom lasted through 1986, when Congress removed the tax incentives. Then the air was let out of the balloon, and nine out of the ten largest banks in Texas were in serious trouble with defaulting real estate loans. The great majority of these loans would have been illegal before 1982. Four years without a sound credit policy in real estate lending became a knife in the heart of the banking industry. We decided we were in for the biggest losses in the history of the FDIC.

The emerging debt binge of the eighties caught up with Texas and its southwestern neighbors first. In November 1986, I spoke in San Francisco at the U.S. League of Savings Institutions convention.

I told the group that "at no time since World War II has the simultaneous growth of debt in both households and business sectors been so rapid. The current escalation of debt in this country cannot be extended for many more years without the potential for unacceptable risk. The rate of increase is just too steep. We must proceed with care. The flashing yellow caution light is operational."

The first part of that talk was sound, but the last part about the yellow caution light was off the mark. It might have endangered the stability of the system itself if I had said what I really felt—that the sirens are screaming and the red light is flashing. The speech was made as a warning to savings and loan executives and was also directed at bankers but obviously neither was listening. The huge accumulation of debt continued, a good part of it in our insured financial institutions.

Following the macro statistics of the economy is a longtime interest of mine. By the end of 1986, it became very clear that U.S. debt levels had reached historic highs. (High in terms of the ability to pay—the availability of income to service the debt.) The most unusual thing about this period was that debt burdens were high in every part of the economy: consumer, real estate, corporate, and at the governmental level. (The government's interest payments on the national debt were growing faster than any part of the federal budget, even defense.) It seemed obvious that the debt binge would mean real trouble for the banking business. But, of course, when things are swinging along, no one likes to have some government man come around and say, "Well, you have to watch out; you are lending too much, the values are too high. There is danger ahead. There is likely to be a crash." As William McChesney Martin of the Fed used to warn, the hard part is taking away the punch bowl just when the party is getting good. While I said what I had to say, it paid to be circumspect about it. Representatives of the government never forget that they cannot just give a personal opinion, and they are listened to much more carefully because of what they represent and not just how smart they are. It means treading a very fine line by trying to warn people without frightening them so much that you could touch off the crash that you are trying to prevent.

The Texas problems did not take long to surface. Early in 1987, the First City Bank Corporation of Texas asked the

FDIC for help. First City was a venerable Houston institution with $12 billion in loans. It was chaired by the respected sixty-seven-year-old son of its renowned founder, Judge J. A. Elkins. The bank was recognized as virtually the ministry of finance for the petroleum business, with the judge's law firm, Vinson & Elkins, as its attorney general. First City had been growing at 20 percent a year during the oil boom. When oil prices fell in 1982, the bank's clients included important names like Parker Drilling Company, from Tulsa; Blocker Energy Corporation, Global Marine, Inc., and Zapata Corporation, from Houston; Western Company of North America, from Fort Worth; and Penrod Drilling Company and Placid Oil Company (the Hunt Brothers) from Dallas. When those companies got into trouble, so did their bankers.

Bank management had already begun to put the brakes on energy lending, and First City might have survived if, like other Texas banks, it had not looked toward the real estate market for new ways to continue its Texas-style growth. In 1982 real estate accounted for less than 20 percent of its loans. By 1987, real estate lending had almost doubled to $3.2 billion, or over 35 percent of First City's loans, and a good part of the increase was in such risky construction and development lending as the fifty-three-story Heritage Plaza, which, largely vacant, later became one of Houston's notorious see-through skyscrapers.

Weeks before we had to do so, the FDIC board began considering a plan for rescuing First City. We discussed it at each meeting, all the while hoping that the situation would not require an FDIC rescue. But it became increasingly apparent that if we did not act, the free market would fail the bank, showing its lack of confidence by withdrawing its funds. Paul Fritts, our director of supervision, had been saying for months that First City would not make it. Finally, on Thursday, September 10, 1987, the FDIC announced it was placing $1 billion in First City's holding company, the legal owner of sixty-two separate banks. The second largest federal rescue in our history was underway, but we decided not to be as solicitous of the interests of the bank's owners and bondholders as we had been in the past. This time as the price of keeping First City open, we for the first time wanted concessions from all the holding company debt holders. So while the action taken would protect all depositors, we announced, "This is no bailout for the old shareholders, or for the old bank management. . . . For their purposes . . . the bank has failed." This was only a slight overstatement because we demanded as a price for putting in our money that the stockholders reduce the value of their shares to a paltry 3 percent of the company, leaving the government with the rest. The bondholders and creditors of the First City Holding Company were required to agree to take a substantial "hit."

Requiring bondholders in the bank holding company to reduce their debt holding became the most difficult part of the deal. In Continental Illinois's failure the bondholders had been protected, even though they were not insured. Most of First City's bonds had been dumped as its troubles became public, and they had been purchased for a few cents on the dollar by Wall Street arbitragers. These individuals from the fast-buck society bought the bonds in a bet that they could hold out for nearly full payment on their cheaply bought debt. They knew that if the FDIC failed to meet their price, we might have to close all of First City's sixty-two banks. They reckoned that the Continental Illinois precedent would force us to cover all company debtors, including them, because we had no other way to handle such a large institution and would recoil from closing it down and risking the panic and huge losses that might occur in the weakened Texas economy. Some of course argued that no such panic would have occurred, but most public officials operate under the banner of "not on my watch" and do not care to gamble with such possibilities.

Although we had no legal vehicle for keeping a failed bank

in operation after taking it over, we had already thought about it and had asked Congress to strengthen our bargaining hand in just such situations by giving us the power to create "bridge banks" to hold and operate the assets of failed institutions until we could dispose of them in an orderly manner. The Congress was considering the proposal even as the First City drama was unfolding. For the moment, though, since we were without bridges, we had to negotiate with the "arbs" to do a backup. We broadcast strong statements about our willingness to "close her down" if the "arbs" would not agree to a reasonable adjustment of their debt claims.

Meanwhile, a First City rescue plan was evolving. A group of new investors, led by Robert Abboud, were going to raise and invest $500 million with the help of the investment banking firm of Donaldson, Lufkin and Jenrette, Inc. Abboud, a sharply dressed Harvard graduate, had a lot of experience in an unusual career. He started at the First Chicago Bank in 1958 and worked his way to the top. He then lost the job in 1980 for failing to keep up with his principal competitor, high-flying Continental Illinois, which was in the process of overextending itself and, as already recounted, failed. After this he went to work for Armand Hammer at Occidental Petroleum Corporation until he again left under duress in 1984. Since Hammer was known to be one of the nastiest and most dictatorial of corporate bosses—a title for which the competition was fierce—it was not a proven minus on Abboud's record. Abboud saw First City as a chance to prove that his prudent banking style was just what Texas needed. With the FDIC's help, he laid out a plan to restore the bank to its preeminent position. We thought Abboud was just what First City needed. It did not turn out to be one of our best calls.

Abboud had some associates he wanted to bring with him. John Stone, our senior supervisor on the case, objected to some of these associates. When we asked him why he objected and what he could prove, he replied, "Unfortunately, nothing for sure." Lacking any hard evidence and believing in innocent until proven guilty, we said nothing. Another bad call! First City came upon hard times again in the recession of 1991, and many of its problems involved loans made by Abboud's associates. In addition and in hindsight, we probably drove too tough a deal with Abboud, which did not leave him enough money to save the bank. Others were bidding, and we took the best bid. It turned out that the bid that gave the most money to the government was too good, because the bank failed again late in 1992, at a cost to the FDIC of perhaps another half-billion dollars.

It took nine months and a few minor miracles to consummate the First City transaction, but in the end the stockholders approved and the "arbs" got more than they deserved but less than they expected. Donaldson Lufkin raised the capital (with a major assist from Drexel Burnham Lambert). Perhaps the biggest surprise occurred on September 11, 1987, when the transaction received the editorial approval of *The Washington Post:*

> As a practical matter, failing banks leave government regulators with very few acceptable alternatives. If a bailout costs the insurance fund less than letting the bank go bust and paying off the insured depositors, then a bailout is self-evidently the right thing to do. The rescue of the First City Bancorp of Texas was a model of good sense and an example of the guidelines that the Federal Deposit Insurance Corp. has worked out through a series of difficult cases.

For the moment we all breathed a sigh of relief. We hoped First City might be the last of the big Texas failures. The complexity of the First City transaction did teach us that failures would be more easily handled by closing the failing banks and eliminating automatic FDIC support for the holding company's bondholders, stockholders, and the troublesome "arbs." The FDIC acted as the receiver of the failed bank and left the bank holding company behind. In addition, we could peel away any claims against the bank, as in any bankruptcy. Then we could construct a "bridge bank" and sell it to a new purchaser as a nice clean institution with no hidden booby traps, such as environmental or lender liability claims. A purchasing bank could pay us for the branch network in a new territory and know exactly what it was buying.

While we hoped for the best, we planned for the worst. The ever-realistic Paul Fritts was predicting many more failures to come across the oil patch in Texas, Oklahoma, and Louisiana. We thought the next catalyst might have arrived on Black Monday, the 508-point plunge of the stock market on October 19, 1987. But after the Federal Reserve flooded the financial system with money, it was clear that no major bank failures would take place as a result of the crash. Banks actually improved their positions because investors moved their money to the safety of insured deposits. The problems in the banking system were different, and deeper, than the overheated stock market. The FDIC conducted an emergency survey of U.S. banks, and three weeks later, on November 9, we were able to report that:

> If people are looking for a domino effect to take place in our economy following Black Monday, there is little evidence in the banking system at this point that the dominoes have begun to fall. In fact, at this time, a number of banks appear to be ahead rather than behind. A survey this week of 215 banks across the country revealed nearly a third took in more deposits than normal since the 508-point plunge on Wall Street, 82 percent experienced higher loan demand from both consumers and businesses, and 94 percent said they expected no additional loan loss.

History proved this analysis correct. Black Monday did not start the depression that many were expecting. It was only a Wall Street correction, and Main Street watched with amusement and some satisfaction as $500,000-a-year, twenty-six-year-old MBAs bit the dust.

Fritts had predicted that the Texas banking system was in for more and bigger problems and, as usual, he was correct. In June 1986, the merger of Republic Bank Corporation and InterFirst Corporation had created the biggest bank holding company in Texas, the First Republic Corporation. It had taken place without federal government assistance, but with the approval of the federal regulators. At the time there were accusations that the comptroller, Bob Clarke, was allowing his Texas roots to influence his decision because the largest shareholder in Republic Bank was a well-known Republican activist, Bum Bright, who was better known as the owner of the Dallas Cowboys football team. Clarke's approval brought accusations from the press of political favoritism.

In fact, there were no political pressures or favors. Clarke's staff had recommended against the proposed combination based on the financial positions of both banks, which had been seriously weakened by real estate. However, Volcker, Clarke, and I agreed that without the merger, both banks were more likely to fail, and that would cost even more than if they failed together. We knew the approval would be criticized, and it was. If all went well, the merger held out the hope of reducing expenses at the two banks by over $100 million per year. New capital would be added by the sale of $200 million of subordinated notes and preferred stock. We also anticipated that after it was merged, the new bank would be more attractive to buyers than two separate banks because it offered complete coverage throughout the state. Thus a new $40-billion-dollar bank was created.

By February 1987, the market was already signaling its doubts that First Republic Bank was viable. It had lost $347 million in the last quarter of 1986, and the capital cushion against bad loans was down to 2.4 percent. The chairman of the bank, Gerald W. Fronterhouse, stated that customer withdrawals of $1.1 billion in January and February were

manageable. The bank began running full-page advertisements denying it was in trouble. There is probably no better
and simultaneously more self-defeating indication that a
bank is in trouble than an advertisement indicating everything is fine. Such advertisements provide many assurances,
but in fact, only raise more doubts. Deposit insurance or no
deposit insurance, a lot of the depositors wanted their money
elsewhere.

Within a week of its February 22nd advertisement, First
Republic, the nation's twelfth largest bank with one of the
largest check-clearing organizations in the country, reported
a record number of depositors pulling their accounts. Some
free-market theorists have claimed that deposit insurance
has an adverse effect on market discipline, preventing runs
on banks; and they long to return to the discipline of the
depositor running for cover. This yearning was soon to be
fulfilled.

The bank's depositors continued to withdraw their money,
and on March 16, 1987, the bank sought FDIC assistance.
While they were not exactly experiencing a full-scale run on
the bank (with lines of depositors in the lobby), something
like a slow walk was underway. People and institutions were
removing their money when their certificates of deposit and
similar instruments matured and taking them elsewhere.

At this time, there was a widespread perception that some
banks were "too big to fail"—that the tidal waves their collapse would send through the financial system would be so
damaging that those responsible for its stability would do
whatever was necessary to prevent such a thing from happening. It was the FDIC's rescue of the Continental Illinois
Bank, its holding company and the bank itself that gave rise
to this clever phrase. After Continental, the comptroller testified before Congress that there were probably ten or twelve
other banks that were also too big to close down. The press
promptly named it inaccurately "too big to fail." It should
have been "too big to allow the banks to close down and

penalize uninsured depositors," but that was not a good sound bite.

Gerald Corrigan, president of the New York Fed, had proposed that we adopt a doctrine he called "constructive ambiguity," which would make it clear that no institution or its depositors could ever be sure that the institution was too big to fail. The regulators agreed to be "ambiguous," but the markets knew that the largest institutions would always be known as too big to fail. No matter how this doctrine might be described, depositors at the First Republic Bank were unwilling to rely on its uncertainties. While the media was predicting the de facto nationalization of the bank through another Continental-type rescue, the market took over, as it so often does.

On Wednesday, March 16, 1987, bankers called from all over the state of Texas and told us that the "walk" on the bank had become an "electronic run." Withdrawals, mainly by smaller banks, had totaled about $1 billion in one morning. It was a real bank run, even if dressed in high-tech garb. I called a meeting of the FDIC board that lasted past midnight to devise a plan to handle the incipient panic. On Thursday, we announced a $1 billion loan to the banks owned by First Republic Bank Corporation and gave an FDIC guarantee to all their depositors, insured or uninsured. It was a holding action designed to calm depositors until we could nail down the terms of the rescue. Unlike Continental Illinois, we gave our guarantee and our money directly to two of the banks owned by the company (the Dallas and Houston banks), but not to the holding company itself and its bond- and stockholders. This difference was of great significance. It removed the safety net from the billions of dollars of holding company debt. It reduced our insurance losses, disciplined the creditors of the holding company for their bad investment, and stabilized the banking system.

Our billion-dollar loan was just a down payment, and we faced the problem of what to do with our new ward. The first thing to do was to find new management to run the company while we tried to drum up a buyer. Fronterhouse, the chairman who had directed the merger of First Republic, was not acceptable. Comptroller Clarke and I settled on Albert V. Casey, former newspaper executive, chairman of American Airlines and U.S. postmaster general. He was an affable man and a master politician with a record of success as a manager. (Not including the Post Office, where success has yet to be achieved by anyone.) He was retired and keeping busy as a part-time professor at Southern Methodist University in Dallas, but he was bored by that job and with his many corporate directorships. Having settled on Casey, we soon learned why he had had a successful and remunerative career. In addition to demanding a good salary of $600,000, he insisted on a signing bonus of $450,000. Our board, with each member paid $83,000 per year, took a big gulp and agreed. We needed the help of a proven manager, even if he was not a banker. Casey had been a director of Republic Bank, but he had had the foresight to leave some years before the collapse. He became chairman and CEO of the First Republic holding company, and we began the search for a private sector solution to what was for all practical purposes, a nationalized organization.

Several bidders appeared, but the first, by months, was NCNB, a North Carolina bank expanding into what now is called a "superregional" bank—one that crosses state lines. Both the idea and the bank itself have proven extremely successful. NCNB was led with absolute determination by its chairman, Hugh McColl, a former Marine who appeared within days of Casey's appointment as interim manager and declared he was ready to make a deal. Our first meeting took place in my office, and McColl made it clear from the outset that this was an acquisition he was going to make and he would allow nothing to stand in his way. He emphasized that he was used to achieving his objectives and that First Republic was one of his most important. Furthermore, he made it clear that he wanted the bank, not the holding company, and outlined in detail how he was ready to take over quickly without disruption to the banking system. By separating a bridge bank from its holding company, we were able to offer a clean bank without the lawsuits and other liabilities of its predecessor.

McColl was a tough bargainer. Twice he walked out of my office during negotiations because he was dissatisfied with our slow pace. He believed that he had a competitive advantage since he had been the first bidder to do his homework on the failed institution—and of course he was right. The last time he roared out of my office he said, "Someone else will have to buy this mess of a bank." He let us know he was withdrawing because we were not willing to keep to his schedule. We bade him a fond farewell.

A week later a call came in from Tokyo. It was McColl (by now labeled by me as the "little general") asking if it was still possible for him to put in a bid. "Yes," I responded, and welcomed him back with open arms. He had been raising money in Japan to back up his offer. I told him we were sticking to our schedule and wished him good fortune in raising lots of yen for his bid. In my dealings with him, he was always a straightforward gentleman and so eager to buy First Republic that no bluffing he tried was at all effective. It was the first step in his desire to expand NCNB, which stood for North Carolina National Bank, into "The Nation's Bank," which is its present name.

Meanwhile, Casey devised a plan to rescue the entire First Republic *holding company* organization, plus the banks. His plan included raising new capital for the holding company from investors. Casey's instrument for raising capital was the investment banking firm of Drexel Burnham Lambert, the home base of the junk bond king, Michael Milken. Drexel had become one of the country's largest providers of new capital, particularly in high-risk situations. Peter Ackerman, Milken's top associate, was assigned to the First Republic account. Drexel apparently wanted First Republic's business not only for the usual reasons, but to obtain a sort of U.S. government seal of approval during a period when Milken and the firm were under an SEC investigation that eventually led to the firm's bankruptcy and Milken's ten-year sentence for securities fraud. Our board indicated it was willing to do business with Drexel until such time as it was found guilty of some violation of the law. Although we were concerned about the possible political ramifications of a junk bond transaction, we were trying to solve the problem at the lowest cost possible to our limited resources.

While many of the best banks in the country looked at First Republic, Casey's Drexel assisted offer, Wells Fargo of San Francisco, and NCNB were the final bidders. NCNB was the declared winner!

On July 29, the FDIC board decided to close the First Republic banks and reopen a bridge bank to be sold to NCNB, because its bid was the least costly to the insurance fund. Actually we had to pay NCNB to take the bank and all its liabilities off our hands, but McColl won because he offered us the lowest cost, which was a capital infusion of $1.05 billion. NCNB put in $200 million and the FDIC put in $800 million. For this NCNB acquired only 20 percent of the bank. We retained 80 percent of the bridge bank and NCNB had the right to buy out the rest. As it became profitable, NCNB bought out the rest and we got our share of the profits, $270 million. If NCNB had not been able to make its new Texas franchise work, we would have been left holding the bag, that is, the bank, and would have had to start again. The structure of the transaction was a direct product of the lessons learned from the Continental Illinois rescue and of the new bridge bank powers enacted in the Competitive Equality Banking Act of 1987.

No one had ever before tried anything like this with a major bank holding company. We devised an hour-by-hour plan of attack. We closed all of First Republic's banks and we put the assets into our newly created successor bank. We thus stripped the holding company—and its stock- and bond-holders—of its prime asset. It was a totally different transaction from the one with First City; without the banks, there was no carcass for the owners, their failed managers, and the vulture arbitragers to argue about. Our general counsel, John Douglas, and our banking supervisors did a marvelous job in effecting an immediate reincarnation of First Republic under new ownership.

When it finally failed, First Republic had shrunk to a $33 billion institution, down from about $40 billion at the time of the merger. We were already estimating the cost of the rescue at $2 billion to $3 billion.

NCNB assigned a team of 250 to take control immediately. The deal was done—and the repercussions began!

Small bankers were no less schizophrenic than those who had criticized us for rescuing Continental Illinois. Hundreds in Texas praised us for saving First Republic because that meant we had saved their funds on deposit there. But hundreds of small bankers from all over the country protested that the rescue gave large banks an unfair competitive advantage over them.

The stock- and bondholders of First Republic were left with their holding company and whatever few assets this shell now contained. The stockholders got nothing, the bondholders far less than the face value of their bonds. The First Republic bondholders screamed. Some unkind letters, to say the least, were received at the FDIC. (It was difficult not to feel sympathy for the thousands of Texans who had bought these bonds for their retirement, trusting the business leaders of their state, and now were left with high-priced wallpaper.) Some on Wall Street looked upon us as lepers. But our board had chosen the best bid, with the lowest cost to the insurance fund. Millions of dollars were saved by leaving the holding company creditors behind, and the government was out of the business of protecting bank holding companies. "Too big to fail" was still alive, but in a more limited way.

Casey was furious with me, the FDIC, and the government, accusing us of double-crossing him. He refused to accept our explanation that his proposal was a more costly solution. His being upset was understandable. At our request, he had taken the job in order to save the organization, and our decision to sell to NCNB meant that he had failed. When I called him to apologize, and said that I hoped he could believe we had done what we thought was right, he told me to get lost.

The problems in Texas were not over. The next major institution to topple was M Corp. Run by Gene Bishop, it had once been Texas's largest bank. M Corp., a holding corporation, owned twenty-five subsidiary banks; many were smaller banks acquired during the previous decade. It was known as one of the most progressive banks, both in terms of technology and personnel. During my tenure as dean of the Arizona State University Business School, M Corp. had been one of the most vigorous recruiters on our campus.

The M Corp. case illustrated a basic defect in the organization of the American banking system. As some of the banks owned by the M Corp. holding company began to get into trouble, it was evident that while some of the smaller banks were sound, the larger ones were not. The holding company accumulated hundreds of thousands in cash from the profitable ones and sat on it, refusing to use the money to support its failing banks with a contribution of capital. The Federal Reserve, which regulates bank holding companies, ordered the M Corp. holding company to release its cash downstream to the banks it owned. This put the directors of the holding company in a dilemma. They were responsible to the stock- and bondholders from whom the holding company had raised money—but they were also responsible to the banks they owned, and many of them also served as directors and officers of the banks. Should they use money to improve the

position of the banks they owned at the expense of the holding company? Or should they protect the holding company's
investors and ignore the banks? They chose to let their weak
banks fail, which meant a loss for the FDIC insurance fund,
while keeping their stronger banks as good assets for their
holding company owners.

Federal Reserve doctrine held that holding companies
were supposed to be a source of strength to their subsidiary
banks through their ability to raise and hold capital. But it
soon became clear that in troubled times this doctrine put
the directors in a conflict of interest because they had to
conserve the holding company's financial resources (to pay
dividends and interest) ahead of the bank's (to increase its
capital cushion against loss). Under the source of strength
doctrine, a director who sat on the boards of both the holding company and a subsidiary bank, as many did, was
obliged to maintain the safety and soundess of the bank. But
by law, the directors of the holding companies found themselves damned if they did and damned if they didn't. If they
put money into the bank, their stock- and bondholders could
sue them for putting it into a failing bank when it should
have been held for dividends and interest. If they did not
put money into the bank, they could be sued by regulators
for not supporting it with the holding company's funds,
which in the case of M Corp. represented a sizable hoard.

This dilemma grew out of the fundamental structure of
American banking. Holding companies came into vogue in
the 1950s, when the Congress enacted legislation to regulate
the institutions that owned banks. Its purpose was to assure
that the banking system would be independent of commercial organizations. The merits of this policy certainly could be
debated—German banks and industry have heavy cross
holdings, and both sides profit from the long-term view their
joint directors can take. But in America it simply would not
do to have General Motors buy Citibank or vice versa. Americans have always been leery of concentrations of economic

power. The bank holding company structure also offered special tax advantages by raising money through debt offerings, and then magically putting it into the banks as capital. It helped bankers get around state laws that restricted one bank from controlling others. No other country uses this particular system; it is cumbersome and inefficient. Nevertheless it was there, and it created a large number of legal problems for the FDIC.

A good, or bad, example was the FDIC suing the directors of the banks of the First Republic organization for declaring dividends to the parent company when the bank was undercapitalized and, we argued, in no position to pay dividends to anyone. The sad fact was that while the bank directors were being sued, the directors of the holding company, which owned the bank and had ordered up the dividends, were not being sued, since they had not in fact violated their duties as directors of the holding company.

The legal problems of the structure became even more diabolical when the M Corp. began to fail. The holding company had a very substantial sum of money that it used to help maintain the solvency of its strong banks but refused to send to the weak banks. The holding company, moving its funds around to keep them beyond the reach of the FDIC, allowed its banks to become insolvent and tossed them to the FDIC to pick up their losses and then held on to the strong ones. We took over most of the subsidiaries, but five—the solvent ones—remained in the hands of M Corp. This resulted in massive litigation. Directors were sued by stock- and bondholders, the FDIC was sued by the holding company, and the FDIC sued the holding company and the officers and directors.

In the end, M Corp. won. The holding company walked away with its good banks and its cash and left the FDIC with a loss of about $2 billion on M Corp.'s failed bank subsidiaries. These unprecedented losses prompted the FDIC to sponsor, and Congress to pass, cross-guarantee provisions protecting the insurance fund. All banks in a holding company had to guarantee the FDIC against losses suffered because of the failure of any bank in the group. In addition, holding companies could not enter into what the law defined as "adverse contracts" draining funds from the banks to the holding companies. In order to obtain this legislative protection for the insurance fund, we had to persuade bankers that cross-guarantee rules were necessary, in fact essential, to protect good bankers from bad, unwise, or dishonest ones who would ultimately cost their insurance fund money.

By 1989, the worst of the southwestern failures had passed. The experience in Texas was unlike anything that the FDIC had ever before encountered. The fund's net worth had been approximately halved to about $8 billion, and the vulnerability of the insurance system to any more Texas-sized disasters became obvious. Nine out of the state's ten big banks failed or were acquired and hundreds of small ones went under, but the FDIC protected the Texas system from collapse. Fortunately—and perhaps precisely because of what we did—the local problems were contained and did not spread into a national disaster. There would be other troubled areas, elsewhere in the Oil Patch and then in New England, but their cumulative effect was to slow the economic recovery in the next decade by making bankers more cautious in their lending, rather than to help plunge the country into a great depression.

We had our critics. Martin Mayer, writing in the March 23 *American Banker,* called our work "amateur hour in Texas" and said, we really didn't understand the problem because I was "only an accountant, after all." Nothing he has written since has changed my philosophy that one is well served to be known by one's enemies. The House and Senate Banking Committees and the General Accounting Office raised questions about favorable tax treatment of the NCNB in its takeover of First Republic. But that was a matter for the IRS; we stayed out of it. Representative Charles Schumer, a New

York Democrat, tried to score some political points with a hearing and report claiming we showed favoritism to McColl of NCNB; it sank without trace.

We even received an occasional congratulatory message. Ross Perot thanked us in a telephone call and a note "acclaim[ing] the FDIC for being willing to step in and do something when disaster was at hand." This was long before the Texas billionaire ran for president. Going into the lion's den, he said in a speech before the New York Bankers Association that I was an unrecognized national hero (along with some Marines and the man who invented FM radio). This was certainly kind of him, and most appreciated. As perhaps is often the case, we acted more from necessity than bravery.

In the end, the Texas experience showed that the FDIC could meet the challenge resulting from the failure of a major part of a state's banking system. Both the system and the FDIC survived, but at a $4 billion to $5 billion cost to the insurance fund. Texas also proved conclusively that our bank supervision system was in need of major improvements. Regulators are supposed to remove the punch bowl before the party gets out of hand. Unfortunately, they, in the spirit of the times, had a couple themselves before they realized that the old rules about drinking were still relevant.

9

New England: "We're Not Texans"

The lesson of the Texas banks had barely begun to sink in when similar signs of trouble started to appear in New England. Many a New England banker had assured me during our Texas torments that no such thing could ever happen in conservative New England—"We're not Texans." So much for regional cultural superiority. *The Rate Monitor,* which lists the institutions paying the highest interest rates for deposits, began listing an increasing number of New England banks. This can be a sign that an institution is trying to grow rapidly and attract deposits from outside its local market, or it can be a sign that depositors fear the bank is in trouble and therefore demand a higher return on their money. Above-market deposit rates are one of the regulator's best tools for spotting financial institutions that are growing too fast—or trying to keep from shrinking too fast—and therefore are likely to be on their way to getting into trouble. I once suggested, not entirely in jest, the installation of an electronic system that would seek out high rates and, upon their discovery, send a small electric shock to the seat of the chair occupied by our director of supervision.

By the middle of 1988 large numbers of New England institutions, particularly the savings banks, were paying rates well above the national average. Savings banks are the New

England version of an S&L, making mortgage loans on one-to-four-family homes. The basic difference is that they have bank charters. Our electronic shock system was not in place, so a directive from the chairman to the director of bank supervision Paul Fritts had to do. He was sent to New England to find out what was going on, and when he got there, he found the result of our looking south and west instead of north and east.

We had depleted our supervisory forces in New England to send them to the Southwest. My predecessor had planned to close our Boston office. But fortunately I had countermanded the order, because I did not like the region being folded into the New York jurisdiction. We needed stronger leadership and appointed a new New England director of supervision, but much damage had already been done, especially among savings banks. Their problems were unusual in that they resulted from too much capital rather than too little. They had been converted from mutual banks owned by depositors to ownership by stockholders, raising substantially more capital in the process. Generally, bank regulators have thought that high capital investment means a low risk bank. The large capital amount serves as a buffer against loan losses. Of course this is sound thinking, but in many cases a stock flotation puts the bank management on a course of unusually fast growth, designed to produce good returns for new shareholders. The newly flush institutions had raised a lot of money and it was burning holes in their pockets. That is exactly what caused the problem for many New England savings banks. They were on a "high."

Their fast growth was based on paying high interest rates to attract deposits and to make high-risk, high-return loans. The FDIC was the primary federal regulator of these banks, and our supervisors should have climbed all over their managements for the risky real estate loans they were making in the booming New England economy. Most real estate operators know their business is a boom-and-bust one, and bankers usually protect themselves by devoting only a small part of their portfolio to this cyclical industry. In the 1980s, real-estate-related loans jumped from less than one-fifth to more than one-third of loans. Unfortunately, we "caught on" too late: high capital levels gave our supervisors misleading comfort while our attention was focused elsewhere. Thirty savings banks in New England and New York failed between 1988 and 1991, when the economic boom collapsed.

When the real estate market collapsed, no state in the nation was worse off than New Hampshire, which was ideologically devoted to the free-market fashions of the 1980s under its governor, John Sununu. "Live Free or Die" is the state's motto—they emblazon it on their license plates—and they almost fulfilled the prophecy. By 1990 over half of the outstanding loans in the state were in failing banks. New Hampshire was losing 4 to 5 percent of its jobs annually, the steepest decline of any state in the nation. Overoptimism and misguided deregulation had done in the once archconservative Granite State. Its speculative real estate markets had been fueled by relatively permissive environmental zoning rules in a state that depended heavily on tourism and recreation for a living. It thus became far easier for builders to build, and banks joined the rush to lend to them. By contrast, Vermont, right next door, maintained very strict environmental and zoning rules, so the same overbuilding opportunities were not as easily available. In the end, few Vermont banks failed because they were not lending in the kind of unregulated environment that helped ruin so many New Hampshire banks.

As the New England economy fell into recession, the vulnerability of the banking system became more apparent by the day. All the largest banks in Massachusetts were on the troubled bank list. The first big bank to fail was the Bank of New England, the thirty-fifth largest in the nation, with $21.7 billion in assets in Connecticut, Maine, and Massachusetts. It had grown rapidly through mergers and partly as a result of a management incentive plan that paid loan officers on the basis of the number of loans they wrote. The loss on the institution was estimated to be over $2 billion. The Comptroller of the Currency had the primary responsibility for supervising The Bank of New England because it was a nationally chartered bank, and the comptroller too had focused on the problem only after much of the damage was done. Once banks make too many bad loans, there is no quick way to cure them through supervision or regulation. Weakness can be corrected only through a long period of adding capital by taking it out of profits or raising it in the market place, and even that may not do the job. In hopes of floating the Bank of New England off the rocks, the bank raised $250 million in a special bond issue in September 1989. Within three months the bank's real estate troubles ended up on the front page of *The New York Times,* and the bonds fell from their face value of $1,000 to $20 or less. No one realized how badly the bank had deteriorated, because real estate values were falling so rapidly in Massachusetts that any financial snapshot would have been wrong promptly thereafter. Even with the new money, the bank soon failed.

It was interesting to note the differences in the way various regions faced economic adversity, and its effect on the banking system. Some parts of the country had no banking or S&L problems to speak of, like my native Michigan. Ups and downs were normal in that automotive-based economy, and bankers planned and lent with that in mind. So real estate speculation was not in vogue, and the financial system was unexciting but healthy.

The farm belt of the Midwest—Kansas, Nebraska, and Iowa—assumed that the government would move in to save the situation because support for agriculture by the federal government during a downturn was an unquestioned tradition. They were shocked when federal regulators, acting as bill collectors for failed banks, foreclosed on family farms.

Our people had some rough times, but in general the attitude was: "we have seen it all before, cycles are part of our life—and this too will pass." In Texas and Oklahoma, people met hard times with a fighting spirit; they were determined to rise again and quickly. There was little crying by can-do governors like Bellmon of Oklahoma and Clements of Texas, although we did receive entreaties to ease the rules so they could put their problems behind them. They almost resented the federal bank rescues, and the FDIC's takeover of banks was looked upon as a foreign invasion.

In New England, when the storm struck, the screams for a federal bailout came loud and clear; but they were delivered almost with resignation in the recognition that real federal help was unlikely. Secure in what they thought was a native prudence, they could not believe that real estate values were falling all around them. As it turned out, the banks had loaned almost as wildly as the Texas banks, especially at the Bank of New England. The two other large banks, the Shawmut Bank and the Bank of Boston, were also in trouble because of the real estate crash, but both have survived. With the exception of the Bank of New England, the big banks in the region did take note of the southwestern experience and moved more quickly to deal with their problems.

New England's politicians screamed for help. Young Joe Kennedy, a representative from Massachusetts and the son of the late Robert Kennedy, led the charge. A very personable young man with the family's political talents, he had, like most of the Kennedys, a first-rate staff. When Massachusetts began to focus on banking problems, Kennedy wanted better treatment for the people of New England, even if it required forgetting about collecting on loans from thousands of overextended borrowers. The fact that such action would cost other U.S. taxpayers was not of paramount importance to him. Discussions became acrimonious at committee hearings. Once he charged me with being uncooperative and inefficient at best, but afterward he sent me a note saying,

"Nothing personal. My people want action." We met for a drink soon after, and the legendary Kennedy charm was in evidence. He sometimes asked me for advice and, unlike many politicians, he seemed interested in my answers. Though we argued at the rap of a committee chairman's gavel, we never had a disagreement that could be considered personal.

Not all of the problems in New England were with the banks. Rhode Island's nonfederally insured credit unions were also in trouble. The cause was mainly the same—bad loans and less-than-adequate supervision. In November 1990, my good friend Roger Jepsen, chairman of the National Credit Union Administration, called to warn me of problems developing in Rhode Island "that you should know about." Jepsen, a former senator, was one of the best and most politically skilled regulators. He knew how to handle his job with a maximum amount of efficiency and a minimum amount of noise, so when he called, we listened. He told us that the private corporation insuring Rhode Island's credit unions was insolvent and the senior officer had disappeared. He also reported that his office had been examining the state's privately insured credit unions, and he warned, "A large number are about to be publicly declared insolvent." Even though all of Rhode Island's credit unions had been insured by private state insurers and not by the national credit union insurance fund, Jepsen predicted that the state's predicament would become a major problem for us, since the state would undoubtedly seek to obtain federal insurance.

We arranged a meeting in Providence with the governor-elect, a handsome businessman-turned-politician by the name of Bruce Sundlun. Bruce had been an acquaintance of mine since our days together at Harvard Law School. The departing governor, Edward R. DiPrete, was also present. Sundlun had spent a lot of his own money seeking the governorship and now had finally achieved success. He was to be inaugurated in four days, starting his term in January 1991.

Before the meeting the FDIC had reviewed the situation. We agreed with the credit union's supervisors that most of the credit unions in the state were insolvent. The potential loss was about $250 million. The credit unions that were in trouble held deposits from over 25 percent of all of the people in the state, many of them working or elderly people who had prudently put away their savings in what they thought was a safe place.

When incoming Governor Sundlun heard this, he responded like the businessman he was, and not the governor he was about to become. He remarked that the depositors had chosen to put their money into these institutions because they would receive a higher rate of interest. While it was unfortunate they would suffer a loss, they had received the benefit of higher interest rates on their investments. The state government's only concern should be closing these institutions in the most efficient way.

We promised that we would help liquidate them. My suggestion, as an old friend, was that penalizing depositors in this situation was not going to be easy to do without a political revolt.

The governor-elect's view was that this developing disaster could be blamed on the previous administration. He said his job was to clean up the mess as quickly as possible.

I replied, "Well, Governor, we sure hope that you can handle it that way, because it doesn't appear that the federal insurance funds can be of much assistance. You might explore how you can protect depositors, at least in part, with state funds. Or even better, you can look for federal assistance through legislation. You know, when things like this happen, governors always go to Washington to ask for a bailout."

The governor said he would be in touch with us as soon as he was sworn in—and he was. Days after the inauguration, his office began a campaign to obtain federal insurance for the failed institutions, just as Chairman Jepsen had predicted. We took a hard look, along with the Office of Thrift Supervision, but no such rescue was possible because the credit unions were not qualified for federal insurance. Taking over insurance losses after they occurred was not our business. Furthermore, our funds were already depleted by large losses on our insured institutions in New England. The businessman-turned-governor began to see political reality. He had a political revolt on his hands if he did not take care of those thousands of small depositors. Within a month Sundlun announced that the state would protect depositors up to the insured amount of $100,000. The problem with this political promise was that it far exceeded the state's ability to pay, probably even to borrow at any reasonable interest rate. Rhode Island's senators, Claiborne Pell and John Chafee, then began a bipartisan campaign to obtain a federal guaranteed underwriting of a special loan to the state. Chairman Gonzalez of the House Banking Committee supported it. Everything was running true to form, both in Providence and in Washington.

While that bill was making its way through Congress, however, matters were getting worse in Rhode Island. One of the three largest banks in the state was nearing insolvency. If it collapsed, a major financial panic might occur in Rhode Island, and the state was now looking desperately for alternatives. It planned to use money from the state pension fund to keep the holding company afloat a little while longer. This was another example of the classic "Russian sleigh theory of survival": Russian sleigh drivers, when attacked by wolves, are said to have thrown out their passengers, one by one, in order to distract the wolves. While the wolves were busy eating the offering, the drivers would gain a little ground. But the wolves always returned to the task. In the end, the technique proved only a delay of the inevitable.

The failure to protect depositors in Rhode Island would

have caused major losses to towns, cities, hospitals, charities, and others within the state, so state retirement funds were deployed. Disaster was averted. The efforts of Rhode Island's senators were rewarded with a provision in the Federal Deposit Improvement Act of 1991 providing a federal guarantee for state borrowing. The depositors got most of their money back, which the taxpayers of Rhode Island, like the U.S. taxpayers in the S&L failures, will be paying for generations.

The Rhode Island experience illustrates how difficult, if not impossible, it is to allow a depositor to suffer a major loss in a bank failure. No matter what free market ideology and our risk-reward system may dictate, depositors will be protected because political careers are at stake. The use of FDIC funds to protect even uninsured depositors is often cited as a major reason for the declining balances in the insurance fund, but actually it accounted for less than 10 percent of our insurance costs. But since the FDIC Improvement Act of 1991, most depositors with more than $100,000 have been forced to take losses above that amount when their bank fails. The average loss per large depositor thus runs about 20 to 30 percent, and the fact that they take losses has helped a bit to stretch the guarantee fund. But it cannot cover everything. The dilemma facing bank regulators has often been framed as the cost of dealing with banks that are "too big to fail." But a more profound dilemma is one that might be framed as "too many to fail," which was the real cause of the big insurance losses.

The banks that were too big to fail hit the insurance fund hard because they were big—not because all their depositors were protected. Protecting the financial system by protecting these big institutions also helps the businesses which make our economy run. Draining their liquidity would force some, and perhaps many, of them to seize up. The case of Rhode Island involved mainly people who are not often regarded as decisive economic actors—until their confidence falters. But the lesson is plain: If banks are businesses, they are a very special type of business. Handling other people's money and providing a way to settle accounts are not like any other services. The idea that they can be left to the mercy of the market—a purist view to which not even Adam Smith himself subscribed—is one that history shows us does not work well. Banks operate on trust, and a loss of trust at the heart of the economy can rapidly lead to a loss of trust in the political system and eventually in the fabric of society. As the FDIC proved in Texas, maintenance of that trust and confidence through deposit insurance did much to save the economy of the state. With all its problems and costs, deposit insurance did the job. Occasionally government does work!!

Wrestling with failing banks in Texas, New England, and elsewhere helped promote the impression that the FDIC and its financial resources had been exhausted by the task. When the General Accounting Office did its 1991 audit of our books, it stated without reservation or equivocation that the FDIC had gone broke during that year. The report stated that we had a *negative* net worth of about $6.9 billion. What a sad development this was for the banks, which were just beginning to recover, and the country, which at last was beginning to face up to the costs of the savings and loan disaster of the 1980s.

If the reader gains anything from this book, it could be one basic insight about accountancy: that figures are not immutable facts, but only one way of presenting reality, and that just as in any other profession, whether law, poetry, cosmology, or bank regulation, reality as seen from one viewpoint is not necessarily what it seems to be from another. Was the FDIC broke, as the GAO opined in its 1991 audit? For official purposes the answer to the question was yes, since by law the accounts of the FDIC must be audited by the GAO— and by their reckoning we were broke. But to give a proper answer to the question of whether the FDIC was *really* broke, a little history is in order.

The GAO is an unusual organization. It is an accounting firm working solely for the Congress, with no competitors and only captive clients. When I arrived at the FDIC, the GAO was in mortal combat with the FDIC over our financial statements. The basis for the disagreement was the GAO's estimate that the FDIC's loss in rescuing the Continental Illinois Bank, the largest failure in the agency's history, would be somewhere around $3 billion. The GAO accordingly wished to reduce the FDIC insurance fund by that amount to reflect the loss. But the FDIC estimated the (eventual) loss at approximately half that, or $1.5 billion. The FDIC had refused to publish its balance sheet with a note giving the GAO estimate, so there could be no GAO certificate clearly stating the disagreement.

It was easy for the previous chairman to leave the dispute unresolved, since he was departing. He could thumb his nose at his official government auditors, which is what he had been wanting to do for some time. As the new chairman, however, I found it easy for me to go forward on the basis of the GAO report, swallow the larger loss, and blame it on my predecessor. Even then we still showed a real worth of over $16 billion in our first year under my chairmanship.

All this proceeded in a friendly and accommodating manner. Charles Bowsher, the head of the GAO, was delighted. After the following year's statement was released, he wrote us a letter saying we had one of the finest annual reports put out by any government agency. Brotherhood among us auditors was at its high point. However, it could not continue, and it did not. The GAO began to receive reports from independent experts that the FDIC was destitute or nearly destitute. They said we were not closing down insolvent banks, and therefore were not recording all the losses that were actually taking place in the real world. Not true, but the newspapers were full of estimates and alarms by professors and pundits, bless their publicity-seeking souls, that the FDIC was nearly broke. Fear quickly swept through the GAO, whose officials wondered what would happen to them if more of our insured banks actually were bankrupt and they hadn't blown the whistle in time to forestall another major drain on the Treasury, thus allowing a crisis to develop that everyone would call "Son of the S&Ls."

In technical terms, the GAO's audit certificate of our accounts would then be in error. No greater sin, no greater condemnation to hell, could possibly take place than for an auditor to have to admit that he had made a mistake on his audited statement. From then on, the GAO decided its motto would be CYA (Cover Your A**). No government accountant was ever shot for *over*estimating losses, only for *under*estimating them. Accordingly, as it moved into the audits of 1990 and 1991, the years that saw the largest problems in the banking system, the GAO began to find great fault with statements the FDIC was preparing. This time the argument was not over what losses were incurred on banks that had actually been closed, but over what banks the GAO thought ought to be closed and had not been closed, and what the losses to our fund would be when they were closed. We reminded them that the banks had not yet been closed and might never be. We especially reminded them how cooperative we had been in the early years of my chairmanship, when we had accepted their estimate of $3 billion for the Continental loss, which finally turned out to be well under $1 billion, even *less* than we had originally estimated. Nothing could budge them. The GAO had become an active player in government, and the combination of CYA and IAR (I'm Always Right) made the agency a real burden on the operation of government. Its staff of auditors descended upon us with instructions to find every loss that was likely to take place in years to come and record them all on our books as of yearend 1990.

The way that they estimated the losses was really quite

ingenious. They took the banks with our lowest rating—there were about a thousand—and declared many of them insolvent. They reached this conclusion by averaging the reserves for bad debt losses of all low-rated banks and applying that average to every one of them. This method ignored the fact that in order to calculate the average, they had to take in not only the half that was below average but also the half that was above. They applied their average to the loss reserves of the better half as well as the worse half, and presto!—they predicted large additional losses. It was rather like applying Garrison Keillor's standard for Lake Wobegon, "where all the children are above average." We at the FDIC by contrast based our judgments on all the reports we received from our supervisors; when they said a bank was actually insolvent, it was so recorded. The difference between the two methods resulted in a huge difference in the net worth of our corporation.

In auditing our report, the GAO insisted that we must provide reserve funds for the future losses. They said they were terribly sorry to have to tell us and that they knew it would shake confidence in the FDIC, but we would have to make an adjustment in our annual report to reflect their pessimistic estimates. We hired an outside firm of accountants to review the matter, and they agreed that the GAO formula was inappropriate. The GAO nevertheless demanded that we allow for $6 billion in future losses. We simply did not believe we should reserve for *future* losses, and in any event, their estimate was far too high. Losses should be recorded when they occur. After a long and tortuous session, we compromised by reluctantly agreeing to carry $4 billion of future losses on our books for the year ending in 1990.

Then began the most interesting part of the exercise, the race to the press. The GAO was determined to release the information on its audit of our books before we could release our own financial statement. We did not think it was appropriate for an auditor to try to see how much publicity it could gather for its role as a watchdog before anyone had broken into the house. The GAO even prevailed upon the House Banking Committee to have one of its staff call us and threaten us with dire punishment if our statement came out before the GAO's adjustments to it. He said that he represented the view of the committee (they always say that) and that the committee would be very upset and look at the FDIC very unfavorably if we released our own report ahead of the GAO's. When informed of this, I summoned Alan Whitney, our press secretary, and said, "Within one hour our financial statements should be in the hands of the press." The GAO statement went out later and fortunately was reported by *The Wall Street Journal* as "containing no new information." For the GAO there is always "next year," and they geared up for our 1991 report with a prediction that the FDIC would be insolvent at the end of that year.

The GAO's 1991 audit was performed after my departure. No surprise, the GAO verified its own prediction of insolvency, showing the FDIC with a negative net worth of $6.9 billion. The GAO's audited statements make it appear that during the period of my stewardship from 1985 through 1991, the FDIC lost $25 billion. By the GAO's reckoning, the FDIC started 1985 with a net worth of $18 billion and ended 1991 with a net deficit of almost $7 billion. But in 1985, the FDIC accounts did not record *any* reserve for future losses—zero (even though future losses would occur). In accounting terms, at the end of 1985 there was no accrual for future bank failures. It was then our and GAO's view that the entire equity of the fund was a reserve for any losses that would take place in 1986 and beyond.

But as we have already recounted, starting in 1990, the GAO had changed its mind and forced us to write down a $4 billion loss for *future* failures. By 1991 this book (read: on paper only) loss had grown to over $16 billion for future losses. If we had disregarded this new and unjustified book entry and used our previous accounting system, the fund would have had a net worth of about $9 billion at the end of 1991. Thus, on the basis of our previous, and in our view correct, accounting system the fund had only been reduced from $18 billion to $9 billion and was not $7 billion in the hole. The GAO's magic accounting was merely playing with the numbers. Any accountant can break any company with paper entries merely by debiting (reducing) net worth and crediting (adding) a loss for a future disaster.

So the real answer to our question, "Is the FDIC broke?" is no, it is not—not in the real world of real money. But the proof lies not in the rival auditing procedures but in the FDIC's bottom line with the U.S. government. The FDIC did not, and never has, used one cent of the Treasury's full faith and credit funding to handle losses by its member banks. When the money is on hand, one need not borrow, no matter what accountants may predict. The FDIC will not need to call on the Treasury for money, either. Future income exceeds all estimates of future losses by a wide margin. The FDIC is not broke, and never was.

It may be that only a CPA and former chairman of the FDIC, would dwell on this point, but it is important for three reasons. First, since the FDIC is not broke and has never used any taxpayer's funds to keep the insurance fund solvent, the tough superregulation of the banks provided by the FDIC Improvement Act of 1991 turns out to be at least in part unnecessary. Second, the large premium increases proposed to be paid by banks for FDIC insurance will not be necessary, and that is good for the banks and the economy. Third, the FDIC did not go broke on my watch. Let's keep the record straight!

10

The S&L Debacle

T he disaster of the savings and loan industry during the 1980s was caused by a series of policy mistakes of unprecedented proportions—mistakes that nearly destroyed the U.S. financial system. The S&Ls were not just comfy isolated institutions where small-town moral dramas played themselves out, as in the movie *It's a Wonderful Life;* they were also an integral part of the flow of savings and investments that powers our national economy. They were the main engine of the housing industry, which is as large and important as the automobile business, farming, or practically any other industry you can think of. We at the FDIC had no direct responsibility for insuring or supervising the runaway S&L industry. This was done through the Federal Home Loan Bank Board. But because of the nation's closely integrated financial system, we were close observers of what was happening in the industry, for several very good reasons.

First, the entry of the S&Ls into commercial real estate lending (a field forbidden to them until the 1980s) had helped fuel a boom in commercial office buildings. This made the S&Ls direct competitors of the banks, which challenge at first glance would seem healthy for both of them. But by making large and imprudent loans for real estate speculation, the S&Ls helped cause the overheated, overbuilt market that produced the subsequent real estate bust. They also presented a real threat to the banks, whose portfolios were newly heavy with construction and development loans.

Another reason to keep an eye on the S&Ls was that competition by so many technically bankrupt S&Ls endangered more solvent institutions. Our calculations at the FDIC showed that our sister fund for the S&Ls, the Federal Savings and Loan Insurance Corporation (FSLIC for short, pronounced by everyone as "fizz-lick") would run out of money if it had to pay for the losses that the S&Ls already were reporting. A majority of the nation's almost 4,000 S&Ls were on their way to bankruptcy by the early 1980s. If FSLIC closed them down and made their insured depositors whole, there wouldn't be enough money left in the kitty, and it would have to call on its presumed full faith and credit government guarantee for the rescue. In the characteristically cruel slang of the financial world, many S&Ls were called "brain dead." These zombies were very much alive when they were turned loose in the marketplace with nothing to lose but the government support that kept them alive. They posed unfair, and recklessly irresponsible, competition to banks. Far from strengthening the financial system, they helped debase credit standards and destabilized the system to the point of threatening the collapse of some of its strongest players.

Congress turned increasingly to the FDIC, and suggestions increased that we take over FSLIC. My predecessor, Bill Isaac, had often suggested that this transfer of responsibility would be sound policy and was inevitable. We resisted the idea, not only because it looked like bureaucratic aggrandizement (of which we were accused anyway by some financial commentators when it was finally forced on us), but essentially because we already had our hands full at the FDIC. We did not need the problems of the bankrupt S&L insurance fund to keep us busy. Besides, if we had wanted the job, the last way to get it was to ask for it. I made more than my share of speeches and testified repeatedly before Congress that we preferred that this poisoned chalice bypass the FDIC, because it would change our agency forever.

Step back for a moment and examine how the S&Ls got into this mess. The industry was born with a congenital defect: its interest rate risks defied the first safety rule taught in Finance 101. They borrowed short (from depositors) and lent long (to mortgage holders); this was the classic recipe for financial disaster. In an environment where interest rates were stable because the government kept them that way, the defect was not visible. But when interest rates became volatile, it was a different ball game. When inflation drove interest rates through the roof, S&Ls' interest expenses far exceeded their interest income from home mortgages. The fatal defect of the S&Ls was fully revealed. Their industry was on the way to insolvency.

How to remedy this problem without blowing the federal budget for government assistance or closing down an industry that provided most home mortgages was the political question of the day. In deadly concert, the lobbyists for the S&L industry, the Democratic congressional partisans of federal help for housing at any price, and the ideologues of the Reagan administration concocted a witch's brew consisting of four equal portions of misguided policy.

First, the S&L industry was permitted, even urged, to move into unfamiliar territory and diversify its investments, collect higher returns on riskier projects, and earn its way out of its interest rate dilemma.

Second, the regulators papered over the industry's bankrupt condition by substituting for traditional Generally Accepted Accounting Principles (GAAP), a new and more lax set of Regulatory Accounting Principles (RAP) designed to accomplish an accounting miracle. Insolvent S&Ls were turned into solvent ones by a number of accounting tricks, such as deferring for years losses on loans sold, and after a merger, writing up goodwill on the books that clearly wasn't there. The government examiners who had to apply these principles did not like them at all; they started calling them Creative Regulatory Accounting Principles (CRAP).

Third, the regulators were ordered to get off the backs of the S&Ls. As a result, not only were the investment and accounting rules relaxed, but supervision was as well. If regulators had been looking more closely at the books, the damage at least might have been controlled.

Fourth, Congress increased the amount of the government's full faith and credit support by moving the deposit insurance limit up from $40,000 to $100,000 for each account, thereby allowing the industry to attract additional funds to lend to new get-rich-quick enterprises. This in effect made the government a full partner in a nationwide casino, first speculating mainly in real estate, later in extremely volatile mortgage securities, junk bonds, futures and options, and similar Wall Street exotica.

Who put this unfortunate brew in the pot? There is plenty of blame to go around. Alice Roosevelt Longworth said it first: "If you haven't got anything nice to say about anybody, come sit next to me." So, move in a little closer, because there is a long list of villains, or at least those who could and should have done much better.

The Depository Institutions Deregulation and Monetary Control Act act of 1980 that increased the amount of money insured to $100,000 per account really started the ball rolling. It gave the S&Ls practically unlimited access to funds through a $100,000 "credit card" issued by Uncle Sam. Investment bankers jumped on board to divide up their clients' money and farm it out to S&Ls offering the highest return. This system of brokered deposits, as they were called, meant that anyone with a spare million or so could spread it around in government-guaranteed packages of $100,000 to some of the riskiest institutions in the country. He could then sit back and collect the high interest payments without worrying, because the full faith and credit of Uncle Sam was behind his money. This was the exact opposite of the original intent of deposit insurance, which was to protect small savers and make them feel secure enough not to yank their money out of the bank whenever they worried about it.

High-flying speculators did not take long to realize that owning an S&L was a key to the Treasury. The S&Ls were an invitation to gamble with someone else's money—the taxpayers of the United States. As a lawyer as well as an accountant, if I had been asked to defend these gamblers in court, I might well have used the defense of entrapment (as some did): a honey pot had been officially created that was irresistible to ordinary mortals.

The thanks for this unfortunate piece of legislation go principally, but not entirely, to the chairman of the House Banking Committee, Henry Reuss, and the chairman of the Senate Banking Committee, William Proxmire, for their part in the 1980 law that raised the limit on deposit insurance at the behest, it is said, of Senator Cranston and the S&L industry's lobbyists. It was a bipartisan effort, done at a late-night conference committee meeting, with none of the normal reviews by the press and public. No doubt the members of the committee were fully aware of the political power of the S&Ls, but the fact is, the legislation was passed with little thought of what its full effect could be.

The S&L operators were very effective lobbyists, if nothing else. (Congressman St. Germain, when he was chairman of the Banking and Housing Committee, was reported to have on a few occasions used a credit card belonging to an executive at the U.S. League of Savings Institutions. When the S&Ls really wanted something done, they did not leave their lobbying efforts solely up to the paid help in Washington. The chief executives themselves came en masse to the capital to lobby their own senators and representatives and to impress upon them in person the local as well as national importance of the S&L industry. Probably no industry discovered earlier the importance of this kind of grass-roots political action.

The U.S. League had a detailed plan to ensure that every elected member of the Congress had a good friend and campaign contributor among the S&L executives. It also put together a coalition that included its traditional partners, the housing and construction industries, realtors, the unions, and consumer groups. All were eager for low-cost funding for homes, and that of course meant subsidized rates. The League was considered the most effective lobbying organization in Washington. Like any good advocate, it put its demands in terms of the general good, focusing on lowering the cost of financing for the average American home buyer. Possibly no single issue is more important to Americans than the prospect of being able to afford homes of their own.

When the crisis arose in 1981, Richard Pratt was chairman of the Home Loan Bank Board. At the time he was hailed as the saviour of the industry. Pratt was the protégé of Senator Jake Garn of Utah, the Republican who became chairman of the Banking Committee when the Republicans won the Senate along with Ronald Reagan's election as president. Pratt, a young professor of economics at the University of Utah, was responsible for relaxing S&L capital standards by changing the accounting procedures. By redefining the way S&Ls figured their capital cushion against losses, his agency made it possible for institutions with no cushion at all to stay in business, all in the name of the doctrine of deregulation.

Remember, Pratt's era was in the early days of the Reagan Revolution. And a battle cry of that revolution was "Deregulate now!" Anyone calling for more banking supervision was branded a "re-regulator" and by extension a disloyal Reaganite, the worst condemnation possible inside the Reagan administration.

Another step down the road to trouble was taken when the Garn-St. Germain Act of 1982 was passed. This law changed the rules that restricted the S&Ls to their traditional home

mortgage lending business and allowed them to get into just
about any kind of lending or investing they chose, no matter
the risk. It was another license to gamble with the full faith
and credit of the U.S. government, supplied through insured deposits. Jimmy Stewart's good old Bailey Building
and Loan would never be the same.

The Reagan years in the White House were heady times.
Much good was accomplished. But sometimes doctrine over-
rode judgment. The enthusiasm to deregulate the S&L industry was a prime example. Economic activities can be
disciplined by the marketplace or they can be brought into
order by government fiat (or a combination of the two). But
in the S&L situation, neither imposed order. The market
players did not care about the soundness of where they put
their deposits, only the return they got. The government, for
its part, was deregulating as a matter of economic faith in the
free market, forgetting that its own full faith and credit had
castrated the market's regulatory strength. So there was little
control or discipline, and an open invitation to gamble with
other people's money.

President Reagan's first budget director, David Stockman,
a very capable fellow, definitely lost track of this problem.
Maybe it was the confidence of youth, maybe the certainty of
the ideologue. (Or perhaps he was just too busy with rising
budget deficits.) But Stockman had no patience with warn-
ings that the Federal Home Loan Bank Board needed more
supervisors. No matter how many requests were made to
him to focus on the troubles of the S&Ls, he passed the problem down the chain of command and, as far as I know, never
took any interest in it.

Another Reagan administration official who did little to
help solve the thrift industry's problems and much to increase them was Donald Regan, secretary of the treasury in
the first term and later White House chief of staff. He was
former chief executive of Merrill Lynch, and his attitude, like
so many others, was that all the S&L executives needed was

freedom to run their businesses; they would work their way out of their problems. In particular, Regan did not want to hear that brokered deposits were dangerous.

To be fair, Regan believed that trying to control brokered deposits by controlling the investment firm that put them together amounted to "shooting the messenger." He argued that the way to control the problem was to oversee the way the S&Ls invested the money, not judge where it came from. This policy made some sense, and I supported it during my early days in office. But it made sense only if the S&Ls were kept under tight control by adequate supervision. Unfortunately, Regan, as chief of staff, denied Ed Gray's urgent requests for additional supervisors for his Home Loan Bank Board to perform the oversight. He was rather offhanded about the whole thing and remarked, "You regulators are like generals: You always want more troops." Regan's commitment to the free market seemed to cloud his ability to see he was dealing with an industry that was not operating in a free market situation.

The FDIC, as previously noted, was responsible for the bank equivalent of the S&Ls—the savings banks (located mainly in New England). The way the FDIC under Chairman Isaac chose to deal with them represented a different philosophy. The FDIC adopted precisely the opposite policy from the one applied to the S&Ls by the Home Loan Bank Board. Instead of allowing them to diversify into fields they did not understand, the FDIC increased its supervision of the savings banks, kept them in the mortgage business, and supported them during the years when they were gasping for air because of the mismatch of interest rates. The FDIC figured that eventually the interest rate cycle would reverse itself and the banks would then recover their financial stability, which is what happened. As a result, while there were failures and losses, there was nothing like the kinds of problems of the S&Ls. Some savings banks, however, simply could not wait out the end of the cycle and had to be closed.

These included the Bowery Savings Bank of New York City, Seamans, and the New York Bank for Savings. But the really big losses in the S&L industry were the result of risky new lending in untried areas, and this practice was forbidden to savings banks under FDIC regulations.

The Reagan administration was not entirely oblivious to the gathering storm clouds. Early in the decade a task force on regulation was formed under the leadership of the then vice president, George Bush, to determine whether the financial system needed reform. Some good ideas came out of that study group, including one that would have required any S&L expanding its lending beyond the traditional area of mortgage expertise to convert itself into a bank, which would bring much tougher supervision and regulation. This could have made a real difference, but the proposals were never pushed by the administration. They went nowhere because the S&L industry opposed the idea, and the administration never really objected.

Did anyone in authority see the huge troubles that were brewing? Shortly after I was sworn in as FDIC chairman (by that great lady from my newly adopted home state of Arizona, Justice Sandra Day O'Connor), Gray came to see me to tell me his troubles. He said the administration was furious at him for trying to tighten supervision, that the industry was ready to kill him because he was publicly outlining its dire shape, and that Congress was upset with him because he had announced he was going to need more money in order to handle the S&L situation. By the time he had finished describing all this to me, a tear or two was streaming down his cheek, and my eyes also welled up in sympathy. I pledged to do whatever I could to help him in his difficulties. On top of everything, *The Washington Post* was on Gray's case for living as the chairmen of the Home Loan Bank Board had always lived. They went to the best hotels and conducted their meetings in the nicest places. With the current condition of the industry and its insurance fund, the papers made a major issue of his extravagant life-style. We both pledged that henceforth we would conduct our agencies in a most monastic manner.

A few prescient experts informed the White House and the Congress of their concerns, but Ed Gray was the only one to raise an official alarm. After only a short period in office, he spoke out on January 31, 1984, with a speech which received good coverage in the press. No interested person could say he had never heard the warning. Gray said, "It is important for the Congress to recognize the possibility of having to cause an infusion of funds from the Treasury to back the credibility of the deposit insurance system." In other words, to back up the system with the full faith and credit of the U.S. Treasury. He told his audience the failure to reform deposit insurance by restricting insurance of brokered deposits "could . . . result ultimately in destroying the federal deposit insurance funds."

Two weeks later, in a speech to the Leadership Conference of the American Bankers Association in Washington, Gray said it again: "Without firm, decisive, and expeditious remedial action, I believe the future viability of the federal deposit insurance system could be gravely threatened—so much so that only massive infusions from the Treasury, and hence the taxpayers, could well be required to support the deposit insurance function."

On March 6, 1984, in another Washington speech attended by top financial writers, this one to the nation's main thrift trade association, he warned that without reform, "it is not only conceivable, but in my view very possible, that at some point in the future, massive infusions from the U.S. Treasury—and hence American taxpayers—may well be necessary to shore up the system." As a result of this particular speech, Senator Alan Cranston chastised Gray publicly for pushing the thrift industry too hard on the issue of brokered deposits.

For his troubles, Ed Gray gained the popularity of a bastard at the family reunion and discovered the correctness of Voltaire's aphorism "It is dangerous to be right in matters on which the established authorities are wrong." Although he was one of Ronald Reagan's California loyalists and had served as his press secretary in Sacramento, his pleas for help fell on deaf ears at the White House.

Gray's great service went unrewarded, as it often does in public life. He completed his term and left office with few friends, many enemies, and no cheers from an appreciative public. Some of the S&L industry leaders went out of their way to prevent his getting a decent job, which he really needed. M. Danny Wall, Senator Jake Garn's administrative assistant and a loyal Republican, replaced him as the top S&L regulator. Possibly the most maligned person in the whole affair, Wall was not really a large contributor to the S&L debacle. By the time he arrived, much of the damage was done. But Danny managed to delay and downplay the magnitude of the calamity, and to delay the closing of Charles Keating's infamous Lincoln Savings and Loan while it piled up millions more losses that would have to be swallowed by the insurance fund and eventually by the taxpayer. To this day it is difficult to understand why he did not step forward early on and raise the warning flag. His treatment of Keating seemed to represent the misguided view many in politics have that big political contributors were to be respected as honest businessmen, no matter what the evidence to the contrary. When Keating's fraudulent empire collapsed, Wall's handling of it came back to haunt him.

Although Garn's vigorous support for Wall with the administration got Wall's job for him at the Home Loan Bank Board, Garn warned Wall not to take the job because he felt the job could destroy anyone who took it. But Danny wanted it and he got it. Wall was confirmed as chairman on July 1, 1987. He immediately moved to cover over the political scars left by his predecessor. Wall was a competent fellow, but his background on the Hill was the wrong training for this job, which, as Garn had foreseen, was really a "mission impossible." Rapidly and rather well he began to deal with the many problems of the industry. He moved to take over and shut down the worst of the rapidly growing savings and loan institutions that were creating the greatest potential losses.

Wall's Home Loan Bank Board was fighting for its life as well as for stability of the industry. The board decided to close more than one hundred sick thrifts holding approximately $100 billion in assets and consolidate them in new and larger institutions by cutting their overheads, increasing their efficiency, and thus making them more attractive for sale. This effort was named the "Southwest Plan." Since the board had no cash to pay off the insured depositors, Wall and his board did what you do when you are out of cash. They used credit—the full faith and credit of the United States Government, and lots of it. The board wrote its own promissory notes to make up the losses in the institutions. To sell them, the board had to pay a much higher rate of interest than the government normally pays, although it claimed that the notes were backed by the government's credit. (This was severely questioned in Congress, but eventually the General Accounting Office ruled the notes were valid claims against the U.S. Treasury.) Further, the bank board also made an attractive offer to those who bought the reorganized thrifts by guaranteeing a top rate of return on the assets they took over. The buyers were not allowed to look at most of their new properties, but they did not need to, since they were really purchasing a government-guaranteed return, no matter what the assets yielded.

The program was designed to keep those assets off the market and thus stabilize the real estate industry. The theory was that if the assets were dumped on a market already suffering from a large oversupply of properties, prices would go down even more. Of course, markets are not so dumb. They knew that the properties would have to be sold some day, so the huge overhang affected prices anyway. The Home Loan

Bank Board ended up with the worst of both worlds—a continually depressed real estate market and the high carrying costs of onerous guarantees on properties held off the market.

Wall was under pressure to act quickly, not only to stem the increasing losses in the institutions that were still alive and operating in the private sector, but also to get the maximum benefit from the special tax breaks for writing off the industry's huge losses—sometimes twice, in what accountants called a double dip—that were due to expire at the end of 1988. There was a wild stampede to buy these reorganized thrifts; the situation gave the buyers maximum bargaining leverage, since they knew that Wall and his board were operating under a self-imposed deadline. Among those who were best at striking the most advantageous deals were Robert Bass of the Texas Bass brothers and Ronald Perlman of Revlon, who probably got the sweetest deal. By coming in at the very last minute, his lawyers virtually dictated the terms of a purchase contract on the last day of the year.

Like all of us in financial regulation, Wall had the unenviable requirement to make his mistakes in public. Unfortunately for Danny, he made one large one with his handling of Charles Keating. If he had asked, we could have warned Danny of the traps. Keating once challenged me to a debate on television, describing me in a speech at the National Press Club as an incompetent, broken-down CPA who had caused the entire U.S. real estate recession and urging that my job be given to Michael Milken, the junk bond king. Frankly, my combative nature urged me toward challenging him to a public debate; but fortunately, the good sense of my press secretary, Alan Whitney, prevailed. You can seldom win a debate with someone who looks as honest as Keating, but who has so little respect for the truth.

Early in his regime Wall apparently decided that he wanted to mend relations with Keating, who was already suing the government on many fronts in what he himself de-

scribed as a personal feud with the former chairman, Ed
Gray. Wall felt a reconciliation would defuse this very heated
controversy, and he met with Keating several times. The supervisors at the bank board's San Francisco office had already recommended the takeover of Keating's savings and
loan for operating in an unsafe and unsound manner. Instead, Wall and his board (with member Larry White dissent-
ing) made the unprecedented decision to remove the
Lincoln Savings and Loan from the jurisdiction of the regional bank board in San Francisco. He assigned Darrel
Dochow, his top supervisor in Washington, to oversee a complete reevaluation and Lincoln's closing was deferred.
Charles Keating and his runaway thrift thus obtained a new
lease on life during the twelve-month review period, further
increasing the eventual losses to the government through
real estate speculation that went sour. The transfer damaged
Wall's reputation and demoralized all the government supervisors. Our bank supervisors were so upset that the FDIC
board publicly assured them that we would not consider
such transfers of jurisdiction in our own operations. Needless to say, Wall was not pleased with our announcement.

One of the most contentious questions in the S&L saga is
why the huge amount of the losses and the enormity of the
problem for the taxpayers was so slow in emerging—especially before the 1988 election campaign. The FDIC had
made its own estimates of the savings and loans' losses from
those recorded on the S&Ls' call reports, the quarterly report that all financial institutions submit to their regulators.
Using the Home Loan Bank Board's own information, we
computed its losses at roughly three to four times the $15
billion Wall was estimating, and within several months after
Wall took office. However, we did not make these estimates
public, although I did tell Wall about them when I knew I
would have to testify on the situation before Congress. He
told us politely, and sometimes not so politely, to mind our
own business.

When Congress then asked us for our estimates on the size of the problem, they became public. To avoid being nailed down to numbers based only on reports by the S&Ls themselves, we stressed that the estimate was unverified and could be low. But the message came across, because it was what many people had begun to suspect. This performance probably did more to convince the press of my credibility than anything else that had been done up to that time. We believed in giving Congress the information they requested if we had it. Any other action would have been dangerous to our health, as anyone will realize who has studied relations between Congress and the government from Watergate to Irangate.

Our report infuriated Wall, and from then on, he believed that we were plotting his downfall. Wall cut off almost all communications with the FDIC. His fortress, in a building a block away from the FDIC, prepared itself against what he thought would be an FDIC takeover move. We had no such plans—and I tried to tell him so—but this only seemed to reinforce his conviction. (Paranoia in Washington is a fact, not a disease.) We were asked to testify on the deals he was making to sell off banks at the end of 1988. Our view was that they would turn out to be very expensive and do little to solve the underlying problems. This helped confirm Wall's suspicions that we were out to demolish his agency.

As the savings and loan problem was becoming larger and better known by the time of the 1988 election, it normally would have been expected to be a contentious issue in the campaign. But it seems to have been mentioned only once, and by one candidate, throughout the bitterly contested campaign. That one mention was made by the Democratic candidate, Michael Dukakis, who described the S&L problem as a big one and the fault of deregulation espoused by the Republican party. The common gossip was that the subject was dropped at the urging of the Democratic speaker of the House of Representatives, Jim Wright, who was heavily

involved with many savings and loan executives. For whatever reason, Dukakis never brought it up again. It was
hardly a desirable subject for the Democrats because they
counted among their supporters, and especially their contributors, the executives of many troubled S&Ls, including
the ubiquitous Charles Keating (he gave to both sides—
whenever it would do the most good), David Paul of Cen-
Trust in Miami, Tom Spiegel of Columbia Savings and Loan
in Los Angeles, and Donald Dixon of Texas's Vernon Savings
and Loan (known to regulators as "Vermin Savings and
Loan"). The biggest swingers in the industry were large political contributors to the Democrats. They supported all
measures designed to help regulators look the other way in
the hope that the industry would heal itself over time.

As for George Bush, all the trouble developed while he was
vice president. He had headed the task force on deregulation, so he had an obvious interest in avoiding any discussion
of the baleful results of misplaced deregulatory zeal. Nevertheless, the Republicans had to be ready for any Democratic
attacks if candidate Dukakis decided to make the S&Ls an
issue. Early in the campaign I met several times with Richard
Breeden, a member of Bush's vice presidential staff who had
been executive director of the regulatory task force (he was
later to be rewarded with the chairmanship of the Securities
and Exchange Commission). He decided that the answer to
campaign attacks would be to attack the Democratic Congress, and we prepared information on the various bills
passed by Congress easing the regulations on the S&Ls and
increasing their vulnerability to trouble. But the attacks
never came. The political parties looked at the S&L disaster
in the same way they assessed nuclear war; it was to be
avoided at all costs because it carried the same risk of "Mutually Assured Destruction."

The issue also never caught on in congressional election
races. While generally favoring Democrats because there are

more of them, the S&Ls also had contributed widely to Republican legislators, especially those in a position to help them. On a policy level, members of Congress found the issue very tricky, since a majority of them had voted for a number of the changes in the law that helped contribute to the disaster. The bottom line was that this was a very nasty and very rare political problem, with neither party as the clear villain. Both parties were agreed on letting the industry run wild, but for entirely different reasons. For the Democrats, easy housing finance had always been a vote-getting ideology they fully endorsed. The Republicans agreed that nothing should be done to restrain the newly deregulated S&Ls' entrepreneurial zeal, which would demonstrate the superior economic efficiency of the market place. Neither party's analysis turned out to be correct, and the public paid the bill.

There is no need to stop at the government in the search for participants in creating the S&L mess. The private sector had its share of culprits. At the extreme were the outright crooks, the ones who used deposit money to line their pockets and buy yachts, jet planes, and mansions. Crooks will always be attracted by the smell of easy money; the S&Ls provided them easy access, and they did a lot of damage. But just plain incompetent management did a lot more by putting money into race horses, windmill farms, pornographic libraries, and other wild investments when the lifetime business experience of most S&L executives had been limited to lending on single family houses within a close radius of their home office. A majority of S&L owners and managers were honest. Some were very competent managers who led their companies profitably during the entire period known as the S&L debacle. These included Herb Sandler of World, Dick Deihl of Ahmanson, and Jim Montgomery of Great Western, who ran California's, and the country's, largest S&Ls. They stayed in their own territory and ran their businesses to meet the challenge of change, innovating when they had to by moving quickly into adjustable rate mortgages. Nevertheless, they later had a tough time separating themselves in the public mind from their unsavory brothers.

Another group that contributed to the disaster were independent professionals working for the S&Ls for fees: lawyers, accountants, appraisers, and business consultants and investment advisers of all sorts. I certainly do not want to impugn the integrity of these professions as a whole, especially since I am a member of the first two, but all too often an unprincipled businessman teamed up with a very clever, well-trained, and equally unprincipled professional; and the public suffered. Consider the way Michael Milken of Drexel Burnham Lambert unloaded junk bonds on the S&Ls; Kaye, Scholer, Fierman, Hays and Handler did questionable legal work for Keating; and Arthur Young performed favorable audits on Lincoln Savings. They and others have been ordered to disgorge hundreds of millions to the government in settlements and fines, which is only fair. If only they had been doing a better job, the public would have been saved many, many times that amount of money.

The pressures on these firms are understandable because, as anyone who has spent years as a CPA doing work for private companies knows, the demands of the client can be difficult to resist. The fact is that, in the case of the S&Ls, too many of the professionals didn't do their job with the required impartiality. They are paying for their failures. Good evidence of this is the settlement by Ernst & Young for $400 million because of the failure of its accounting for the S&L industry, the largest settlement of its kind in history. When the magnitude of the S&L problems made it certain that the RTC would be suing CPAs for hundreds of millions, I spoke with the leaders of the profession about their problems with the S&L industry. It was certain that accountants were going to take a terrific beating, both financially and in public reputation. We told them they needed to start making large and comprehensive settlements quickly—and to get the disaster behind them. The Ernst & Young settlement is the first evidence that they are moving in that direction.

Incidentally, it is nice to know that my former firm, now known as BDO Seidman, has not as of this writing been involved in any lawsuits in this area. Being long separated from the firm, I do not know whether they had just been lucky not to have been aggressive in attracting the wrong kind of S&L clients, or they had learned their lesson from the Equity Funding scandal.

Finally, our friends in the fourth estate often like to credit themselves with dogged persistence in bringing important if obscure issues to the attention and understanding of the public, but they certainly did not do so in this billion-dollar scandal. Granted, the S&L crisis was not a good media story, particularly for TV. It was too dull, too complex. It required an enormous amount of effort just to be able to speak the language, not to mention understanding the issues. There were a few good early stories when the problems started to unfold, but they did not comprehend the size of the problem and there was little of the follow-up that would have been essential to keep the story alive. Some exceptions were some early warning pieces by Mike Binstein of the Jack Anderson column. But the media didn't stay with it, and therefore neither did the public. More could be said, but I have made it a lifelong principle never to make war with someone who buys ink by the barrel.

Toward the end of the Reagan administration, under the leadership of Treasury Under Secretary George Gould, the administration did turn its attention to the problems of the S&Ls and their insurance fund, and a plan for bailing out the industry began to take form: a $15 billion rescue to be financed by the industry. It proved to be highly controversial because it imposed higher premium costs on the industry and forced closure of insolvent institutions. The thrifts opposed the plan through the U.S. League of Savings Institutions, which heatedly denied the size of the problem.

The U.S. League was effectively able to beat back the effort with substantial support from Speaker Wright of Texas. Our FDIC projections showed that if the administration could have pushed its plan through Congress, losses from the thrifts gasping for life would have been cut substantially. But analysis also made it quite clear to us that the loss was going to exceed the administration's projection of $15 billion by at least $30 to $40 billion. The plan as ultimately passed provided just under $11 billion and contained a series of restrictions on supervisors that limited their ability to close failing thrifts.

Of more importance was what the new Bush administration would do about the S&L problem. I knew Bush from the Ford White House days, when he headed the CIA and it reported its findings to our Economic Policy Board. We used to have lunch at the White House or the CIA to discuss economic topics. Bush was a better politician (in the best sense) than a spook, and he was a great representative of his agency. I was surely one of his strong supporters. Bush seemed to represent the kind of leadership the Republican party needed. I had come from its liberal side, the Romney/ Rockefeller wing of the party. Bush was identified with that part of the party, as opposed to the Goldwater/Reagan conservatives. Looking back, I ask that history please forgive me for getting on the wrong side of a good many of those issues and not supporting the Goldwater conservatives. Goldwater would have made a great president. He was a fiscal conservative and really would have brought government spending under control; he truly believed the free enterprise system worked best when the government restricted itself to policing it. Also, he was a real libertarian on social questions and thought there were many private matters the government should simply stay out of.

After Bush's election in November of 1988, the FDIC worked feverishly with his staff and the staff at the Treasury Department to design a rescue plan that the administration could initiate promptly after the inauguration the following January. We thought that the size of the problem involved somewhere around 350 or 400 insolvent institutions, with $200 billion in assets. Most would simply have to be taken over and liquidated.

The incoming Bush administration decided to remove the Federal Home Loan Bank Board as the insurer of the savings and loan industry and to transfer that function to the FDIC. The Federal Home Loan Bank Board had simply grown too close to the industry it had been charged with regulating. It acted as both a charterer of the S&Ls and their insurer, but it also acted as a cheerleader for the industry as much as a regulator. Restructuring was in order, and so was political retribution. The board's functions as the principal federal regulator of thrifts would be transferred to a new Office of Thrift Supervision (OTS), which would not be independent but a part of the Treasury, much like the Comptroller of the Currency. Meanwhile, the board's insurance role would be passed to the FDIC. Later, when we took over these responsibilities, we decided to give the new fund a name with the comforting acronym of SAIF, the Savings Association Insurance Fund, to remind people that the government's full faith and credit still backed the deposit insurance fund, no matter how much that had cost us in the past. Ultimately, the proposal meant that we could chalk up one of history's largest victories in the Washington turf wars. However, we were less than overjoyed, since our victory in that perpetual game meant that our little agency would never be the same again. The proposed legislation also would create the Resolution Trust Corporation, which was designed to take over, dissect, bury, and dispense with the sick and dying S&Ls. Bringing this new monster to life was an experience that was a great, if not totally enjoyable, affair, as described in the next chapter.

Danny Wall, the captain of the now sinking Federal Home Loan Bank Board, had been a good and loyal member of his party during the election, never saying anything, even though he must have known that he was sailing a ship that could not make it to shore. Shortly before the president was inaugurated, Wall and I were called to the White House's West Wing, where he got the bad news from Richard Breeden that his agency was to be dismantled. It was small consolation that he might be receiving the appointment as the head of the new Office of Thrift Supervision under the wing of the Treasury. Aghast, he launched a furious tirade, alleging in colorful language that the FDIC and particularly its chairman had plotted his downfall and the destruction of his agency. We let him go on for a full thirty minutes, and then he began to repeat himself. At that point a comment from me was in order. "We've heard it all, Danny," I said. "You may believe whatever you want. Believe it or not, the FDIC would prefer not to take over your agency. We've got enough trouble of our own. So why don't you keep quiet, and we'll try to work this out as smoothly as we can." That ended the conversation. Before we left, we both pledged our support for the administration's program. In the end, Wall was a loyal soldier, perhaps too loyal.

The S&L crisis was born in the economic climate of the times. It was nurtured, however, in the fertile ground of politics as usual and the political mentality of "not on my watch." The system may have given rise to the crisis, but human beings, with all their faults, ultimately determined the scope of the debacle. The S&L mistakes resulted in the closing down of one-third of the industry, destroying the agency charged with promoting and insuring it, and costing the American taxpayers around $200 billion, plus interest on that amount, probably forever! No larger financial error appears to be recorded in history. And all because the use of the full faith and credit of the U.S. government was not treated with the respect and fear that must be accorded it.

In King Solomon's words, "He that is surety for a stranger shall smart for it" (Proverbs 11:15).

11

The Resolution Trust Corporation: The World's Largest Fire Sale

T he Resolution Trust Corporation (RTC) took its name from a financial term: to "resolve," which in bankruptcy means to dispose of the firm's assets and settle things once and for all. Like most goals of government, this proved easier to promulgate than to perform. This resolution was unprecedented not only in the variety but the size of the assets. At its peak it would deal with about $400 billion worth of assets from failed institutions. About half of this historic figure was in home mortgages, and other loans, most of which were good, solid loans that yielded regular interest payments. But the other half of the S&Ls' investments were the problem. They averaged only 60 to 70 percent of their face value, and some raw land was worth only about 10 percent of the money loaned on it.

The RTC was set up by the Financial Institutions Reform, Recovery and Enforcement Act (FIRREA), signed into law on August 9, 1989.

The RTC was supposed to contain, manage, and "resolve" failed savings associations that had been insured by the FSLIC before the law's enactment. The RTC was directed to sell off the assets of the S&Ls at the maximum value it could realize in the market, and at the same time it was also directed to minimize the impact of dumping all this already dubious real estate, junk bonds, stocks, and other question-able financial paper on a glutted market. It was also directed to minimize losses wherever possible, but at the same time to make much of the S&Ls' bankrupt property available for low-cost residential housing, which by definition would have to sell at below market prices. The goals set for the RTC would be forever in conflict, but Congress went away happy at having tried to salvage something good for the country out of the disaster.

The new law reflected the bureaucratic warfare that had fathered it. The drafting of the legislation was a classic exam-ple of a battle between agencies and a good example of how badly Washington can work. In this case the FDIC and the administration were at war.

The problem of putting together the RTC arose from an attempt by the administration to retain control of the way the very substantial funding would be spent. We had already testified in the autumn of 1988 that the costs would be $50 or $60 billion, warning that they might go higher but we could not prove this without more information. During the follow-ing spring a joint estimate by the FDIC, the Treasury, the Bank Board, and outside consultants was about $50 billion. That was far lower than the eventual cost (and far higher that the Treasury's previous estimate of $15 billion), but the point is that no one could really know until we got a look at the books of the sick thrifts.

Before the RTC was created the president had asked the FDIC to take over a number of failing thrifts. In place of the soon to be defunct Home Loan Bank Board, we were sup-posed to "baby-sit" the failed institutions. We argued long and hard that the FDIC should not be the agency entrusted with this mess. It would make our job as *bank* insurer and regulator much more difficult, and banks needed our full attention at the moment. We would be undertaking a pro-gram for which there would be no thanks and heaps of abuse, and it could change the way our agency was viewed by

the citizenry. If we were to be involved, we wanted the full
authority for cleaning up the mess.

Our arguments fell on deaf ears. We did not know what
was going on behind the scenes, but the message was clear.
The administration did not want the FDIC to run this entire
operation. It wanted us to do the day-to-day administration
while somebody else controlled the money and conducted
the high-level strategy—a perfect formula for blurring responsibility and deflecting blame. A new board headed by
the secretary of the Treasury would control the money and
decide strategy. Insult of insults, the chairman of the FDIC
would not be a member. While we would be allowed to pull
the oars, we were not to be in charge of the navigation.

Some of my colleagues at the FDIC wondered if all this
had anything to do with my personal standing in the administration, where my independent behavior was apparently
not held in the highest regard. It did appear that the White
House, Treasury, and OMB had already decided that in no
way was the FDIC to run the operation because of our long
history of independence. On this sour note, we began a long
courtship for a marriage that was doomed to years of domestic strife.

We sat down to try to negotiate a practical operating structure. For the administration, the matter was turned over to
the secretary of the Treasury's new deputy, John Robson,
who had been a fellow member of the Ford administration. A
charming, tenacious, energetic bulldog of an ex–business
school dean and corporate executive, John had a career that
spanned government, corporate America, and education,
much like mine. None of this helped as we began the unpleasant task of drafting the legislation for the president's
new S&L plan. Occasionally, Under Secretary Robert Glau-
ber and others from the Treasury pitched in, but poor John
had to deal with the crotchety chairman of the FDIC on a
daily basis. We argued that the experienced personnel of the
FDIC should set up the RTC as a separate organization, out-

side the control of the Treasury. The strategy would be to let the FDIC handle the start-up, and after a year turn it over to the administration to run like any other of its efficient government operations.

Negotiations ran hot and heavy, and a good friendship dissolved into something considerably less cordial. Every time my secretary announced that Mr. Robson was on the phone my groan could be heard all the way down the hall to C. C. Hope's office at the other end of the building. The administration proposal defied all rules of organization: strategic planning and decision making were completely separated from operations, and everything conspired to cut the channels of communication from boss to line worker. Any ex–business school dean should have been appalled, and this one certainly was. A separate RTC oversight board was to be created. It would consist of five members, three from the administration. Various officials were considered, including the director of the Office of Management and Budget, the attorney general, the secretary of Housing and Urban Development, and the chairman of the Federal Reserve Board. As I noted earlier, the chairman of the FDIC was definitely not a choice.

Finally, the administration decided to go with an oversight board made up of the secretary of the Treasury as chairman, the chairman of the Federal Reserve System, the secretary of Housing and Urban Development, and two other members representing the public, one a Democrat and one a Republican. This board would "make policy and oversee the operations." Separately, the FDIC board would reconstitute itself as a second board to run the RTC, charged with the task of "administering" the cleanup of the failed savings and loans.

Thus, a two-headed creature was to be created. As a last-minute compromise, we suggested a good way to achieve some coordination between boards would be to reconsider putting the chairman of the FDIC on the Oversight Board. This was vetoed by the White House, which, like every White

House, was already very unhappy with its inability to call to heel the government's independent agencies. Relations became more acrimonious. The problem was both personalities and substance. Robson let me know that if I wished to resign over the matter, the board would be able to survive the shock. For our part, we were demanding the authority to do the job we were being assigned, and we did not want to be caught in the classic trap of being assigned responsibility for a difficult and unpopular task without authority to deal with it. We were of course not without some leverage. The administration knew that the FDIC's views on the legislation would be asked by members of Congress and that we would not be shy about expressing them. So it insisted that we agree on a plan to put before Congress.

The organizational battle raged on, and at one point it was deemed necessary for the FDIC to change its negotiator, since the chairman was losing his cool on the subject. In fact, the thought of resigning in protest occurred to me on a daily basis, but was rejected as cowardly and not good for the country. Besides, I must confess, the challenge of trying to make the RTC work intrigued me. It certainly was going to be a world-class managerial challenge with the organizational setup they were handing us.

While strange compromises are not unusual in government, we ended up with an all-time classic. The legislation turned out to be, in effect, a contract between the Oversight Board and the FDIC. The powers of each party were laid out as though we were independent private contractors. It set forth in some detail the agreement on how we would operate.

The agreement is still very hard to understand because it is almost irrational. Three separate decision-making organizations were involved: the RTC Oversight Board, the FDIC, and the RTC itself. The Oversight Board's job was to set strategy and manage funds. The RTC's job was to take over the failed savings and loans and liquidate them. The FDIC was the operating manager of the RTC—and the boards of the two organizations were identical. The books of the S&Ls were regularly examined by a fourth agency lodged in the Treasury, the Office of Supervision. When the OTS found an S&L to be insolvent, it was turned over to the RTC for liquidation.

Each of the four organizations had an assignment related to the others in a hierarchy that defied logic. But there were political and bureaucratic explanations for this contraption. The RTC Oversight Board was going to be responsible for the billions spent cleaning up the S&L mess, and it was only reasonable to fill that board with individuals who would be accountable to the administration. (On it sat five people, four of whom were answerable in greater or lesser degree to the administration: two cabinet members, the secretary of the Treasury and the secretary of Housing and Urban Development; two public members named by the president, and the "independent" chairman of the Fed.) The board, which could set policy, review, and audit, could have nothing to do with administration and operations. The RTC's day-to-day manager was therefore kept off the Oversight Board, since he was supposed to be accountable to it and could not, in effect, play a role in overseeing himself.

On the other hand, the actual process of liquidating the assets of the failed S&Ls would be a difficult one, and it had to be done by an organization with experience. The old Home Loan Bank Board was being put out of business for botching the S&L problem in the first place, so that left us. The FDIC would administer and operate the cleanup, but could not participate in strategic planning or budgetary control. The administration was stuck with using our independent talents, which it had already discovered it could not fully control. So it did so through the budget process. The money to close the failed S&Ls would be supplied only with the approval of the RTC Oversight Board.

When the bill got to Congress, there were a few protests,

mainly by Senator Bob Kerrey of Nebraska and Representative Bruce Vento of Minnesota. But the issue was too complex for political advantage, so Congress passed the legislation as presented; and the two-headed monster was to be created. The RTC was distasteful legislation at best; no one likes to appropriate funds for dead horses.

As chairman of the FDIC I headed the RTC, which had as its board the same people who were board members of the FDIC. Robson was designated temporary president of the RTC Oversight Board. That board soon found it difficult to make its decisions without any input from those of us in operations (as even a first-year business school student could have told them). We at the FDIC were invited to each oversight meeting to discuss problems, but not to stay and participate in making decisions.

To show our diligence, the secretary of the Treasury promised that, upon the passage of the legislation, the RTC would promptly liquidate three small savings and loans. But operating rules had not yet been put in place and approved by the Oversight Board. We at the RTC had to get all of our funds from the Oversight Board, and we asked for money to pay off the depositors of the three S&Ls. The Oversight Board requested a detailed plan covering everything from pencils to paper clips. Because we were just setting up, no such plan existed. So the board decided that no funds could be made available.

I was about to appear on the *MacNeil/Lehrer NewsHour*. Robson was informed that when the question of why we were deferring the promised liquidations was raised, "lack of funds" would be given as the reason. As I was settling into one of the interview chairs across from Jim Lehrer, a note arrived stating that the Oversight Board had changed its mind and would provide the necessary funding. Given the PR disaster that it would have created if no funds were available, there suddenly was found a sufficiently detailed plan for "this early case."

Shortly thereafter, on the recommendation of John Robson, the Oversight Board hired Daniel P. Kearney as its first president. An experienced investment banker and financial man (Salomon Brothers) who had also worked in the Office of Management and Budget during the Ford administration, he appeared an ideal choice, with both government and private sector experience. Dan was easy to work with, made quick decisions, and was determined to make the awkward setup work. He delegated authority where he thought appropriate and took the responsibility for the many difficult decisions he had to make to get this complex bureaucratic contraption to work. But he soon found that his job was not what he had understood it to be. Robson as secretary to the Oversight Board wanted control over daily operations. Designated as president, Kearney had assumed that he would be a real chief executive officer working under a board that was independent of the Treasury. He found that he was at best a top staffer, and the Oversight Board was really an arm of the Treasury. After learning that he could do little without Secretary Robson's approval, he resigned in protest. A real gentleman, he bowed out gracefully and restrained his desire to explain what a mess the RTC organizational structure was.

David Cooke, the executive director of the RTC who had been my deputy at the FDIC, had already testified before the Congress on some of the difficulties of getting this huge operation under way. He said that it was hard to know where and how to get a decision out of the system, and that he spent much of his time trying to find out who had the authority to give him an answer. This public testimony did not of course endear us to the Treasury. (Brady was reported to have gone into a towering rage.) When Kearney resigned, he turned the attention of Congress, and everyone else concerned, to the fact that something was wrong with the setup.

William Taylor, chief of supervision at the Federal Reserve (and later chairman of the FDIC), was brought in as a temporary replacement for Kearney to act as president of the

RTC. Since Taylor was an experienced bureaucrat and had seen what had just happened to Kearney, he knew how to handle the situation—that is, he knew how to mollify the Treasury while at the same time trying to get something done. He also had the benefit of Kearney's resignation, which made the Treasury far more willing to find ways to make things operate more smoothly lest it be blamed for two successive resignations. We at the RTC thanked Dan Kearney for having made the ultimate sacrifice. In terms of bureaucratic valor, he had thrown himself on an enemy machine-gun nest and taken it out at the cost of his job, and to some extent his reputation. Unfortunately, there is no equivalent of a Medal of Honor for bureaucrats who sacrifice themselves for their country. We should create one, and Dan Kearney should be the first recipient.

Kearney's story, however, leads to some observations about government jobs and their occupants. When David Cooke was made executive director by the RTC board on my recommendation, many observers thought we should have gone outside the government and hired a proven private sector manager. David was a very bright young fellow, a certified public accountant who had worked in the FDIC for his entire career, and was recognized as a bureaucrat of real talent. If the RTC had been a standard organization, with a board of directors and a president/chief executive officer designated to run the operations, the private sector might well have been a good place to tap management, but no high-powered private sector executive would last long in the bureaucratic morass created by the RTC legislation, as Kearney's fate proved. We needed someone who was experienced in the bureaucratic maze that only the government can create. Experience hardens the "bureaucrat" to be able to deal with the delays, frustration, and inefficiency of a highly visible public job.

Some excellent people prove my point. Bill Roelle, head of our Knoxville, Tennessee office and a twenty-five-year FDIC veteran, was put in charge of the savings and loan "gas chamber," where insolvent institutions were put out of their misery, a skill he had learned in dealing with the failure of the notorious Jake Butcher's banks of Tennessee. (Butcher had perfected the scheme of moving assets between his various banks to create the illusion of solvency in order to fool bank supervisors.) Lamar Kelly was brought over from the FDIC's Division of Liquidation to head the RTC's mammoth task of disposing of the junkpile of assets we inherited from the failed S&Ls. But not everyone worked out as well, and correcting personnel mistakes proved to be one of the disadvantages of bureaucracy.

The RTC's Western region was headed by Tony Scalzi, a top bank examiner but with no experience of bank liquidation. A wonderful public representative and a fine fellow, he was no administrator. Our Western region was an important one: California was the home of some huge S&Ls, and in Arizona all but one of the state's S&Ls had collapsed into the arms of the RTC. Scalzi remained in the job for over a year while problems mounted. Why did we leave him there so long? Government managers are not used to taking drastic actions about personnel. No one is fired or suffers a salary cut. David Cooke handled difficult relations with the Oversight Board and the Congress, but he did not have the experience, training, or heart to take quick and decisive action to shift his old friend Scalzi. Finally, we prevailed on Cooke, and Scalzi was transferred to the kind of job he should have had to begin with—one involving supervisory skills.

One of government's greatest difficulty is in changing its ways. All big organizations have this problem, but in government there is no bottom line, no pay incentive to motivate people and force change. This is not to say that people in the bureaucracy are not well intended. By any standard, almost all of them are, but they respond to the system in which they live. The inability to force change requires them to adapt in order to save their sanity. They have learned well not to try to fight City Hall.

We were not past Thanksgiving Day of 1989 before it became certain that the number of savings and loans that were going to have to be taken over was far in excess of the number originally estimated. The problem was far worse than anyone in the government had envisioned, including me, and it was getting worse every day. The economy was beginning to slide into recession. Real estate was in a real depression in some parts of the country, particularly in Texas, where the savings and loan problem was the largest. We were faced with taking the most politically unacceptable action of all, having to admit that we had made a big mistake. In government, as in business (to a lesser degree), there is nothing that causes more consternation than an admission of error.

The Bush administration's original estimate—far higher than anything ever estimated by its predecessors—had been that more than 400 S&Ls with over $200 billion in assets would be turned over to the RTC, and that this operation would cost the RTC $50 billion. In less than a year, the estimate had grown to 700 or 800 S&Ls with assets worth over $400 billion and losses exceeding $100 billion to the RTC— which meant the government and eventually, of course, the taxpayers. We would also need billions more to pay off depositors and carry the weak assets of the institutions until they were sold and we could recover the funds we had invested.

It worked like this: If the institution had $6 billion in loans on the books and $6 billion in deposits, we would have to pay off the depositors. That would demand $6 billion of our cash up front, but as we sold the $6 billion in assets—loans on empty office buildings, desert land, or whatever harebrained schemes in which the S&L had invested its depositors' money, we would probably realize only about $4 billion. Thus, even though the loss might be only $2 billion, we would still need $6 billion in cash—working capital of $4 billion, plus the additional $2 billion to meet losses, in order to close and dispose of the institution. The funds we needed to do the job were far larger than the final cost, and they had to be borrowed from the government.

Fortunately, Bill Taylor was president of the RTC when the administration decided to face up to the huge underestimate it had made. Taylor had reviewed the situation with the staff of the Oversight Board. He agreed with us that the cost of the bailout was going to far exceed anything previously estimated. New testimony was drafted for Secretary Brady, increasing the estimated loss to somewhere between $110 billion and $160 billion. We all agreed with that estimate, and for once, we made it high enough. Adding in the cost of 1988, Danny Wall's FSLIC deals of about $60 billion, the total could exceed $200 billion.

Congress was shocked, and the statement was received with great consternation, but at least the administration got high marks for finally having come clean about the cost of the problem. One of Congress's pet peeves is slanted testimony that belittles the scope of a problem or misleads. But coming clean about past errors is not easy. If you have made an honest estimate and it is wrong, you can still be accused of not coming clean. If you make a higher estimate than you really believe is likely or even possible and it turns out to be too high, no one protests. But Lord help you if you set it too low, and it turns out your estimate is wrong.

The Resolution Trust Corporation was growing like a bureaucratic weed, and the end was nowhere in sight. In a year, it had 8,000 employees and thousands of independent contractors. It prosecuted more than 150,000 active lawsuits, and employed over 1,500 people in its Legal Division. The RTC also hired more than a thousand outside law firms, and its legal bill was approaching $1 billion a year. Some of the top firms had been paid in excess of $20 million in fees in a single year. The assets that the RTC hoped to dispose of were primarily mortgages on one-to-four-family homes, but also included golf courses, marinas, condominiums, uranium mines, ranches, windmill farms, coin collections, works of art (and items claimed to be works of art), and office buildings— anything that anybody wanted to put up as collateral at a friendly savings and loan.

When Taylor returned to his job at the Fed, Peter Monroe took over as president of the Oversight Board. His background was in real estate and he had worked at the Department of Housing and Urban Development. An experienced bureaucratic operator, he realized the job's limitations and operated with deference to Robson and company. He did his best for us at the RTC as well, a tough act to pull off, and was a leader in promoting the RTC's pioneering securitization of commercial mortgages program. Anyone who undertook the job of running the Resolution Trust Corporation Oversight Board could count on wearing the scars for the rest of his or her political life.

But my job as CEO of the RTC itself was even less rewarding. The job combined all the best aspects of an undertaker, an IRS agent, and a garbage collector. Being alert to offending any of the foregoing operators, let me add, that any one of those jobs is exemplary and desirable. It is the combination of all three that causes the problem.

A major task of the RTC was collecting hundreds of thousands of loans made by defunct S&Ls, an occupation that never produces many friends. Our lawsuits, most of them to chase individuals who were in no rush to repay money borrowed from institutions that had vanished from the map, further diminished our popularity. Politically, this assured screams of protest by the borrowers to their elected officials. We sued officers and directors for negligent behavior, and we also defended ourselves in court against the outraged borrowers who were no longer allowed to draw on loan commitments made by the brain-dead S&Ls in our mortuary.

Further public outrage was stirred by the billions of dollars of property we wanted to sell in markets already waterlogged with sales from surviving banks, S&Ls, and insurance companies. Buyers complained that the RTC did not operate like a private seller, and it was impossible to make a deal with its bureaucracy. Other sellers meanwhile complained that we were ruining their market by dumping our property on it—they did not want us to sell at all. The Arizona superintendent of banking, a somewhat eccentric fellow, declared that the RTC was not only illegal and immoral, but it was destroying the Arizona economy. Since the RTC owned so much Arizona real estate, an allegation of this nature was not surprising—but we did not create the glut, we just inherited it.

Running the RTC had become a far greater challenge than anyone had expected, and would have defied the abilities of Sloan of General Motors, Henry of Ford, or Herbert of Hoover. Each savings and loan arrived with records in disarray, key personnel gone, lawsuits by the hundreds, and a management that was still mismanaging or had departed and left the cupboard bare. Never in human history has so much garbage been dumped in such a small spot by so many diverse organizations. It was a most unbelievable mess.

Our new computer systems were overwhelmed by the avalanche of assets. There was an ever-present conflict between allowing managers to act independently and therefore rapidly, and our internal controls, which demanded every transaction be checked and rechecked against fraud.

Operations are bureaucratic in any government agency. However, there is a dilemma peculiar to any agency that has been set up to liquidate property, one that we faced in the FDIC and never completely solved. All the people we hired knew that every asset they sold brought them one step closer to being out of a job. This created a truly perverse incentive. Furthermore, playing it safe was a part of the operation by its very nature. Almost all of our people were hired fresh off the street, and many were scared to take responsibility in their new job as "government agents."

Of the thousands of new employees, we knew that some

were likely to be crooks. But how do you know which ones? We had six different agencies auditing RTC operations: two independent inspector generals, our own inside internal control team, the Oversight Board staff, the congressional committee staffs, and the General Accounting Office (GAO). There were times when there would be more auditors than participants present at RTC transactions. Naturally, when employees have to justify every step to several auditors and overseers, and then later, maybe, to congressional committees, caution becomes the watchword of operations.

Occasionally, we gathered up our courage and decided to move in a bold and imaginative way. I made the decision to schedule an international auction to sell hundreds of millions in real estate in one record-setting and eye-catching transaction. The RTC would put on the world's biggest real estate auction and prove we could move with unaccustomed, ungovernment-like vigor and (we all hoped) attract more clients for our huge inventory.

David Cooke and his team developed a typical bureaucratic checklist designed to pick the best qualified auctioneer. It gave hiring points to the handicapped and minorities and to the performance of good works in the past, but very few points for past relevant experience in the field. As is often the case, the government people, moving in a new area and unfamiliar with auctions, turned to the private sector for advice. They seem to have received too much help in the design of the checklist from one of the potential bidders. From the RTC point system emerged an auctioneer named Gall, from Miami. His previous experience did not include auctioning any large pieces of property. Gall and his associate, the formidable Washington public relations firm of Hill and Knowlton, seem to have overwhelmed our bureaucrats. A number of people who had worked on a similar but much smaller auction at the FDIC had warned us that there was no way on earth Gall could handle an international auction of large pieces of real estate. Cooke was informed and asked to take a second look at his selection process. He pronounced himself satisfied that the process had been fair and efficient. I told him, "David, my good friend, the responsibility is yours."

The RTC went forward with the auction plan. But the RTC believed that Gall had failed to live up to his contractual commitments; he was supposed to invest $1 million in advertising and other preparations for the auction but never came up with the money. Cooke quickly came to the conclusion that the auction would flop. He asked for a delay, which was agreed to. When even the delay date was missed, we decided to cut our losses, cancel the auction, and take the criticism that we knew would come our way. The Congress once again accused us of incompetence and inefficiency. Gall also blamed us and filed suit. It took a year to settle, very favorably for us as it turned out, but the incident gave us more than enough of the kind of press coverage we didn't need.

The "big auction" taught the RTC several lessons: Walk before you try flying. Do not try to show off with a big splash unless you know there is water in the tank. Most important, when the government asks for bids, remember that the name of the bidders' game is to get inside the bidding operation and set it up to win. Protecting the integrity of the bidding process is essential, and the only way to do it is with a hands-on approach. While Cooke was running the big auction and took the heat for its failure, the fault was really mine for trying to put us on the map by suggesting a big show to begin with. A dumb idea with predictable results.

The problems had no end. Thousands of prospective buyers made offers for property and then received no response for weeks and sometimes months. After we published a rule that every bid had to be answered within one month, the bureaucracy often took the easiest way out and turned down bidders at the deadline. Our statute required that every possible operation had to be performed by private contractors; and suddenly we had a list of more than 60,000, all seeking work ranging from appraising and selling properties to providing paper clips and fax paper. Most were honest citizens seeking to perform diligent work at a modest profit, although some surely were not. On my desk I had a small plaque that read, in Latin so as not to offend the honest visitor, "Never underestimate the ability and desire of certain citizens to rip off their government."

Every contract had the potential for fraud or gross mismanagement. Our Contracting Division moved slowly, seeking not only honesty and efficiency, but a path through the congressionally mandated mine field requiring us to be fair to everyone no matter what race, creed, and sex—and moreover, being able to prove it if challenged. Even-handedness was not enough; affirmative action required even more, the righting of past wrongs through the contracting procedure. Jesse Jackson called upon us to explain what he viewed as an insufficient number of contracts with minority firms. A very persuasive individual, he convinced us to hold a special seminar for African Americans and other minorities at which he, I, and our staff would explain to them how to obtain their fair share of our work.

This had limited success, in part because it soon became clear that the ethnic groups no longer considered women equal participants in what they regarded as a minority coalition. Not entirely an inconsistent argument, since women are, at least by the numbers, a majority. The seminar turned into a heated discussion between the representatives of the women and of the ethnics over which group had a better claim to being preferred in our contracting process.

Our affirmative action plan gave minority firms a special break on bidding. If their bid fell within about 5 percent of the best bid, it would be accepted as the winning bid. But what was a minority firm? One successful bidder who profited from the affirmative action advantage consisted of a woman who was the owner of record with 51 percent control, and her husband, a property manager by profession, who owned 49 percent. A year before it had *all* been owned by the husband. A number of firms came to us with a minority member in charge, at least nominally, and a suspiciously large number of whites comprising the rest of their organization. This was not exactly what we intended. There are some very sticky problems involved in determining the gender or racial makeup of bidders. Are the blacks truly African Americans, the ladies truly female? Employees were known to claim to be Hispanic and Native American to obtain preferences for job promotions. Once you get into racial preferences in bidding, it makes managing an art and not a science, and not one that satisfies any of the groups involved.

Our inventory of "affordable housing" posed another problem. Our statute did not allow us simply to sell our low-priced homes to the highest bidder; we had to offer them for first refusal to certified low-income buyers. In a twist on the usual definition, "financially qualified buyer" meant someone who had little other money or income. We devised financial means tests for eligibility and made sales only to those designated under the statute. Here was an invitation to those who were willing and able to con the government. Soon a television special presented rich citizens bragging that they had beaten the system and bought housing bargains for resale at a large profit. The buyers used straw men to purchase the homes, and the real buyers were millionaires. TV helped us find the fraud, though I do not think they were trying to aid us.

Our Affordable Housing Division redoubled its efforts to find real low-income buyers while fending off the crooks, but many of those whom we wanted to purchase our affordable homes could not get financing. By definition, their income was not sufficient to satisfy lending institutions. Through state housing agencies we structured creative financing for low-income buyers; by the end of 1992 the RTC had closed deals on close to 14,000 single-family affordable housing sales. Many people are now living in houses they could never have aspired to without the bankruptcy of all those misman-aged S&Ls. If we ultimately received no bids, we would give the homes to a state housing authority or even a local char-ity. Needless to say, setting this up to the satisfaction of the various groups was impossible. One group known as ACORN, the Association of Community Organizations for Reform Now, a nonprofit organization involved in housing and banking issues, never ceased complaining about our ef-forts.

In an unusually friendly segment, television's *60 Minutes* showed a deliriously happy couple that had bought a three-bedroom, two-bathroom house in Colorado Springs, with a great view of the mountains to the west, for $31,000. There were few satisfactions in operating the RTC, but the look on the faces of the couple as they settled into a house that had been priced at $90,000 was a winner. It is an ill wind that blows no good.

We were liquidating six to seven S&Ls a week, and with them came billions of dollars worth of assets that had to be valued. We needed to record them on the books at their real worth, rather than at the much higher value they had car-ried on the books of the institutions (which is one reason why they failed). We had to be able to value every kind of loan and real estate holding imaginable. Only then would we know how to price them for sale. We needed to know exactly what an acre of desert between Tucson and Phoenix was worth. What were the values of chunks of the Alaskan tun-dra? How do you value the world's largest magic collection, and a liquor store's wooden Indian? What was the price for marinas without water, golf courses without greens, and of-fice buildings without tenants. Valuation is not an exact science. Markets fluctuate. We asked the Oversight Board for policy direction, and they bucked it back to us as an operating problem. Consequently, we hired appraisers by the score, and reappraised continually.

The General Accounting Office was quick to highlight our problems. What else is an auditor for? They said our asset valuations were so uncertain that they could not provide an audited statement. Worse, in our Denver office we had closed down defunct S&Ls' computer systems without getting our own system properly on line, and about $7 billion worth of assets disappeared from our books, to be found again only after substantial accounting fees and a considerable amount of embarrassing publicity.

Most of these problems could have been avoided if we had slowed the process of taking over the S&Ls until all accounting systems had been tested and put on line. But delay would have cost hundreds of millions in losses that were accumulating daily on the books of the S&Ls, so we had to move fast and inevitably made mistakes. Not surprisingly, what we considered to be cost-effective management decisions were hardly acclaimed by the GAO, whose ability to criticize is without peer. Yet another example of the old Washington adage that where you sit determines where you stand.

From the beginning of its short life, my message to the RTC was "Never forget you are primarily a sales organization—selling to the private sector. You are not a government agency doing the usual task of administering the laws of the Congress." On average, over half the assets of a failed S&L were home mortgages and were easily sold into an established market, the government-guaranteed Fannie Mae (the Federal National Mortgage Association) market. (Potentially, another huge full faith and credit liability.) The rest of the assets were harder to sell, and that was the heart of our sales challenge.

In mid-March 1990, while preparing for testimony on the RTC operations, I did some back-of-the envelope calculations. If the RTC sold $1 million in assets a day every day of the year, it would sell $365 million per year. At that rate it would take about three years to sell $1 billion of its assets. But the RTC had an inventory of about $40 billion in difficult assets—commercial mortgages, nonstandard home mortgages, problem real estate and so on. So even at sales of $1 million a day, it would take more than 120 years to clear our inventory, and it was still growing. The obvious conclusion of this little bit of arithmetic was that only by selling large pools of assets would the RTC complete its job in its legal lifetime (it was mandated to close down on or before December 31, 1996).

Our strategy of selling in bulk was born on the back of that envelope. To implement the program we created a national sales office to deal with large customers. A potential big buyer would be assigned his own sales representative just as IBM has one salesperson concentrating on a Fortune 500 client, or Boeing on a big airline. The RTC developed a bulk sales program. To sell big packages we needed to pool assets and sell the pool to one buyer in a single portfolio, or to several buyers by turning our mortgages into securities. Within a few months our securitization program, led by David Cooke, Michael Jungman, and Ken Bacon, became the most innovative new securities effort seen on Wall Street since Salomon Brothers invented pooling mortgages—securitization—years before.

The success of our sales effort depended on the obvious strategy of selling big piles of assets, which required rich buyers. As usual in government operations, there were those who opposed the idea. Some in Congress felt the program favored the big buyers such as GE Capital and Morgan Stanley, but who else had such huge amounts of cash and how else to get the job done? Local salespeople, both in and out of government, objected to having properties put in pools that eliminated the inventory they could push. They took their complaints to their congressional representatives, and undoubtedly will continue to do so until closing day.

To facilitate sales, the RTC developed a graduated basement pricing system for small properties not suitable for pooled sales. After three months the price went down by a certain percentage. The longer the holding period, the lower the price, down to 50 percent of the original sales price—which was the appraised value as of the time we first put it on the market (and not the inflated book value at which we often inherited it from the blue-sky promoters of the failed S&Ls). Again there were protests that we were "giving away the store," but how else were buyers to be found, except to copy the famous methods of Filene's basement in Boston? We never found a buyer who wished to purchase our assets out of patriotic duty.

In a speech to the National Press Club on March 21, 1990, I laid out our marketing strategy and discussed our priorities for stemming RTC losses. "Bad assets" were no longer to be known as such, but would instead be known by the more appropriate term "opportunity asset inventory." Buyers for large packages of assets would be sought through our new national sales office. Starting in April, we would make our inventory available in an easily updated data-disk format. I closed with our 800 number and a reminder that Visa and MasterCard charges would be accepted.

The flood of liquidations meant that the RTC was running out of money. We had expected to have $80 billion in losses by the end of September 1991. Our worst case estimate was now somewhere near double that amount. But the political climate was not encouraging for more congressional appropriations. The RTC was being blamed for almost every conceivable human transgression—defrauding the poor, enriching the rich, bureaucratizing the bureaucracy and, above all, bailing out the thrift industry. (We were really bailing out depositors and liquidating the failed part of the industry, but no one ever seemed to describe it that way.) Congress had reluctantly appropriated the last $30 billion, and the thought of having to dig into the taxpayers' jeans for billions more, with hardly a voter understanding and even fewer appreciating what they were doing, was more than most congressmen could bear.

Charles A. Bowsher, chief of the General Accounting Office, testified that the RTC books were unreliable and that they had found mistakes in the records. With that report, the Oversight Board panicked. We suggested that the best thing to do when someone's accountant says you have a problem is to send your accountant to talk to his accountant and let the matter progress. Instead of that, the board wrote a letter to the General Accounting Office begging for any examples of the bad accounting practices they had found at the RTC. Who could resist that kind of invitation? The General Accounting Office happily unburdened itself of fifteen or sixteen real horror stories: an account with a law firm that was not in balance, a bill that had been paid twice, etc.—examples not hard to find in an organization with assets of $300 billion, and especially in one that had been created only twenty months before. We promised to do better, and we did. In its 1991 audit report, the ever-vigilant GAO removed its objections to our accounting records, an accomplishment attributable to Cooke's great job.

As we came to the time when additional funding would be required, many in Congress, including Senator Riegle and Senator Garn (the chairman and senior minority member of the Banking Committee), indicated that improvements must be made in the structure of the RTC and the Oversight Board. The general mood in the Congress ranged from negative to ugly. Philip Searle was a politically connected, retired, second-level banker from Florida and head of the RTC

Advisory Committee who had once been in line for a seat on the FDIC but refused when he could not be assured he would soon replace me as chairman. He demanded that we find a strong private sector real estate entrepreneur to re-vamp the RTC's operations and make them "user-friendly" —a tall order. It is hard to see how, even in the private sector, people in the business of collecting debts and dump-ing real estate onto already illiquid markets can be very friendly to anyone, let alone users of their services. His pro-nouncements were also somewhat irrelevant to the facts, since he seemed to believe that the RTC was mainly in the real estate business. Less than 15 percent of the RTC's inven-tory was real estate, the rest being notes from various debtors of the S&Ls, which we were trying to collect. But these com-ments only illustrate the mood of the moment, and his re-port did not help with Congress.

A chorus of complaints came from the dissatisfied, and some complaints had justification. Senators Garn and Riegle were right: the organization needed improvement. I wrote an Op Ed piece that perhaps overstated the problem, so it was never submitted for publication. It asked:

> Who is the Chief Executive Officer of the S&L cleanup? Please answer from the following list: 1) Nicholas Brady, Secretary of the Treasury; 2) John Robson, Deputy Secretary of the Treasury; 3) Peter Monroe, President of the Oversight Board; 4) David Cooke, Executive Director of the RTC; 5) William Seidman, Chairman of the RTC and FDIC; 6) Philip Searle, Head of the Advisory Committee of the RTC; 7) None of the Above.
>
> The correct answer to the question is No. 7, "None of the above." There is no one Chief Executive Officer of the RTC cleanup, and there can't be under current law. The players are in fact as follows: William Seidman is chairman of the Board of the FDIC and CEO of the FDIC. He is also Chairman of the Board of the RTC and has appointed David Cooke as Chief Ex-ecutive Director of the RTC. However, the FDIC is by statute the "exclusive manager" of the RTC. Further, the statute provides that the FDIC's responsibility will be to handle liquidations,

property sales, and otherwise be in charge of day-to-day operations. This charter is clearly one of a Chief Operating Officer, not a Chief Executive Officer. It is thus clear that no matter what the FDIC/RTC might desire to do, it can't appoint a Chief Executive Officer since its total powers are limited to being the Chief "Administrative" or Operating Officer.

Where is the rest of the CEO? The RTC Oversight Board is chaired by Secretary Brady, and its President is Peter Monroe. This institution has many of the responsibilities normally designated to a Chief Executive Officer. These powers include setting basic strategy and policy, approving budgets, and generally being ultimately responsible for the operations of the institution. However, by law it cannot interfere in day-to-day administration of the RTC.

Trying to identify a true Chief Executive Officer of the RTC highlights the fact that part of those responsibilities are within the Oversight Board, these being divided between its Chairman, Secretary Brady, and its President, Peter Monroe. With operations controlled by the exclusive management contract of the FDIC (David Cooke under the delegations of the Chairman of the Board, Seidman, and the Board) and the ultimate responsibility in the Oversight Board (Peter Monroe under the delegations of Secretary Brady and the Board), no one is in charge of the RTC.

The Treasury supported Searle's message to get rid of the bureaucrats and turn the mess over to a new private leader. John Robson, one of the architects of the RTC Oversight Board, indicated that he thought we should look for someone with private-sector experience to head the RTC, given my approaching retirement.

A new and simpler organization with one strong CEO was needed. It was my view that statutory changes were required to get the job done. The complex organization of the Oversight Board and the FDIC/RTC Board may have been justified in the beginning, when the FDIC's experience in bank liquidation was needed to get operations going, but no longer. The RTC could and should have become a separate organization, freeing the FDIC for its traditional responsibilities of bank inspection and supervision.

Thus, when the RTC requested additional funding in 1991, we also suggested separating the two agencies. Immediately and perhaps inevitably the Treasury Department objected, arguing that the present organization was working and that there was no need to change it. If a strong CEO was needed, the Treasury said, the Oversight Board and the FDIC could simply delegate their responsibilities to one individual, who would become a strong CEO by delegation of increased authority. We felt this would not work for two reasons. First and most obviously, delegation from two boards still meant two bosses over the new CEO, hardly a recipe for decisiveness. Second, by law the FDIC was the exclusive manager of failed banks, and while it could delegate that function, it still had the responsibility of ensuring that its chief operating officer was performing properly.

We met in Treasury Secretary Brady's office to discuss the situation. The argument was heated. Robson opposed the separation of the RTC and the FDIC, and Brady just listened.

At a subsequent Senate hearing, Brady testified that restructuring was not necessary in order to name a single CEO. We would fix things, he promised, by delegating to the new executive all the power that everybody shared. Unfortunately, the secretary's testimony indicated that we at the FDIC agreed with him, which can be charitably described as a misunderstanding. He called me after the testimony and said, "Please don't make any comments on the testimony until you read what I said." I said, "O.K. My position was stated in my appearance, and for once I'll say no more."

Then Steve Labaton, a Washington financial reporter for *The New York Times*, called to say that on the basis of a leak from the administration, he had written a story reporting that the FDIC was going to fire David Cooke and replace him with an executive from the private sector. We said there was no such agreement and that Cooke had done an excellent job, given the organizational tangle in which he had to operate.

This is the kind of governmental conflict that makes enemies out of friends. It was an unhappy situation. I called Brady and said, "My friend, *The New York Times* will run a story tomorrow that we are in basic conflict. I'm afraid the record shows that we are. What's to be done?" He said, "Well, doctor, what do you want me to do?" I replied, "Why don't you support a structural change that will allow us to set up a true CEO and get the FDIC out of this act. We can start looking for that person right now in expectation of getting that legislation." He thanked me for my views, said they would work on the matter, and promised to send me a proposed joint statement. We could never agree on one, so it never was made.

This controversy was an honest disagreement. Treasury supported the present structure, mainly because it was Treasury's own creation, but also because reopening the question might pave the way for Congress to impose all kinds of draconian strictures designed to embarrass the administration and undermine what we had already accomplished. It was a classic example of the urge in public life to defend what you have done against all odds, no matter whether it is right or wrong, virtuous or evil.

As the end of my term as chairman was near, the matter was more of academic than practical importance to me. Should we simply go along with the Treasury view so that my retirement could be accomplished with appropriate amiability? Let the matter be worked out by whoever succeeded me? Although it was tempting, that alternative was eliminated by the Congress. The Senate Banking Committee drafted a bill that essentially followed the FDIC's recommendations: a new and separate CEO position was created along private sector lines. The Oversight Board was reduced to oversight, and the FDIC was to have no RTC responsibilities.

The matter came to a head in July 1991, just as I was about to go hiking along the John Muir Trail in Yosemite National Park. My FDIC associates asked me to cancel the trip and return to lobby for the bill. I declined. My presence in Washington proved unnecessary. Despite my dereliction, a bill reorganizing the RTC was enacted pretty much the way we had proposed. Once that passed, the search for that single and powerful CEO began. Cooke decided he wanted out. A number of well-qualified people were interested. We had been talking for some time to an ex-Chrysler executive, Gerald Greenwald, who was the closest thing we could get to Lee Iacocca. Ultimately he was passed over, and he ended up helping to bail out the bankrupt Olympia and York real estate empire, a failure so large that it was a kind of mini-RTC. The favorite became our old friend from the First Republic transaction, former American Airlines chairman Al Casey. What goes around comes around. He swallowed his antipathy toward me and agreed to become the new "strong" CEO. His performance thereafter had its ups and downs, and he departed with a push from the new Clinton administration.

As of December 31, 1992, the RTC had accomplished a great deal with its new streamlined organization and the strong Al Casey in control. The RTC had protected approximately 22 million deposit accounts in closed thrifts, worth $197 billion. It did not just save big fish; the average account balance was $9,000. It did not bail out S&L owners.

A total of 734 nonviable S&Ls with about $400 billion in assets had been seized by the Office of Thrift Supervision and sent to the RTC. Ninety percent of them were sold or liquidated by the RTC, and two-thirds of their assets sold off to help defray the salvage costs. By and large, these were not fire sales. Recoveries by the RTC from sales, and collections of $305 billion in thrift assets have averaged 92 percent of their book value at the time the government took them over.

Virtually all of the overhang of below-standard S&Ls had been transferred to the RTC. As of September 1992, only thirty-one institutions with $28 billion in assets were "critically undercapitalized" and would have to be wound up. Another eighty were on the OTS "watch list," some of which will probably fall below the line in 1993 and 1994 and will also have to be wound up. By the end of July 1992, the RTC had successfully closed over 652 thrifts. It controlled only one-third of the $400 billion in assets it took over and was selling them off at the rate of better than $8 billion a month. Naturally the rate of sales and the proportion of value recovered for the taxpayers will slow as RTC reaches the final stages and gets down to its hard-to-sell assets.

The RTC initiated more than 3,000 enforcement actions. More than 1,000 indictments have been handed down, with more than 900 convictions as of this writing, a conviction rate of more than 90 percent. The key indictments and convictions have included: Charles Keating (Lincoln Savings); David Paul (CenTrust); Tom Spiegel (Columbia Savings); Don Dixon (Vernon Savings); and Ed McBirney (Sunbelt Savings). Nearly 2,000 civil actions have been launched against directors, officers, accountants, and lawyers who defaulted on their trust or, in some cases, clearly defaulted on their professional responsibility. This coordinated government-wide effort to recover ill-gotten gains was undertaken by Justice, RTC, FDIC, and OTS. Recoveries through fines, judgments, awards, and settlements already exceed $1 billion, with several billion in total claims pending.

After four years of losses, the S&L industry returned to profitability. At the end of 1992, less than 1 percent of the industry was insolvent. S&L profits for the twelve months ending March 1992 were $2.8 billion; profits for the first quarter alone were $1.6 billion. As of September 1992, average tangible capital had increased to 5.82 percent, well above regulatory requirements. It will be the economy, interest rate changes and real estate market conditions that will dictate the future performance of the thrift industry.

Not bad for a government agency with one of the worst assignments in history. Be encouraged; occasionally government does work. Or perhaps the first RTC chairman is a bit biased.

12

Trying to Get Money Back from Keating, Milken, Neil Bush (and Thousands of Others)

L awsuits follow closed banks and S&Ls like weeds popping up after a summer rain. After the failure of thousands of banks and S&Ls, claims for damages, negligence, and fraud occupied an increasing amount of our energies at the FDIC and RTC officialdom. Nothing was harder to control than the bureaucracy's sheer delight in litigation. Litigators want an unending supply of people to sue lest they become unnecessary to the agency and are forced to seek new employment.

We were the custodians of a financial casualty ward that provided the perfect environment for litigious souls. Our proud record of cutting the number of our lawsuits by half was obliterated when the S&Ls became our problem and brought with them hundreds and sometimes thousands of new legal actions to collect money on outstanding loans. Once the banks went belly up and passed to their reward under the care of the taxpayers, many debtors did not seem to believe they owed anything any more. We farmed out cases to more than a thousand law firms in cities across the country, creating prosperity for lawyers in the midst of recession, if for no one else.

Every recovered dollar reduced the taxpayers' bill for the S&L failures. We tried to reduce the collection costs, but that would have been possible only by changing the American legal system. A few intriguing suits involved defending dead S&Ls against borrowers who claimed they had been promised a line of credit and suffered business losses because they did not receive the money when they asked for it. But by far the most challenging were those that sought damages from some of the best known of the S&L failures—Charles Keating of the Lincoln Savings and Loan; Neil Bush of Silverado; and Michael Milken, junk bond salesman to the industry.

Charles Keating's S&L was *the* example of how the industry had spun out of control. Keating had been put into business with the help of a junk bond underwriting led by Milken of Drexel Burnham Lambert. The Home Loan Bank Board had advised him to diversify his investments. Lincoln took that advice and ran with it. Keating dropped entirely the business of making home mortgages, formerly the sole business of savings and loans and the reason for which they had been chartered. In five years the only home mortgages Lincoln made were to its favored employees. But during that period, Lincoln grew tenfold from approximately $600 million in loans to near $6 billion.

Growth was funded primarily by brokered deposits. The insurance fund fought to eliminate insurance on these deposits but lost in the courts and in Congress. (At the FDIC, we then controlled the problem by instructing banks to notify us whenever their brokered deposits exceeded 5 percent of their total deposits. That substantially reduced the number who were willing to engage in this kind of funding.) Keating's S&L used its new money to purchase high-yielding junk bonds from brokered deposits syndicated by Milken and to become speculative land developers.

One of Keating's largest ventures was the Phoenician Hotel, probably the most costly and luxurious hotel ever built in the United States. After the RTC took it over, I had the great pleasure of staying there a number of times, not on pleasure trips, I hasten to add, but to speak to our customers who had conventions there. At a cost to build of half a million dollars a room, it was a palace of unparalleled conspicuous consumption. It was an extraordinary display of what fun you can have spending other people's money. It was filled with marble statuary. Each bedroom was large enough to hold a small convention. It was not really done in bad taste, just excessively expensive. Keating was particularly proud of it, and various dining rooms in the hotel were named after his wife, himself, and his children. A monument to Keating's ego, its opulence guaranteed it was never going to be profitable unless the hotel could charge the unattainable sum of $500 a night for every room in the house. The standard guideline for hotel rates says that the nightly room charge should be one percent of the total capital cost of the room. The Phoenician's rooms each cost $500,000, so the hotel had to average this $500 a night for at least 70 percent of the year for it to make money. No hotel in Arizona (which has some classy hotels—like the Arizona Biltmore) ever came close to that price at that occupancy level. Even after the RTC inherited it, cut overhead, and improved operations, it still lost millions on the basis of its original cost.

Keating decided at one point to cut his losses and sold 40 percent of the hotel to the Kuwait Investment Trust, which operates out of London as an arm of the Kuwaiti Government. It had veto power over the sale of the hotel, and we would have been delighted if they had either bought the remaining interest or allowed us to sell it to others, but they would not allow us to do either. We were trying to persuade them at the time the United States was rescuing Kuwait from Saddam Hussein, but the Kuwaitis proved very uncooperative partners. Either they were traumatized by the war or, equally likely, they were holding out for the lowest price they could obtain for total ownership. At one point we got so aggravated that I suggested, perhaps not entirely in jest, that we call on my friend Secretary of Defense Dick Cheney to use some of his vast naval power to persuade the Kuwaitis to behave in a more responsible manner. After the Gulf War was successfully completed and Kuwait was free, we expected to find the Kuwait Investment Trust more responsive and helpful, but in the end they treated us as they would any business partner, not as their nation's saver. Finally they bought out our retreat at what we believed to be a fair price.

Another of Keating's ventures was a huge new planned city outside of Phoenix on the highway to Los Angeles. He bought thousands of acres of desert and pronounced that when finished he would have fathered a new city of 20,000 people. When his business collapsed, he was on his way to putting in roads and lakes. We later asked real estate experts to judge the city's potential. They thought that it might take ten to fifteen years to develop and would probably make back only half its projected costs. Two experts guessed that it might work better if it could somehow be considered a suburb of Los Angeles, some 400 miles away. It stands as a tribute to what happens when an individual gets the unstructured opportunity to spend unlimited amounts of the government's full faith and *credit* for whatever his imagination may conjure up.

Keating also lavished his unlimited funds on his employees. Many of his secretaries were paid double the normal rate for the Phoenix area. At one point, upon seeing one young lady whom he thought was performing her secretarial duties well, he invited her into his office and pronounced her performance so exceptional that he doubled her salary on the spot. The highest paid employee aside from Keating himself was his son, a twenty-nine-year-old former bartender who was running the real estate operation and earning just under $1 million a year.

Keating also had special ways of dealing with his accountants. His accounting firm, Arthur Young and Company, had assigned Jack D. Atchison to the Lincoln account. Atchison found no problem in giving Keating's savings and loan a clean audit in his final year at the accounting firm. Within minutes after signing the audit, he resigned from Arthur Young and joined Keating at approximately four times his former salary. It was his audit that helped cost Arthur Young its settlement of $400 million with the government. Atchison was barred from the practice of accounting in the state of Arizona.

Keating's operations gained distinguished professional support. In a 1985 report he must wish he had never written, Alan Greenspan, then a private economic consultant in New York but now chairman of the Federal Reserve System, commended Charles Keating and the Lincoln Savings and Loan as a soundly operated institution. He pointed out that it had diversified entirely out of old-fashioned home mortgages and thus had eliminated the interest rate risk inherent in the traditional savings and loan business. The Greenspan report failed to note that Keating's savings and loan had simply exchanged interest rate risks for much greater asset quality risks—that is, the old-fashioned, hair-curling risk of speculative real estate investments.

Keating also used his money to buy influence with the government through political contributions, stating openly that he certainly hoped the money would influence government decision makers when he needed help. In this he was nonpartisan. In one instance, Keating sought an appointment to the Home Loan Bank Board, the chief regulatory body for the S&Ls, for Lee R. Henkel Jr., Lincoln's former legal counsel. With the support of Donald Regan, then chief of staff of the Reagan White House, and of Senator Dennis DeConcini of Arizona, a Democratic beneficiary of Keating's largess, Henkel received an interim appointment to the Bank Board. At his first board meeting, he introduced a proposal to protect Lincoln from regulatory foreclosure. It was buried in a long resolution he presented on other matters. Fortunately, the special provision was spotted by Chairman Edwin Gray and was not adopted. Henkel was never formally confirmed as a member of the board. In 1992 he finally settled the government's suit, which charged that Lincoln paid him off by buying his business and forgiving his loans, and was banned from the banking and thrift industries.

Five senators received substantial sums from Keating, and they became known as the Keating Five—DeConcini, Alan Cranston of California, Donald Riegle of Michigan, John Glenn of Ohio, all Democrats, and John McCain, Arizona's Republican senator. At a famous meeting with the five senators, Ed Gray, the Home Loan Bank Board chairman, was questioned about recommendations from his examiners in the field that Keating's S&L should be closed down. Gray later told me how unbelievable it was for a group of senators to get together and talk to a regulator, not just about regulations in general, but about one particular case, and with the senators' requesting that "no staff be present." In this case Gray felt he was being pressured to change the rules to favor Keating's Lincoln Savings. It amazes me that five such astute politicians did not realize how they could be hurt when all this would be replayed in public, as it eventually was. Gray asked my advice on how to handle it. I said, "Go public with the problem. Make it clear that you are not going to be influenced by that kind of activity."

But it is easier to advise someone else to blow the whistle on five U.S. senators than to do it yourself. Gray said he did not feel he could confront the five because he needed their votes in the Senate to obtain new funds for his failing insurance fund. Furthermore, his term on the board was expiring and he felt it was his successor's problem. He urged Danny Wall to close down Lincoln Savings, but Wall did not take that sound advice.

Keating's highly paid law firms, accounting firms, and appraisers were also very much a part of what turned out to be a huge fraudulent operation. Federal Judge Stanley Sporkin asked where were the professionals when all these improper activities were taking place? The agencies regulating the thrifts sued all the accounting firms including two of the Big

Eight, Arthur Andersen and Arthur Young, and two big law factories, Kaye, Scholer, Fierman, Hays and Handler and Jones Day Leavis and Pogue, for being asleep at the switch, or worse.

Before the Keating Five hearings took place, I said that from a senator's viewpoint, it was not unreasonable for them to make an inquiry about how regulators were treating their friend. After all, Lincoln had already been certified a few years before as sound by Greenspan, a respected former White House official. Further, a major accounting firm, Arthur Young and Company, had written that regulators were being unreasonable. With this background it would have been perfectly reasonable for a senator who had been contacted by his constituent, to make an inquiry of the regulators. Senator DeConcini used my statement in his presentation to the Ethics Committee, which was reviewing his conduct along with the other senators.

Senator Riegle had been a key supporter of the FDIC's fight against the White House for its independence, and we appreciated his help. At his request, we prepared a statement citing his diligence in helping us resolve the savings and loan problems. My staff advised that it would be wiser to decline to make any statement to the committee unless subpoenaed. But we submitted the statement. First, because it was true, and second, because one cannot expect to receive support when it is needed without providing support in return. My press secretary, Alan Whitney, feared the immediate reactions in the press and counseled me to be careful. As a matter of fact, my statement supporting Riegle went largely unnoticed, to my surprise.

Suing Charles Keating's Lincoln Savings and Loan became the favorite activity of a legion of lawyers. The RTC's investigation provided most of the evidence for its civil suits and similar actions by holders of its notes and by California and federal authorities. But Keating appeared to have gone broke after his splurge, or else he had hidden his assets, so there was not much left to collect. California authorities put Keating in jail for criminal fraud, and it appears he will be there for a considerable amount of time. It could not have happened to a more deserving gentleman! He defrauded depositors in one of the more heartless and cruel frauds in modern memory. His tellers were told to persuade depositors, many of whom had lodged their life's savings with Lincoln, to move their money from insured deposits to the bonds of Keating's holding company, which even at that time the regulators adjudged insolvent. Thousands of people were swindled in Keating's crass and unsuccessful attempt to save himself.

Another criminal sued by the RTC was Michael Milken of Drexel Burnham Lambert. A phenomenon that mystified me when I was dean of the Arizona State University Business School was: How did Drexel Burnham Lambert and its star partner Michael Milken roll up an unparalleled record of successes in selling junk bonds? As far as we could determine, his underwritings never failed and appeared to be marketed successfully, no matter how suspect the company or how risky the buyout deal that was being financed. Other investment houses had some failed junk bond offerings, but Drexel's record was near perfect. We directed our faculty to research the matter. (Actually you cannot direct faculty, you can merely suggest.) The faculty came up with no plausible explanation; like so many others they fell back on the thesis of the junk bond king's unique genius.

But as we at the RTC examined the financial carnage of the savings and loans later in the decade, I was struck by one thing. Some of the S&Ls that had suffered the heaviest losses were also the largest holders of Drexel-created junk bonds. They not only included Charles Keating's Lincoln, but Cen-Trust, run by David Paul in Miami; Tom Spiegel's Columbia and Denver's Silverado, where Neil Bush, son of the president, was a director. All were Drexel clients. Columbia almost completely abandoned using its deposits for home financing to concentrate on buying these high-return bonds. As I discussed this with John Borenzi, my deputy, and Al Byrne, our new general counsel, the light of simple revelation suddenly flashed on. An S&L could be a near-inexhaustible source of funds for buying junk bonds. S&Ls could raise nearly unlimited amounts of funds through brokered deposits at low rates because the money was insured by the government. They could then buy these high-yielding bonds and make their profits on the spread between the low and high rates of interest. And that is exactly what they had done until the recession came and the companies could no longer earn enough to pay the high rates of interest; they went down like a row of bowling pins, defaulting on their payments and turning the bonds into wallpaper.

Thus we framed our suit against Drexel Burnham Lambert and its star junk bond king, Michael Milken, alleging that several S&Ls had suffered huge losses by buying his bonds. It was not illegal for them to buy junk bonds, and he had not guaranteed they would hold their value. But we charged that Milken had bribed purchasers to buy them by giving warrants or rights to S&L managers. We also charged that he rigged the market by operating a sort of daisy chain among the S&Ls to trade the bonds back and forth across his famous X-shaped trading desk at his headquarters in Beverly Hills. By manipulating the market, he maintained the facade that the bonds were trading at genuine market prices and therefore worth more than they really were. When he was brought down, and his trading operation with him, so were the S&Ls that depended on the value of his bonds to stay afloat. The dean's dilemma was solved. With captive purchasers, you cannot fail to have successful underwritings, especially when the buyers have an unlimited source of funds guaranteed by no less than the full faith and credit of the U.S. government.

It was apparent that we needed heavy legal artillery if we hoped to carry the day against Milken in court. From his prison cell he commanded the services of four or five of the largest legal firms and could easily pay their fees from the hundreds of millions of dollars still left in his personal fortune. He represented an unprecedented challenge to the government's lawyers, who were experts in the minutiae of regulatory cases but had never battled fraud on this heroic scale. We would be up against some of the most talented law firms in the United States. As I said to our chief counsel, Al Byrne, "We're not going to go into this NFL contest represented by the East Grand Rapids High School football team. We have to have comparable pros."

In order to make the case more palatable politically and still appealing to top firms, we decided to ask for bids on a contingent fee basis. Our award went to Cravath, Swaine and Moore, a blue-chip New York firm offering the services of two of the nation's finest trial lawyers, Thomas Barr and David Boies. Under our agreement they would charge about half their regular rates, but we agreed that they could charge their full rates if they recovered $200 million. Below that, the lower rates applied. The top rate of Messrs. Barr and Boies was $600 dollars an hour, about the highest quoted rate in the profession.

When word got out that the government might be paying these rates, it was the political equivalent of the Pentagon's $900 toilet seats. A legal fee of $600 an hour was something that everyone everywhere could understand and be affronted by. Congress and the press fell to it with glee. As the case finally turned out, our choice of lawyers showed that we had made a sound business decision, though without being sufficiently sensitive to the political repercussions. Later we trimmed such top fees somewhat, but what we should have done at the start was to have offered the lawyers a smaller hourly fee and a larger percentage of what they recovered.

Milken's response was to launch a vigorous public relations campaign led by Linda Robinson, wife of James Robinson, then the head of American Express; she was a gifted professional who had also fronted for some of the toughest gunslingers in the takeover battles of the 1980s. The Harvard lawyer Alan Dershowitz, who won an acquittal for Claus von Bülow in the celebrity murder trial dramatized in the movie *Reversal of Fortune* and celebrated his successes in a book called *Chutzpah,* was engaged by Milken as an adviser and promptly began proclaiming the outrageousness of our suing his client. The battle lines were clearly being drawn, and many who had benefited from the sale of junk bonds rallied to defend their hero. *The Wall Street Journal* published a long editorial bemoaning the fact that the FDIC was attempting to destroy junk bond markets, which, it argued, had served as a rich source of capital for business. Without doubt these bonds have served as a useful tool in capital markets by raising money for new and small entrepreneurs who could not raise it through the banks. Used (and sometimes misused) in corporate raids, they shook up the self-perpetuating boards of all-powerful insiders that were running down some of our nation's most important companies. But they were being traded in a way that deceived their buyers; Milken had corrupted his own marketplace.

Our lawsuit was a great success, partly because we settled rather than deciding to go for broke. Going ahead in court would have been difficult because we were suing on behalf of the S&Ls as their successors, and they had cooperated in the fraud. Unfortunately our victory appears to have left Milken with more than $1 billion, even though I told the press my goal was to leave him with only "his lunch money." We asked for $6 billion recovered $1.3 billion, of which the FDIC and the RTC will get slightly in excess of $500 million. We received another $500 million in the bankruptcy of Milken's firm, Drexel Burnham Lambert. Cravath, Swaine and Moore advised us to settle (they could have made millions more in fees by advising us to pursue the suit); as far as the taxpayer is concerned, our top lawyers were paid about $32 million overall, and earned their $600 per hour, and then some!

Among the thousands of potential law suits, one presented more political mine fields than any other. Neil Bush, the fourth child of the president, was a director of the Silverado Savings and Loan of Denver, Colorado. Silverado had been one of the highest fliers of the S&L industry. Michael R. Wise, chairman and chief executive of Silverado, was active in Republican as well as charitable circles and had served as chairman of a 1987 political dinner in Denver that raised $300,000 for Mr. Bush's first presidential campaign. Wise had already recruited Neil Bush as a Silverado director in 1985, when the then vice president's son was a thirty-year-old newcomer in the oil-exploration business with no experience in banking.

Silverado collapsed in late 1988 at a cost to the government of about $1.5 billion. The Office of Thrift Supervision alleged that Neil Bush had a conflict of interest as a director because his two business partners in an oil drilling venture were large borrowers from Silverado. The partners supplied all the funds for the drilling venture, including young Bush's salary, mainly from this borrowed capital. Following charges by the Office of Thrift Supervision and the FDIC's own routine review of a failed institution, our professional staff recommended a suit against Neil Bush and his fellow directors to recover the fund's losses. In Neil's case, the suit was based on a conflict of interest between his board position and his partnership with the S&L's large borrowers. Any decision on whether to file this or any other suit would normally be made by the professional staff without the chairman's participation, unless there was a special reason to bring it to my attention. In this case John Bovenzi, my deputy, wanted me to know about it ahead of time.

I decided that it would not be proper for me to take part in the decision, to "recuse" myself, in Washington jargon. My personal problems with the administration over the independence of the FDIC might prejudice my view, so I stayed out of it. The case was referred to the FDIC board for approval of the suit. Somehow every member found some reason to recuse himself; the matter should be handled in a normal way with a decision by the staff. The staff decided that the Silverado directors were liable for the losses, and it authorized a suit. The word went out to our Denver office to be prepared to file the papers the next day. That evening ABC News ran a story prepared by its investigative reporter Allen Frank, reporting that the decision to sue young Bush had been made. Someone on our staff had leaked the story. While we thought we knew who did it, leaks are almost impossible to prove without phone taps. Since final authorization to sue had not been given, we decided to let ABC be wrong, and look for the leaker. We wanted to treat all press people equally and time the announcement to suit ourselves. The announcement to sue for damages came some time later, and it was coordinated with the Office of Thrift Supervision's separate disciplinary action for conflict of interest as a director.

While the OTS was preparing to call a hearing for Bush on Monday, October 1, 1990, we decided to file the FDIC suit for damages late on the previous Friday, so that the matter could be seen as part of the same activity, rather than a separate proceeding. In this way it would not look as though Neil Bush was involved in two separate improper incidents. After the announcements, we heard that Barbara Bush was most upset with me for announcing our suit at the same time and thus, it seemed to her, gratuitously piling it on her son.

A note arrived from my friend Charles Bartlett, a former newspaperman who knew everybody in Washington and had been around the town forever—so long that he is said to have been the one who introduced the young Jack Kennedy to one Jacqueline Bouvier. Charles's note indicated that Barbara Bush had been informed that we had plotted the case against Neil in such a way as to bring him maximum embarrassment. This idea seems to have originated in Treasury or the White House; but wherever it came from, it showed that the Washington use of rumor for attacking one's foes was very much alive. I gave Bartlett a detailed explanation of how we had handled the matter, which he then summarized in a note and sent on to the president's wife, the ever-popular Barbara.

It was my effort to let her know that I really felt badly about Neil Bush's problems, that we were trying to ensure that he was being treated fairly. At the same time, it was my view that Neil had to be sued under our obligations as a trustee of the failed institution, of which he had been a legally responsible director. So Bartlett wrote a very heartfelt note to Barbara. In it he said, "Please believe that Seidman has the deepest compassion for Neil, and for the anguish that his problems are causing his parents." That was certainly an accurate description. As far as can be determined, the note had little effect on the way an angry mother felt about anyone who was suing her son.

Once the Neil Bush matter became public, the White House was very careful not to try to influence how the FDIC dealt with it. What little communication we had with the White House ceased. Later when reviewing the pleadings in Neil Bush's case, I felt real sadness. Although an adult, he was young and immature and had set out to prove that he could make his way in the world. But he fell into the hands of charlatans. They used him in a most unfortunate way for their own advantage. Neil appeared to be well meaning, but he certainly was unsophisticated and unwise. Anyone with children who have had similar problems can sympathize with the parents and understand their concern. For the children of presidents, the risk is greater because a perceived relationship with the White House is often worth a lot of money.

Presidents probably need a new type of bodyguard designed to protect children, brothers, sisters, and family from exploiters, a difficult assignment at best.

Young Neil was fighting mad and unwilling to settle the matter. He believed that he had done nothing wrong. If he had been given a lie detector test, it is likely that he would have passed it with his veracity unchallenged. But whether he knew he had done wrong was not the question; it was whether he had in fact been negligent as a director and had a conflict of interest. The ultimate decision in the OTS action would be made by its director, Timothy Ryan, and not by me. The FDIC's case would be resolved in the courts because our's was merely a civil suit for damages.

Late one afternoon, just before the Christmas holidays, I was getting ready to leave the office when Chief Counsel Al Byrne stuck his head in and said he wanted to talk to me about something. We did not know much about Al when we hired him as general counsel six months earlier, except that he had managed a large law department, knew banking, and was a partner in the Washington office of Dechert Price & Rhoads. He was a good-looking friendly man in his mid-forties, with a take-charge personality but little political experience. He also had the merit of having been referred to us by the White House personnel office. We were delighted to inform them that we had picked one of theirs for this important (and thankless) job. Byrne turned out to be a very smooth operator and an excellent lawyer, but early on he suffered from political naivete.

On this particular occasion Al said he wanted to discuss the length of my term as chairman. There was some ambiguity in the law about the date on which my term officially ended. One reading of the law suggested that my term would not expire until 1993, while the common view was that it ended at the end of six years (in 1991). At my request Al had called C. Boyden Gray, the president's lawyer, to discuss the matter and now wanted to tell me about the conversation. According to Al, Gray was aware of the ambiguity and thanked us for the "heads up."

I figured this was all Al had on his mind, so gathering up the plastic grocery bag full of paperwork which was my brief-case of choice, I started toward the door. But Al caught my arm, "Gray has a question about the Neil Bush matter." I had been around Washington long enough to know that whatever Al was about to tell me meant trouble. Boyden wanted to know if there was any legal process to move the Neil Bush case out of the administrative process and into a federal court. I told him it was a matter to stay out of, a loser, and none of our business. "Give Gray whatever legal counsel you can find in the statutes, and nothing more."

I left Washington the next day to spend the holidays at our family's ranch north of Santa Fe. I did not think much more about Al's conversation with Boyden Gray. Neil had done some very dumb things while he was a director of Silverado Savings and Loan Association, and as a result, an OTS ad-ministrative law judge had ordered him to "cease and desist" from doing them again in the future. Although that decision represented little more than a slap on the wrist, Neil was either too proud or too young to admit he had made mis-takes and he was not about to accept even this minor repri-mand. His associates were reported to be advising him to settle up and get out, but he was convinced he had done nothing wrong and he was outraged. (The president, I am told, refrained from trying to direct his headstrong son. I don't think I could have done any better as a father in deal-ing with a very difficult problem.) As far as we knew, Neil's only appeal was to Timothy Ryan, the top man at OTS, and Ryan would most likely enforce his own administrative judge's decision. Was it less clear that a federal district court would uphold the OTS decision if Neil Bush continued to challenge it? Who knows? But the question was academic since the law required him to exhaust his administrative remedies before he could take his case to court.

This was an OTS matter. The FDIC had filed its own law-suit against Neil Bush and the other directors of Silverado in the hope of recovering some $200 million for the insurance fund. It was not our job to determine whether or not Neil should be restricted in his future banking activities. This was Tim Ryan's call, since he supervised the thrift industry. Con-flict of interest rules, in any case, had prevented Al Byrne from taking part in any aspect of the Bush case because his former firm had represented one of the directors of Silver-ado, even though he did not handle the case personally.

On January 2, my first day back in the office after the holidays, Tim Ryan informed me that Al had called him about Neil Bush and the possible change of venue. Ryan was upset and wanted to see me in person to tell me the tale of Byrne's call. Byrne had called Ryan right after he had left my office on December 20 to repeat Gray's question about how to get the Neil Bush case out of OTS and into a federal court. Ryan informed me that he had referred the matter to the Treasury's independent inspector general. This official, a kind of in-house policeman, works independently of the agency to which he has been appointed and is free to investi-gate illegal or questionable activity without interference from anyone.

It was not clear to me on what basis Tim Ryan would refer the matter to the Treasury Department's IG because we had our own. Since Ryan was an FDIC board director and since Al Byrne was an FDIC employee, it seemed to me that if an official investigation was necessary, then the FDIC's IG should conduct it. While at first I did not believe the matter called for an investigation, it turned out to be necessary to get all the facts. Inspectors at the Treasury Department in-terviewed everyone concerned. They collectively mulled it over for four months.

Before all this got under way, I called in Al Byrne for an explanation. He confirmed that he had called Ryan, but he said it was only to consult with him on a "procedural issue" raised by Gray. I asked him, "Did Boyden ask you to make the call?" He answered, "No." "How can a very smart lawyer like you pull this kind of a stunt?" His answer, a weak one, was that he believed he was acting appropriately.

In addition to an investigation by the two inspectors general, the Department of Justice made its own inquiry through the local district attorney and decided it had insufficient evidence to prosecute. In the end, Byrne got a rap across the knuckles from the Treasury IG, and our board docked him his bonus for the year.

Here was a neat little story for some investigative reporter, and I could even write the headline: "White House Tries to Influence Neil Bush Case." Considering its potential for political scandal and the large number of people involved in the investigation, it was miraculous that the press never got wind of it. That could have been a public relations disaster, to say the least, for the FDIC, the administration, and the president. To the credit of all, for once, there were no leaks to the press. The only explanation I can think of is that it would have been in no one's interest to do so, neither Byrne's nor Gray's nor Ryan's. The only other source could have been the inspector general's office, and its officials don't deal with the press.

Neither agency recommended disciplinary action against Boyden Gray, nor did they find he had done anything wrong. Al had taken full responsibility for his call. He may have been reprimanded, but he may have gained Boyden's eternal gratitude and he learned a valuable lesson.

The more interesting question was why Al Byrne, who is a brilliant lawyer and went on to serve the FDIC very well, would make the mistake of calling Ryan in the first place. Byrne said he was only trying to respond to a White House inquiry. An extraordinary effort to act in anticipation of the wishes of the president and his staff is a far-too-common Washington occurrence. Such behavior can often lead to disastrous results. Just ask some of those who tried to help Richard Nixon and his staff in the Watergate cover-up. Now the entire incident is of no consequence except for what it can teach us about how Washington works and the ill-advised knee-jerk response that is too often caused by *White House* requests.

13

Dealing With (and Being Dealt With By) the Bush White House

E very part of the Washington experience indicates that anyone operating in the political scene should have the highest respect for, and fear of, the White House chief of staff. Moreover, one should stay on his good side at all costs. When President Bush appointed John Sununu, the former Republican governor of New Hampshire as his chief of staff, it was a bit of a disappointment. Not because I disliked Governor Sununu, but because he was one of the few people appointed to a high position in the Bush administration who had not been a member of President Ford's administration. (Secretary James Baker, Secretary Dick Cheney, CEA's Alan Greenspan, Trade Representative Carla Hills, Security Advisor Brent Scowcroft, OMB's Dick Darman, top White House staffer Roger Porter, Secretary Nicholas Brady, and Secretary Jack Kemp, to name a few.)

John Sununu, a strong conservative, had been a big Bush supporter and was credited with helping him carry New Hampshire. My view of Sununu was so positive that when talking with Bush's chief political counselor and pollster, Bob Teeter, about possible vice presidential candidates, I'd had two names to suggest: Senator Pete Domenici of New Mexico and Governor Sununu. I thought either one would bring good ethnic balance to the ticket. Like everyone in Washington, I hoped to meet with Governor Sununu once he took up his duties as chief of staff, and to establish a good working relationship with him.

Even before the new Bush administration was in place, it was struggling with the magnitude, the likely cost, and the possible political fallout of the savings and loan industry problems. At the same time the administration was facing a huge budget deficit, which had averaged about $200 billion a year throughout Ronald Reagan's eight years in office. With the cost of paying off insured depositors of the busted savings and loans, the deficit was going to get larger under George Bush. Candidate Bush had run on a defining pledge of "Read my lips. No new taxes," but as president he was looking for money to keep the deficit from spinning further out of control. New taxes were ingeniously called "revenue enhancers."

The Treasury staff decided to fly some of these kites on the Hill to test the wind with some members of Congress. This was equivalent to putting them in a full-page ad in *The Washington Post*. Soon Kathleen Day, a *Post* reporter, called to ask my reaction to the administration's proposals. She said the most controversial one, and the one that might be the greatest interest to me, was a proposal to charge bank and S&L depositors a fee when they opened a new savings account. The proceeds would be used to pay for deposit insurance losses. I told her that the FDIC had not been consulted. Without thinking very much about it, I remarked brightly that this new fee was a real reversal from days past when a depositor could expect to be awarded a toaster for opening a new account. Now, instead of receiving a toaster, a new depositor would have to buy one for the bank. The idea was not taken seriously, because in my opinion it had about as much political viability as a 50 percent cut in Social Security payments.

The remark caught the fancy of those who lived inside the Beltway, who promptly labeled the administration proposal as the "Reverse Toaster Tax." It was mentioned on television talk shows and in editorials, where it usually was noted that my comment had killed the idea. It had literally been laughed out of town. This apparently infuriated Governor Sununu. When he showed up at the White House staff meeting the next morning, he was reported to have announced that he was going to do something about that fellow Seidman, and he thought it might require taking a toaster and shoving it in a spot that only he would mention.

Sununu's threat was promptly leaked to the press. Did I have a comment? We did not really think that the suggestion was being given serious consideration by the administration, since it involved the FDIC's premiums, which could only be set by the FDIC board, and we had not been consulted. However, with regard to Governor Sununu's suggestion about inserting a toaster in my anatomy, I said it would be a pleasure to meet him with my seconds and a pair of toasters any morning he desired. Toasters arrived as gifts at my speaking engagements, and to Governor Sununu my remark became an irritating symbol of the FDIC's independence and the limits of the White House chief of staff's power. The toaster tax was never a seriously promoted proposal of the chief of staff or the secretary of the Treasury, but my glib remarks about it were to reverberate throughout the remainder of my term as chairman.

Of course, Chief of Staff Sununu was just trying to do his job. He had an unusually abrasive way of handling his position, which eventually led to his demise as chief. For some that came before him, the eminence of the chief of staff's position was the last view from the top before a steep return to the reality of private life.

Despite my best efforts to be a good team player, my relationship with the Bush administration continued to deteriorate. The administration proposed that members of the FDIC board would serve at "the pleasure of the president" like any cabinet or subcabinet officer who can be removed with a telephone call if his decisions or anything else displeases the White House. My first knowledge of this came in a call from a staff member of the Senate Banking Committee indicating that, immediately upon passage of the administration's bill, the president could terminate my role as chairman. The White House had neglected to inform me of that provision, so my surprise was evident. Independent boards had long been in disfavor with Republican administrations, and Attorney General Edwin L. Meese, keeper of the Reagan administration's ideological conscience, had suggested eliminating various independents lest they deviate from the writ from on high.

The best known example of an independent board in Washington is the Federal Reserve Board. The independence of the FDIC board was somewhat more prescribed, but still its members did not serve in the same status as members of the administration. We served fixed terms and could only be removed "for cause," which was usually taken to mean something beyond the whim of the president. When the issue of independent status was raised, it was a testing time for us at the FDIC.

Should we become team players and give up our presumed position as an independent, one that had helped give our agency credibility and respect for half a century, or should we oppose the administration and risk the retribution that being out of favor with the administration might bring? My fellow board members urged, and we decided, unanimously, to oppose the administration's proposals. Secretary Brady summoned us to his huge office in the Treasury for a discussion. We argued that the FDIC's independence had long been central to its success in avoiding political influence and scandal; our agency was not broke, so it did not need fixing. Secretary Brady indicated that the matter had already been decided by the administration, and no appeal would be entertained. The matter was closed. When asked if we might argue the matter before the president, he said the matter had been settled and that he expected me to support the administration's position.

One never knows if such a message is really true or whether it simply conveys the impression that the cabinet member may have wanted to provide to one of the lesser lights in government—that his word is as good as the president's. It so happened that some weeks later I was at a small cocktail party at which the president was present. It is very bad practice to talk shop with a president at a social affair. I nevertheless took advantage of the opportunity and made some comment about the importance of the independence of the FDIC and our view of why it should remain an independent agency. As an experienced politician, he did not want to discuss substantive matters at a cocktail party. But in a somewhat annoyed way, he made it very, very clear that the decision had indeed been made and that it was his decision.

As a result of this exchange, the FDIC found it even more difficult to buck the administration because now we knew the proposal to reform our agency came right from the top. Nevertheless, we decided that our duty lay in opposing it, and this we proceeded to do in testimony to Congress.

In its infinite wisdom—and after hearing our arguments—the Congress decided to scrap that aspect of the reorganization. A bipartisan committee recommended that the status of the FDIC's board should not be changed and that the present chairman should serve out his term. This represented a total defeat for the administration. Obviously our victory did not endear me to the president, to Governor Sununu, or to Treasury Secretary Brady.

It was not long before the political pundits were printing the rumor that the administration would like to get rid of me. The stories usually were cast in the terms that the Bush administration wanted to replace a Reagan appointee with its own, a policy that was being applied selectively. It is a well-known Washington technique to let the world know through the rumor mill that the president is dissatisfied with an official's performance and thus get rid of the offender without having to confront him directly. Many times these rumors alone are enough to make the individual involved decide that resignation is the better part of valor. If the stories continue that this or that cabinet member is not up to snuff and he does not take the hint, he is likely to be called in and to suffer the indignity of being ordered to resign. This being the recognized pattern, most political appointees will take to the hills when they read that the president is displeased with their performance.

My friends in the press were telling me that Treasury was saying that the chairman of the FDIC was on his way out. They also stated that White House Chief Sununu hardly missed a cocktail party opportunity to make some derogatory comment on my job performance, my independent behavior, and my unlimited willingness to meet with the press. Given these little nudges, it seemed the right thing for me to do was to request a meeting with the president to discuss my future plans and, more important, to report on the current status of the banking and S&L industries and what we believed ought to be done about it. In retrospect, it was unwise for me to have made such a request unless I wished to resign on the spot. It is wise not to raise the subject of resignation with the president unless you want to leave at once. Unless the president loves you like a brother, once you put in play the idea that you may be leaving, you are already on your way out. If you stay a while, you are a wounded duck. In this case my objective, beyond reporting on the deteriorating condition of the economy and the financial system, was to assure that my departure would be made on a friendly basis at a time that was mutually acceptable.

When Secretary Brady was asked about the matter, he indicated that he thought the president would be pleased to see me but probably so that he could tell me that he wanted his own person in the job. In a two-minute conversation with Brady he said he had no problem with the way I was performing my assignment, but he did not urge me to stay. We called the White House and requested a meeting with the president. There was no response from the president.

I turned again to my good friend Charles Bartlett, a close friend of the president's, who suggested a new approach: the back channel. This was a private method of communicating with the president directly without having to go through the White House staff, and particularly the chief of staff. The president had given his private secretary, Bridgett Montague, the names of special officials, old colleagues from the CIA, trusted former campaign workers and old friends of his and Barbara's whose messages he might not necessarily want exposed to his official staff, and instructed her to put correspondence from them on his desk. No one else would see them. The existence of this channel usually aroused paranoia in the chief of staff, and woe be it to anyone caught using this private communication system to speak ill of the chief of staff.

Charles sent his back channel message on January 25, 1990, urging George Bush to meet with "Bill Seidman, who has requested an appointment for some time and is hearing through the grapevine that your chief of staff has vowed that he will never allow such a meeting to occur." Shortly thereafter, a White House meeting was arranged for February 2— not with the president, but with his chief of staff.

On the morning of February 2, 1990, I walked by one of the President's Marine guards, who snapped to attention as I entered the West Wing of the White House. The receptionist greeted me as a long-lost friend from the days of the Ford administration. I had met Sununu once, months before, for a couple of minutes, when I went to the White House to discuss some problems in the industry with Richard Breeden, who was heading the White House staff on banking and S&L problems. It had been a very cursory discussion, during which Sununu indicated above all that he wanted the regulators to follow the administration's line in publicly praising its S&L rescue package. The FDIC was lending its support, totally unaware of the attack on our independence to be hidden in the final language sent to the Hill. He then prepared to leave. When Sununu stood up, he seemed to expand by two or three inches as he said, "I'm going in to see the president." Clearly we were supposed to be impressed into total subservience.

For this meeting, I waited only a few minutes and was ushered in to meet Governor Sununu. We shook hands, and my first impression of the chief that morning was that he had the limpest handshake of any politician that I had known. Since the meeting had been at my request, I suggested three topics for discussion—the S&L and banking problems facing the administration, candidates for the FDIC and RTC Boards, and my own plans with the FDIC. He made no comment.

I continued, "A survey by our Division of Supervision shows hundreds of additional S&Ls—above those already on the Office of Supervision's list—are expected to fail. The problem is far larger than has previously been forecast. It might reach a level of 800 to 900 institutions with over $400 billion in assets. On this basis, the RTC will be out of funds by January 1, 1991."

Sununu appeared totally uninterested, asked no questions and expressed no concern. He replied, "The industry is going to improve its position. Interest rates will decline and property values will increase." His response on the approaching problems with the banking system and the economic problems of the debt problem was the same. I provided him with papers on the subject, which he said he would put on the president's reading pile.

On to the second subject. "It is my view, and the view of our board, that the president should consider appointing a banker, preferably a community banker, to our board. We need the viewpoint of one who has been in the business. It is particularly desirable, since the FDIC is the primary regulator of approximately 8,000 banks. With the help of the banking associations, an outstanding candidate could be found. We will be pleased to suggest names." No response.

And then to the third: "With respect to my own position, my term ends in October of 1991, and I do not want to be reappointed, nor do I plan to finish out my term."

Sununu suddenly perked up and took an interest in the meeting. He said, "The president would like to appoint someone for the long term. I expect you to leave as soon as possible and not to take more than sixty days, ninety days at the most."

He repeated, "We would like to see you resign in not more than ninety days at the outside. The president has no problem with you personally or the job you've done. He wants someone who will serve out the presidential term."

I responded, "I would have to talk with the president personally about this matter."

I finally attempted to establish ground rules: "Governor, is this to be a private meeting about which neither of us will speak to the press?" He answered, "It will be entirely between us, Secretary Brady, and the president. There will be no leaks from the White House."

My notes of our meeting concluded: "In general the meeting was calm and unemotional between two fellows that obviously did not like, and had no great respect for, each other." We parted without setting another meeting date. Leaving the West Wing, I thought what a lousy way this was to handle things. It may have taken place inside the White House, but the style was that of Versailles and Louis XIV. Besides, the FDIC was an independent agency, and orders to the chairman were not the way to get results. The fact that Sununu was obviously enjoying delivering the message did not help matters at all.

Before passing through the White House gate, some fifty yards away, I had gone through hurt feelings, disbelief, and anger. Another fifty yards along 'Pennsylvania Avenue toward the FDIC headquarters on Seventeenth Street, it seemed to me that the conversation should be ignored until I heard from the president personally. My job was to get back to the FDIC and keep working. Upon reflection, which included recollection of my experience in the Ford White House, I realized that the message Sununu delivered probably came from the president. Presidents often have their chiefs of staff convey unpleasant news. No matter, there was much to be done. I went ahead with my speech to the National Press Club, outlining the basic marketing strategy to promote the swift sale of all RTC property to the private sector. We also kept up the work of putting in place a major program to liquidate 130 institutions by June 30 and to carry out our first big program for selling hard-to-sell assets.

We got on with our work, and while my visit to the White House had not been handled with much courtesy or finesse, the White House was expecting the usual courtesies from my office—even if Sununu could not wait for me to vacate it. We received word from the Treasury, the White House staff, and even from some lobbyists that a young man named Bob wanted a job with the RTC in our new RTC National Sales Office. He had applied four months earlier, but nothing had happened. We were asked to expedite his application and were told, by the by, that his wife Bridgett was a personal secretary to the president, and that the president had an interest in the matter. We followed up quickly. Our sales office felt that young Bob was indeed qualified for the job, and they were considering his application, which moved ahead with speed. Of course we could have taken the view that this was inappropriate pressure on an independent agency, and we could have justified stiff-arming the White House and even telling the press. But even under the current relationship with the White House that would have been inappropriate and petty. Certainly the president's views about people that he would like to see employed in his administration should be treated with respect, so Bob got his job. We reported to Undersecretary Robson at Treasury, "The young man has been hired."

We went about our business as though the meeting with Sununu had never taken place. When asked about the meeting, I said it was "not for publication." In a speech in Chicago I did say I expected to leave before my term expired. While true, it was probably a mistake to cast a doubt on my term as chairman. It starts people thinking about the successor. We decided that as far as Sununu was concerned, we would wait and see what happened.

During the next month, April of 1990, word came to me in one of those strange routes peculiar to Washington, that Treasury Secretary Brady had decided who he wanted as my successor. It was William Taylor, the Fed's chief of supervision. It seems that a reporter from *The New York Times* was playing tennis with a Treasury official. During the game, the conversation came around to me and my future. The reporter, in a wild guess that might produce a story, asked, "Have you decided that Bill Taylor is the person that would be acceptable as Seidman's replacement?" The Treasury official said nothing, but his look indicated that the reporter's supposition had struck gold.

When all this was relayed to me, it appeared that the administration was prepared and determined to proceed. Bill Taylor was a good friend, a first-rate regulator, and a very capable person. At my request, we met in my office in the middle of April. Would he be willing to take my job? He said he had thought about the matter and he would, even though it would mean a substantial cut in pay. From the tone of the conversation, it was clear that Secretary Brady had already discussed it with him. It was a done deal.

As the administration's plan unfurled, it became obvious that the sixty-day ultimatum was part of the agenda of Sununu and Brady. The grapevine said that it was Brady who asked the president to support a change and the president was willing to go along with his old friend—but only he knows the real story.

Later in April Governor Sununu's secretary called. The president was ready to meet me. The meeting took place in front of the fireplace in the Oval Office, a spot that I had occupied many times as a member of President Ford's White House staff. President Bush indicated that he knew of my talks with Sununu and wished to follow up on them. He thanked me for my work at the FDIC and indicated that he would like me to consider being "special ambassador" to Panama and Nicaragua to direct the new Central American Aid program of $750 million. The United States had recently established democracy in Panama and signed a peace agreement in Nicaragua. He said it was a very important job, not a make-work position.

I told the President that the RTC was in the middle of a major program closing 139 S&Ls that could not be completed before June 30, and that any announcement of changes in our leadership before then would not be good for the operation. My suggestion was that we could announce my departure after that date, effective on October 15, 1990, which would mark the completion of my fifth year on the job and allow time for a smooth change in an amicable manner. The president seemed to agree but indicated the Central American job would probably have to be filled before that. No agreement was reached on my departure.

The next two or three minutes were spent discussing the constantly rising estimates of loss from the savings and loan disaster due to the debt-induced real estate recession in the country, the fact that the FDIC insurance fund was suffering significant losses, and the fact that the RTC would be out of money by the start of the next year. Bad times were ahead. This two or three minutes of talk was the only discussion I had with the president on banking and S&L matters during my active tenure—which covered some of the most difficult times in U.S. financial history!

The president indicated that Sununu and Brady would talk more with me on the subject. As the meeting ended, the president complimented me on my great service to the country and my unquestioned integrity. It was my impression that he really meant it and that he felt somewhat awkward in the position that Brady and Sununu had put him. All present agreed that the conversation was to be confidential, off the record, and top secret.

Within a day, a call came from Jerry Knight, a senior business reporter at *The Washington Post,* asking me what had happened at the meeting. Was it true that I had been offered an ambassadorship and was it true that the president wished to have me leave my job promptly? In accordance with our agreement and in contrast to my usual willingness to talk, I told Jerry it was a confidential meeting. In any event, it was inappropriate to speak about private meetings with the president. He indicated that it was a White House source that had given him the story that I had been forced to resign.

I told him, "No comment, Jerry."

He said, "That's not like you, Bill. You usually have some kind of comment."

And I replied, "Well, this case is different, Jerry."

The next day *The Washington Post* duly reported that White House sources were saying that the president wanted me to resign soon. The attack by leaks was under way. Rough sailing was ahead. Identical stories appeared in other papers, which indicated that the information was coming directly from Sununu's office. Since this was probably my last job in public service, I had no desire to end it this way. Why pick a fight when an amicable departure could have been arranged? The answer was simple: One does not tell Chief of Staff John Sununu that his ultimatum will not be complied with in every detail without consequences.

Now the world, or at least the self-absorbed world inside the Beltway, was waiting to see me resign under pressure. In the tradition of "The king is dead, long live the king," the major interest in Washington was the identity of my successor. Secretary Brady came to see me in my FDIC office and asked, "Would you agree that Bill Taylor would be a good choice as your successor?" I said that I could not think of a better one. "So that speculation can be quelled, he should be named now," Brady suggested. He wanted to know if I would publicly support him now. Given that no plan for my departure had been agreed upon, I declined.

Then Brady called from his car and said he had spoken with the president, who was anxious for me to suggest Taylor as my successor if I approved. Brady urged me to call the president and talk with him and ended by saying, "The president is eager to talk with you." Against my better judgment, instead of waiting for a call, on May 3 I called the president and said, "Secretary Brady has suggested that Bill Taylor would be a good replacement when I leave. Taylor is a good man and I can support him. But the leaks that are coming out of the White House will hurt us all." The president agreed.

Shortly afterward the president was preparing for a press conference. One of the obvious questions would be why I was being pressed to leave. An account of the practice session reached me via the grapevine, and the president was said to have replied: "I do not want him to leave. I like Bill Seidman and I am not asking him to leave. He is an old friend and I think he is doing a good job." Sununu then spoke up: "Mr. President, you should not say that. Say that Seidman wants to leave, we are going to accommodate his wishes and that Taylor is going to be his successor."

The president held his press conference on May 3, and the following exchange with reporter John Mashek of *The Boston Globe* took place:

> Q. It appears now the administration has acknowledged what your FDIC Chairman, Bill Seidman, had been saying all along, which is that the savings and loan bailout is going to be a lot

more expensive than you initially anticipated. Why, then, are you so anxious to see him leave, and how are you going to accommodate his increased costs at a time of fiscal restraint?

THE PRESIDENT: Hey, listen—I haven't told you I'm anxious to see Bill Seidman leave.

Q. Aren't you saying that you wouldn't be unhappy to see him leave?

THE PRESIDENT: Bill Seidman asked to see me a while back, came to see me. Said he was not going to fulfill the rest of his term, and we discussed that. He asked to see me to tell me that. Today, he called me with the name of a successor that he enthusiastically supports. And he's done a good job. We have a significant project that he's in the middle of handling—we call it the June 30th Project—to get a lot more done with a lot of these savings and loans in a short period of time. He's agreed to enthusiastically tackle that. And he also said, look, I understand if you might want to put your own person in there. But it's his initiative with me. And today, he suggested the name of a Bill Taylor who we're very high on to take over his responsibilities. So it's one where everyone wants to have winners and losers, and I don't think there are any. I think Seidman has conducted himself with extraordinary grace and great ability. I've known him for years, worked with him way back when.

Q. Mr. President, the costs. How to deal with the increased costs of the bailout?

THE PRESIDENT: We've got to work with the Congress on how to deal with the cost. And right now, there's a significant review going forward to see what the costs are. The figures change all the time on you.

Q. Mr. President, if Bill Seidman has done such an outstanding job at the FDIC in overseeing the savings and loan bailout, why didn't you prevail on him to stay on to assure continuity and an independent voice at that agency?

THE PRESIDENT: Because I think that his decision was a personal one and he's entitled to make it, and that's why. And I support it, and I salute him again.

Q. He didn't bring bad news about what the cost of that bailout might be, did he?

THE PRESIDENT: Listen, if all the people who brought bad news in here were asked to do something else, it would be a little lonely. No, that's not the reason for this at all. I would ask you that you talk to Bill about it.

The text of the press conference seems to support the fact that the president was playing it straight in saying he did not want to force me out—but only he really knows. It was apparent above all else that Sununu felt his authority had been undermined by my unwillingness to accept his order to leave on his schedule. But by my mentioning Taylor to the president, as requested, I had given them the signal to make me a lame duck. As many friends told me, it was not my best day. Agreed!

Leaked stories continued from both the White House and the Treasury, indicating their desire to have me leave office. By planting these stories, the administration was unintentionally raising the visibility of the S&L problem. Throughout the country, there were reports that my willingness to "tell it like it is" had cost me my job. On May 6, the columnist Mary McGrory wrote:

> . . . Seidman did not refuse to do the White House bidding on any aspect of the [thrift] cleanup. It's not as if anyone had a different or better idea of what to do. It's just that Bush wants the problem to go away—or at least be quiet—and Seidman thought the country ought to know more about the trouble it's in. And that is why he got the grisly, quintessentially Washington treatment of assassination by newsprint. He deserved better.

Numerous editorials and columns appeared saying that people who try to tell the truth as they see it don't last long in Washington. One protest to the president came from no less a party loyalist than my long time friend, Representative Guy Vander Jagt of Michigan. One of the strongest supporters of the president in Congress, he wrote George Bush privately that he was "disappointed" that I was leaving because my presence at the FDIC at this crucial time provided "a degree of credibility and confidence which is absolutely essential."

In a way, the good governor, Chief of Staff John Sununu, had done me an unintended favor by providing me a national platform to present my views. When John Sununu was forced to resign as chief of staff, someone said, "Poor John is his own worst enemy." My answer was "Not while I'm alive."

In accordance with the president's request, Sununu and I met to talk about the proposed job as ambassador in Central America.

Sununu said that Lawrence Eagleburger, the under secretary of State, was the key person for me to talk to. He promised to set up a meeting. He said he wanted to announce the matter by the end of May and "I assume you can adjust your schedule to leave by then, Bill." I did not reply.

Then, quite unexpectedly, Sununu said, "This whole affair is not my battle. It is a Treasury and not a White House initiative." He reasserted that position in an interview on May 13th with Garrick Utley of NBC, who asked him about my charges that the White House wanted more authority and control over the FDIC. The following exchange ensued:

> SUNUNU: The people that we interact with is the Treasury. Whenever somebody gets into a situation that they feel uncomfortable with, the White House is the easiest target to suggest as manipulating it. Treasury is the one that interacts with Bill Seidman. And the RTC relationship, the FDIC, the new OTS structure, that's operated out of Treasury. The fact is that Bill Seidman himself has recommended his successor. . . .
>
> UTLEY: Yes, we all know that, as important as Treasury is, that department, the White House is also standing behind the Treasury. Isn't the fact true that the White House would like to have greater control over this whole S&L process?
>
> SUNUNU: No. We want to make sure that the president's policies and Congress's policies that were put together in the legislation are followed constructively. I think Treasury and all those folks over there have different responsibilities and the fact that somebody doesn't want to finish out their term—and so the

President was notified of that by Bill Seidman—doesn't mean
that we're pushing him out.

UTLEY: And you have had no role in this yourself?

SUNUNU: No. I've met with Bill Seidman and talked about it,
but to say we initiated it is just not right.

Charles Bartlett provided a Washington insider's view,
writing in his newsletter that I had incurred the wrath of
both Brady and Sununu, and that one way Brady retaliated
was to deny me a seat on the Oversight Board which set
policy for the thrift bailout. His newsletter continued:

> Relations at the working level between Treasury and the FDIC
> were worsened by a "turf game" which developed from criti-
> cisms that Brady had let the State Department and the Office of
> the Trade Representative wrest away functions traditionally held
> by the Treasury. Responding to criticisms that he was presiding
> over a diminished department, Brady determined to stake out a
> dominant role in the bailout machinery. It was frustration over
> this encroaching Treasury posture that caused Daniel Kearney,
> experienced in finance but not in government, to resign only a
> few days after he had been cheerfully installed as Chairman of
> the Oversight Board.
>
> A similarly inspired frustration caused Seidman, long known
> for his candor, to threaten that it was time to return to his ranch
> in New Mexico. These threats were irritating to the Treasury
> Secretary, as were Seidman's publicized (and unhappily valid)
> assessments that the cost of the bailout would exceed the Trea-
> sury estimates.
>
> Having marked Seidman as an enemy instead of as a collabo-
> rator in cleaning out this Augean stable, Brady found fuel for his
> hostilities. Seidman was perceived to be exaggerating the size of
> the problem in order to cast himself in a more heroic light. His
> testimony on the Hill was closely watched for intimations of hos-
> tility to the Treasury. And finally Sununu called Seidman to the
> White House to say bluntly that the President wanted his resig-
> nation so that he could put his own man in the job. Seidman, no
> amateur, said he would be pleased to do whatever the President
> wanted but only after he had heard it from the President . . .
>
> Confronted with the first raucous personnel squabble of his

good-humored administration, Mr. Bush took steps to put a happy face on the situation. Brady visited Seidman's office in a conciliatory gesture, the President minimized the contentious aspects of the affair in his press conference, and Seidman may well in the end remain a member of the Bush administration. But this was a remarkably silly, personalized triumph of vindictiveness over the enormous challenge of putting the thrift scandal to bed. . . . So the problem must be dealt with swiftly by capable men working as a team. We did not see that largeness of spirit in the campaign against Seidman.

Within a couple of days I decided there was nothing to do but stay the course. I did not want to be pushed out of the job, not only for personal reasons, but because it would be very bad for the institution. An independent regulator should be independent and exercise that independence, especially in the face of pressures from any administration. Further, the time to leave is when things are pretty well in order. Leaving a mess for someone else to clean up would only delay the cleanup and cost the taxpayers more money.

Concern about the independence of the FDIC was obvious, and we had fought for it several times before. The effort to force an agency chairman out of office through leaks seemed to me to be an insult that should be resisted. One article in *The New York Times* said that I emerged from a congressional hearing seeking only to maintain my dignity in the face of reports that I was a goner.

Many had suggested that I would be smart to leave before my reputation was ruined. To tell the truth, that did not seem to be of paramount importance at the time. Not all of the suggestions to go came from my administration "friends." Some columnists called me a folk hero for my candor, rare as it was in Washington, and urged me to quit while I was ahead. Others counseled me to stay, saying the job needed to be finished. For example, there was the very kind note my deputy David Cooke sent me, "I know you are trying to decide your plans so I wanted to give you my thoughts. You should stay."

Old too soon and smart too late. I stayed on; and from then on it got tougher. The next time I was questioned about another leak on my departure, my response was "Tell Governor Sununu that for each statement he makes about the president wanting me out of the FDIC, I'll stay another month." Apparently he insisted on cutting off any graceful way for me to exit from my job. To no one's surprise, nothing further was heard about any ambassadorial job to administer aid in Central America.

The unpleasantries continued for a while and then good fortune ended the verbal exchanges. Peace came not through brotherly love and forgiveness, but through the failure of the Silverado Savings and Loan out in Denver. Once the word got to the White House that the president's son might be involved in a suit with our agency, all efforts to give me a push terminated. The possibility that such activities might be construed as an effort to influence the "Neil Bush case" was not something the White House wanted to risk.

While I was never invited to White House parties— Sununu saw to that—the FDIC was free to operate independently. The chief of staff pointed his guns in other directions until he was finally removed by presidential order after a storm of protests from all sides on his conduct of his duties. From my point of view, it was better to be lucky than smart.

But the question of how long I could remain as chairman arose again in a different and unexpected way. Our general counsel, Al Byrne, had studied how the new financial reorganization law applied to the FDIC, and he informed me that in his view the statute did not call for my term to end after six years, in October of 1991, as we all thought, but rather in February of 1993. The law itself was ambiguous; one section said the chairman would leave at the end of his regular term, another that the term itself would end in February of 1993, after the next presidential inauguration. My main interest in this arcane legalism was that it would make the term uncertain enough to enable even the lamest of ducks to walk upright. It might also dismay Sununu if he discovered that I had the right to stay until 1993.

Research on the matter continued, although I recused myself since it involved my term. I was not concerned about the outcome, but just raising the question had given me breathing room. If your troops are not sure when you are leaving, you can exercise the authority to do your job without their being preoccupied with your successor. In due course Byrne provided a well-researched opinion concluding that my term extended until 1993. He said he wanted the opinion of an outside law firm. I told him to check with the board. Later he presented the board with a fifty-page opinion from Cleary Gottlieb, which also happened to be the top law firm to which our former general counsel, Jack Murphy, had returned as a partner. It held that my term lasted until 1993.

Then I read in *The Washington Post* that the FDIC had agreed to pay a legal fee of $50,000 for the opinion. Always ready for a good political shot, Chairman Gonzalez of the House Banking Committee was enraged by the expenditure and said that if anyone wanted to know the length of the chairman's term, they could ask him, since his committee had drafted the legislation. Actually, his opinion after the fact would not carry much legal weight, but my friend Chairman Gonzalez did not necessarily care about the finer technical points that engaged the legal profession. My reaction was unhappiness, also, but for a different reason. While $50,000 might have been a reasonable fee, paying for an outside opinion at any price was no way to use FDIC funds.

The story ends sadly. My special counsel (and ace speech writer) Jacqueline Pace went to our good friend Jack Murphy and told him how upset I was. She persuaded Murphy and his partners to provide the opinion to us pro bono. Not good for them, but very good for the FDIC.

Ultimately, the matter was bucked to the Justice Department by the board of the FDIC for a definitive opinion. Perhaps at the request of the White House, they responded that the law was clear: There was no question that my term ended in 1991, not 1993. Since it was not going to make any practical difference when all this was going on in 1990, the matter was dropped. But when we reached the autumn of 1991, the FDIC again asked the Justice Department for its opinion on whether my term expired on October 16, 1991, or later so that they could determine whether I had "served my full term." This time the Justice Department backed away and opined that the length of my term was a matter for the agency to decide, not for them.

I have often wondered what would have happened if President Bush had called me up, indicated that he wanted me to leave, and explained that he felt it was for the good of the country. Such a call never came. Through all of this controversy, it seemed to me that the president, like most presidents and executives everywhere, hated to see fights among people working for him. He wished that squabbles, turf battles, and policy disagreements would all disappear, and that his aides would kiss and make up amicably. (Anyone who has run an organization knows the feeling.) I received calls and letters from bankers, political leaders, and ordinary citizens in almost every state in the country telling me to stay in Washington and finish my job. Many of them said that the main point in my favor was that someone in Washington was telling the truth about what he was doing. One letter, which I shall never forget, said, "You are a breath of fresh air. At last, an honest man in Washington. Don't back down." They reflected a view, later seen in the presidential election of 1992, that too many Washington politicians were arrogant, wasteful, and untruthful. Many, but certainly not all, politicians were getting too self-important to play it straight with the American people. In politics, as in life, that attitude will eventually be deleterious to one's health.

14

With All That Experience, What Have You Learned?

A s my term neared its end on October 15, 1991, the time had arrived to leave the FDIC and the RTC. Bank failures were declining, bank profits were escalating, the RTC was up and running. The Bank Insurance Fund was recapitalized (and really was not broke) and the S&L industry, or what remained of it, was profitable. And incidentally, John Sununu was being forced out of his job as chief of staff at the White House for overreaching his powers, abusing his "perks," and essentially for throwing his weight around. Time for me to declare victory, hoping it really was so, and go on to other things.

As I packed my office furnishings from Arizona and New Mexico and boxes upon boxes of my papers, it was time for reminiscing. Because I have reached the age of seventy and served ten years in senior positions in the U.S. government, entitled or not, here are some observations and reflections on working in our nation's capital and conducting our nation's business.

The Banking System: Long May It Loan

Our banking system is totally different from those in the rest of the developed world, with both detriments and benefits. The events in this book illuminated some of its detriments, but the benefits are often overlooked. They are an essential support for our decentralized economic system. This decentralized system fosters individuality and initiative, which are reasons we create more new companies than any other country in the world. Judgments on credit are made at a local level by people with the information that is likely to result in better loans. One of the reasons that the United States is about to enter what I predict will be the most successful economic period in its history is that our kind of flexibility and innovation is not reproduced anywhere else in the world. These are the keys to success in the new world we are entering.

Our decentralized lending system, with over 30,000 lending units, means that many, many more new and different ideas are funded in the United States than anywhere else in the world. This is part of the reason that the United States leads in industries like biotech, finance, software, communications, and media, which are the brain businesses of the future. Microsoft, the world's largest computer software company, is already bigger in market value than International Business Machines Corporation, the hardware company that gave its entrepreneur, Bill Gates, his biggest opportunity. We have developed a system that is more responsive to individual initiatives than any other. Our great challenge is to protect it. One way to do so is to protect small banks and allow them to compete.

We have a remarkable, resilient system. The kind of disaster we have just come through would have brought down the financial system in most countries. Our system survived. We are recovering, and one of the reasons is the diversity of our financial institutions. The ability of the U.S. financial system to take punishment and survive (with some government help of course) was surprisingly good. Despite misjudgments about loans to Latin American countries, leveraged buyout artists, and construction and development entrepreneurs that cost billions, the banks and even the majority of the S&Ls survived. As they pulled back from their mistakes, both the financial system and the political system overreacted and a credit spree became a credit crunch. The pendulum of regulation and deregulation swung back and forth over time as it has in the past and will in the future. By 1993 it was pointing at regulatory overkill rather than deregulatory license.

While our banking system has survived, it has not grown. It continues to lose market share to uninsured competitors. The record failures and the loss of competitive position in the 1980s indicates the need for fundamental reform of our financial system. *Here is my advice to future presidents and politicians.*

Provide the U.S. banking and S&L system with the tools to be a strong and effective competitor. It must have the ability to provide a full line of financial services to its customers. To achieve this, regulated financial institutions need to be allowed to provide new products—just ask any big bank. I recommend "two-window" banking: one window for insured deposits yielding safe and predictable returns (often called the Core Bank), and another window for deposits that will offer the risk of higher returns from the markets, but without insurance. The insured funds will be carefully supervised and their use restricted to the safest of investments, mainly government securities and consumer credit. The uninsured window will offer its customers a full line of financial services from life insurance to stock investment to mutual funds. Customers will have a choice of both windows and will be able to switch their money between them at will. This two-window system will help us regain a banking system that will be both vibrant and rigorous. We cannot sustain a growing economy without one, and sick economies have been the cause of more presidential defeats than wars or abortion rights—ask former presidents Ford, Carter, and Bush.

Deposit insurance has proven its worth and is here to stay. But in any form, deposit insurance backed by the full faith and credit of the U.S. government is a dangerous business, comparable to a nuclear energy plant. Well designed and supervised, it can benefit mankind. Poorly run or designed, it can melt down and take the financial system with it, as it almost did in the S&L disaster during the 1980s. Further improvements to our present system include limiting the ever present demand to expand coverage and allowing the insuring agency to operate as nearly as possible like a private corporation.

Governmental controls of our financial institutions are complex, inefficient, outmoded, and archaic. They need to be reformed under a single independent federal regulatory agency. Do not bother to ask regulators about it; their only message will be their turf.

Do not try to achieve social goals such as community reinvestment, minority lending, publicly supported housing, etc. through private-sector financial institutions. It only weakens their ability to support private economic activity. They must behave in an ethical nondiscriminatory manner, but not as engines of social change. Social engineering should be done through institutions set up specifically for that purpose, so they can be monitored to determine whether they are successfully accomplishing their public goals—and abolished if they are not.

Do not underestimate the ability of private-sector bankers and financial executives to do dumb things—for example, loans to less developed countries, leveraged buyouts, and the risky commercial real estate lending of the 1980s. Instruct regulators to look for the newest fad in the industry and examine it with great care. The next mistake will be a new way to make a loan that will not be repaid.

The status of the full faith and credit commitments of the U.S. government will determine our ability to manage our budget and your government. We must watch these commitments like a hawk because they don't go on the books until they go sour, and then they go on in a big way, as deposit insurance did. Many interests would like just a nice, small government full faith and credit guarantee to help their businesses grow. Resist! Resist! Resist!

Please do not shoot the messenger if he comes bearing ill tidings from the world of finance. Listen carefully, for the tale he tells may be your salvation.

The Fourth Estate: No One Ever Overestimated Its Power

The power of the fourth estate is seldom underestimated by anyone who has reflected on the Washington scene. You are what the press portrays you to be—because most people have no other way of knowing you. Of course this does not mean that the press runs the process, because there is no one entity, even though it is called the press. The press is made up of hundreds of different reporters and organizations. As an example, even a partial list of the press people who dealt with the FDIC during my chairmanship extends from the business reporters for newspapers, magazines, and television whom you would expect to be covering a financial regulatory agency; to general reporters representing newspapers in Texas, Florida, and California; to talk show hosts like Bryant Gumble, Larry King, Ted Koppel, Paul Duke, John McLaughlin, and Pat Buchanan; to columnists like Evans and Novak and Mike Binstein of the Jack Anderson column, one of the early reporters on the story.

Since the press comprises a large variety of people doing their jobs in different ways, speaking of the press as though it has a single mind is a mistake. The press has many minds. Among themselves, reporters are very competitive in seeking out news and encouraging "leaks." They compete in one of the totally unregulated free enterprise systems in the United States—one with no holds barred. At one time it would have been considered inappropriate to sit outside the door of a presidential candidate and report on the women who visited him during any given period, especially if that did not seem to be affecting his ability to make political decisions. However, things have changed.

In a seminar in Washington after the ill-fated Gary Hart escapade, members of the press were asked, "If you were able to get a great story by disguising yourself as a waiter and slipping into the bedroom to deliver an order to a gentleman and his lady who had ordered room service, would you pay the hotel a thousand dollars to be able to exercise the opportunity?" Every major publication represented answered that it would pay the money. When the moderator raised a question about the moral issue involved, the answer was "If I don't do it someone else will." This attitude is making it more and more difficult to operate in a government that has always been based on the need for civility and compromise.

When I arrived to work in Washington twenty years ago, my initial impression of media coverage was that it often was detrimental to good government: a continuous barb in the side of those serving their country in a selfless manner. My impression changed. The fact is that it would be difficult, if not impossible, to keep our government honest if the press were not considered to be unseen members of every secret meeting that takes place in Washington. Anyone who does not treat a meeting, no matter how secret it is, as likely to be reported, will learn to his or her sorrow that the press was there! The press keeps many of the crooks at bay as it searches to uncover any and all possible news. The press makes evaluations, some sound and some unsound. The citizens have the benefit of its work—good or bad, right or wrong.

The media must judge credibility on a regular basis. Often

quick judgment is necessary, since stories that are written for the newspapers or recorded for television are usually made public on the very same day they were begun. Working as a reporter for dailies or wire services means incredible time pressure. When a reporter makes an error, it is out before the public right away, for everybody to see and comment upon. So one's credibility as a public official, and theirs as journalists, can be enhanced by helping them to be accurate. From time to time, this might mean journalists produce copy that you would rather not see, but that is one price for official credibility. If credibility is lost, an official's line of communication with his public is destroyed. Lying or intentionally misleading or withholding information will do the job in a hurry. The press is aware that officials are trying to use it to carry their message, but they expect it to be done fairly.

Media people, as a matter of self-preservation, judge everyone on his perceived veracity. Like virginity, once lost, its reincarnation requires a miracle.

When the media reports incorrectly, it is important to correct the report promptly by whatever means possible: a letter to the editor, a press release, or a telephone call. A false story that is not rebutted is assumed to be true. Furthermore, the author of the piece needs to know that when he makes a mistake, it will be publicly rebutted.

Learn to live with and love the people in the media, no matter how much you may wish they would vanish—and if you do not want to see your memo on the front page of *The Washington Post,* don't write it.

Credibility—the Only Hard Currency in Town

There is no limit to the suspicious nature of the populace when contemplating the politicians and bureaucrats of Washington, and rightly so. Their suspicions usually can be

WHAT HAVE YOU LEARNED?

fully justified. The propensity of some public servants to use public monies for private enjoyment is too frequent and well documented to be denied. The fact that almost all of those on the taxpayers' payroll are honest, hard working, and conscientious about their responsibilities does not assuage a general suspicion that they are "all crooks." The recent behavior of members of Congress misusing their own House of Representatives' piggy bank has again added to this belief. To find the few who are dishonest, however, requires a thorough and relentless examination of all who feed at the public trough.

Many a good and honest person gets caught in the press's zeal to find the guilty. The rewards available to reporters who uncover the misdeeds of a public official are substantial, extending to being paid to appear on television talk shows and becoming celebrities themselves. Looking for a "cover-up" not only invigorates the press but alerts politicians to the possibility of great political gain. The sole purpose of many congressional hearings is exposing cover-ups. For example: Are the bank regulators hiding a banking collapse until after the election? Did the administration finance Saddam Hussein's Kuwaiti offensive? Did the regulatory authorities know about the nefarious activities of the Bank of Credit and Commerce International, and who its real owners were? Was the lavish expenditure made for travel really justifiable as a public expenditure? Was the visit by your friend an important factor in influencing his company's success in winning a government contract?

My exposure to ethics in Washington began during the Ford administration, which replaced the scandal-scarred Nixon-Agnew regime. We did not need to be cautioned about our behavior because all of us occupied offices formerly used by gentlemen who were now wearing striped suits, or in the process of obtaining them. So, when we arrived to serve President Ford, office redecoration consisted of a review of the cast-off furniture stored in the attic of the

old Executive Office Building. The decorators employed by
the previous administration were forced to redeploy to the
private sector.

The FDIC chairman was a prime target for ethical examination. Many reporters were lured by the possibility of nail-
ing the nation's chief bank insurer with extravagant
expenditures. All my personal investments were placed in a
blind trust. My expense accounts were available to all under
the Freedom of Information Act. My office redecoration,
complete with Arizona artifacts loaned by the chairman, was
a great disappointment to those reporters who searched for
imprudent expenditures. We ran our business with the aus-
terity of a Dominican monastery. We aimed to keep our ladies safe from harassment and our life-style was designed to
be beyond reproach.

One certainty about Washington is that it is not a place to
make money. If wheeling and dealing is an addiction or if
other resources are not sufficient to supplement your government pay (which incidentally has become quite high), do
not accept the call to government service. Good people, like
ex-Attorney General Ed Meese and his wife Ursula were always getting into difficulties trying to make ends meet while
in public service. It has often been said, "If you do not want
to see any of your financial activities reported on the front
page of the papers, take care not to participate." This takes a
lot of the fun out of politics! But it is certainly good for the
Republic.

The Congress—Friend or Foe?

Relations with the Congress are always an important factor
in determining your political health, and getting along with
its members is a sine qua non for surviving as a part of any
administration, particularly as chairman of a federal agency.
Whether you can do your job or are done in by it depends

on your congressional friends and foes. The Congress creates agencies and it can condemn them to death, or worse, to impotence. Every member of the Congress has a vote and is important, but the committee with jurisdiction over your agency is of paramount importance. The chairman and the ranking minority member lead the list of members who must be given deference—and full information on all activities of your agency. Many times my public responses to a statement by these ever confident and wise congressional leaders was "if the chairman says so," or "I never disagree with the chairman, but with great sadness in this case. . . ."

Each and every member of Congress is different in personality, ability, reliability, and constituent interests. Some are in safe districts, and some face a battle every two years. Thus, like dealing with the press, dealing with the Congress is a misnomer. Dealing with individuals—Chairman Gonzalez or Congressmen Schumer, Leach, or Wylie—is a more accurate way to describe the challenge.

For example, Congressman John Dingell of Michigan, always described as the "powerful" chairman of the Energy and Commerce Committee, is one of the most feared of the breed, as a relentless pursuer of those who have in his view misbehaved. When he is "on your case," you have real trouble. Fortunately for the FDIC, he and I had worked together during the Ford administration and developed good communications and mutual credibility. This allowed me to go to my first hearing before his committee with less trepidation than most. When the chairman actually got down from the high platform, where members of the Congress sit to look down upon their witnesses (victims) and welcomed me, his staff took note of the greeting. It was a most appreciated courtesy and one not often extended by the gentleman from Michigan.

Why Washington Works—the Dispute-Resolution Mechanism

The question most frequently put to me by friends outside of government goes something like this, "Isn't our government a disaster, and isn't the whole system an unfixable mess? How could you stand working at the FDIC for six years?" To the surprise of a good many, the answer is, "It works surprisingly well, considering the kinds of problems it has to deal with." My old mentor, Governor George Romney of Michigan, a good Mormon, used to say to me that "the Constitution of the United States is a divinely inspired document." My reply always was "Well, Governor, you may be right. It seems to be a great document, but divine, really?" Now, having dealt with it in the real world of government, I believe that the governor was probably near the truth. Here is what changed my view.

Under our Constitution, our government in Washington does not, for the most part, govern. Instead, it provides a dispute-resolution mechanism through which conflicting interests can be resolved. Thus, when Tip O'Neill said as speaker of the House of Representatives that "all politics is local," he was, as usual, right on target. Almost all politics revolves around people's parochial interests, much more so than around the major issues of the day. The government is organized to find a compromise among the various competing demands of the people so that it can maintain a government supported by the people. This is one of the keys to the successful operation of our government. Of course, there are a great many who feel that compromise is immoral. If they are correct, then our democracy is condemned. But they are wrong!

Thus, our democratic government does not hand down orders in the tradition of yesterday's kings or today's chief executive officers. It produces compromises among the conflicting interests presented to it. Our Constitutional Convention itself produced a series of compromises centered around many local and regional interests. Compromises were achieved to solve various differences, and bargains were made everywhere: between the Northern states and the Southern states, between the coastal states and the inland states, between the big states and the little states. Those who believe compromise is disgraceful and immoral will gain little support from American history. Of course, as stated in the Declaration of Independence and the Bill of Rights, some principles are not up for grabs; but day-to-day problems seldom involve these lofty principles.

The U.S. Senate's membership was a compromise, allowing each state two senators, no matter its size. In the House the compromise was between the slave states and the nonslave states. In determining how many representatives each state should be entitled to, the states of the South wanted to count all their slaves. The North rebuffed that on the argument that the slaves were not allowed to vote and therefore should not be counted. Eventually a compromise was reached and each slave counted as three-fifths of a person. (Fortunately that compromise was ultimately eliminated from the Constitution.) If one recognizes government as an essential vehicle for compromise, one might ask how the country ever achieves any national purpose. Are there principles that are above compromise? Of course there are—high principles such as equal treatment under the law are always used as a basis for decisions about specific issues. If congressmen deal with satisfying the needs of their constituents, is anyone looking out for the people as a whole? That is the primary job of the president and his administration, because he is the only one elected by all the people. His job is to guide the many compromises that must be made in the national interest. If we have a weak president, our government does not work well.

The hearings held by Congress become an essential part of the process of exposing and reconciling opposing parochial views. The paid lobbyist is a part of this process. On many issues a particular representative or senator will not have a constituency that has a large interest in a particular battle (for example, lighthouse funding in Kansas). That is when senators and congressmen can more easily rise to the level of statesmanship and vote for what they think is good for the Union. There is no one at home to defeat them in the next election for having taken the high road.

No government faces a governing challenge like that of the government of the United States. Every ethnic and religious group in the world is represented within our borders. We are a large country of mountain states, border states, small states, and big states. We have a wide diversity of wealth and education, and one reason we have been able to maintain this diversity is the very existence of our government as a mechanism for the resolution of disputes. It allows people to believe, and prove, that they can have an influence on what our government does at all levels. In fact, with the Soviet Union gone, there is no nation that even closely approximates the diversity of the United States—or the potential for violent unrest.

We have our problems, but given the challenge of our situation, we continue to show improvement, though often by fits and starts. We have safety valves that allow various points of view to be brought to the attention of those who make governmental decisions. While this does not work perfectly and some people are left out for a time, our society does allow—and the Bill of Rights encourages—its citizens to assemble in groups and go before their elected representatives to state their views.

In the end, the collective judgment of the people has proven to be far superior to that of any small group of governmental officers. How can this be true? How can the average citizen know what is the appropriate nuclear defense? What is the appropriate size of the federal judiciary? Obviously, the average citizen cannot, does not, and, probably for the most part, could not care less. But the average citizen has a few things about which he cares greatly. Are officials telling the truth, are they stealing from him as a taxpayer, and are they protecting his interests? In the ordinary course of affairs people spend their lives determining whether they are being conned. As a result, the average citizen is good at determining who is giving him the straight story and who is not. Throughout the Watergate hearings, when the question of the day was whether the president had lied, the majority of the American people decided almost immediately that there was lying; and they made it clear by two to one in the polls.

In electing their representatives, as in daily life, the basic standards applied by people are the integrity of the individual's character and the truthfulness of his statements. Although there are those who have tried to carry judgments into a candidate's daily life, the American people seem fairly forgiving about most of their politicians' personal indiscretions as long as they have not been lied to or stolen from.

The accomplishments of the United States of America are unmatched. Our future is bright. We have the American advantage: We are the freest people in the world. There is more opportunity for our people to move up economically and educationally than in any other country in the world. We have the skill and abilities of a multiracial nation. Our innovation and flexibility make us the leader in the industries of the future. If we do not allow ourselves to be destroyed by voting more from the federal treasury than we are willing to provide in taxes, our successes will continue.

It was my idea from the time I stepped off a destroyer alive and well after two wartime years in the Pacific that I owed the world a debt. Serving in the government was one of the great ways to meet that obligation, and one of the rewards of a lifetime. So let me close by saying that it was a great privilege to serve my nation. It was something that very few have the opportunity to do, and I feel most fortunate to have had my chance—my chance to contribute to the chaos in Washington. Properly viewed, the creativity of our chaos can be our true American advantage.

Index

Comptroller of the Currency
(cont.)
  and Bank of New England,
    163
  as bank regulator, 68, 117,
    118
  creation of, 119
  and new capital standards,
    132–33
  see also Clarke, Robert
Conable, Barber, 51
Conference on Inflation, 18–20,
  22
Conference on Productivity, 63–
  64
Congress
  FDIC relationship with, 107–
    16
  importance of staff, 50–52
  lobbying before, 50–52
  ombudsman role of, 115–16
  Seidman view of, 107–8, 278–
    79
Conover, C. Todd, 139
Continental Illinois Bank, 76,
    82, 104, 139, 144, 145,
    149, 153, 170
Cooke, David, 86, 139, 205, 206,
    207, 212–13, 218, 220, 221,
    222, 223–24, 225, 265–66
Cooke, Peter, 132
core deposits, 103
Cornell University, 42
Corrigan, Gerald, 150
Cranston, Alan, 179, 184, 233
Cravath, Swaine and Moore,
    237, 238–39
credibility, importance of, 276–
    78
credit unions
  regulation of, 118
  in Rhode Island, 165–68

Darman, Richard, 43, 247
Dartmouth College, 42
Davis, Jim, 99
Day, Kathleen, 79
Deaver, Michael, 24
debt, foreign, 36–39
Dechert Price & Rhoads, 242
DeConcini, Dennis, 232, 233
Department of Housing and
    Urban development
    (HUD), 3–4, 5
Department of Justice, 85, 268
deposit insurance
  argument against, 149
  history of, 65–66
  for S&Ls, 66, 118, 178, 195
depositors
  big, losses by, 75–76, 168
  in large vs. small banks, 75–76
  proposal to charge fee, 248–49
  protection of, 168
  uninsured, protection of, 168
Depository Institutions
    Deregulation and Monetary
    Control Act of 1980, 178,
    179
deposits, core, 103
deregulation movement
  amount of supervision
    required, 83–84
  as anti-inflation measure, 20,
    23
  blind adherence to, 89–90
  in Carter administration, 23
  in Reagan administration, 23
  and S&Ls, 23, 180, 181
  start of, 20, 22, 23
Dershowitz, Alan, 238
developing countries, *see* Third
    World debt problem
DiConcini, Dennis, 234
Diehl, Dick, 191
Dingell, John, 279

DiPrete, Edward R., 165
directors, *see* bank directors
dispute-resolution mechanism, 280–84
Dixon, Donald, 190, 226
Dochow, Darrel, 188
dog's name, 77–78
Dole, Bob, 110
Domenici, Pete, 247
Donaldson Lufkin, 146
Douglas, John, 154
Drexel Burnham Lambert, 146, 152–53, 192, 229, 235–36, 238
Dukakis, Michael, 189, 190
Dunlop, John, 28

Eagleburger, Lawrence, 263
Economic Policy Board, 24–28
  and international finance, 35–39
  and Kissinger, 34–35
  and petrodollar recycling, 37–38
  and recession, 30–32
Edwards, Mickey, 109
Ehrlichman, John, 5
Eizenstat, Stuart, 43, 51
Elkins, J.A., 143
Enders, Thomas, 34
Equity Funding scandal, 72–74, 76
Ernst & Young, 192, 193

farm banks
  and capital ratio, 128–30
  failure of, 163–64
  and forbearance, 128–30
  and recession, 81, 110–11
FBI, 5, 70
FDIC
  aftermath of Texas experience, 158–59
  assets of, 68, 100, 174
  and bank failure forecasts, 112, 139
  and bank holding company protection, 144, 146, 147, 154
  bank supervision function, 58, 68, 81, 83–84, 97–99
  and big depositors, 75–76, 168
  booklet for bank directors, 58, 94, 95
  breakfast meetings at, 108
  budget for, 82–83
  Congressional Relations division, 81, 108, 109
  as debt collector, 91–92
  defined, 118
  and deregulation, 83–84
  estimates of S&L losses, 112, 188, 189
  favors for Congressmen, 113–16
  and First City Bank Corporation, 143–47
  and First Republic Corporation, 150–55
  and GAO audits, 170–74
  history of, 65–66, 119
  impact of interstate banking on, 61–62
  independence of, 67–68, 83, 84–89, 250–51, 265
  lawsuits by, 91–95
  liquidation function, 81, 99–104
  loss of limousine service, 109
  and M Corp., 157–58
  and new capital standards, 132–33
  as observers of S&L problems, 175–76
  and OMB, 82–89
  organization of, 81–82